The Thermidorean regime and the Directory 1794–1799

The Thermidorean regime and the Directory 1794–1799

DENIS WORONOFF

Translated by

JULIAN JACKSON

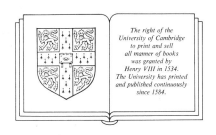

The right of the
University of Cambridge
to print and sell
all manner of books
was granted by
Henry VIII in 1534.
The University has printed
and published continuously
since 1584.

CAMBRIDGE UNIVERSITY PRESS

Cambridge

London   New York   New Rochelle   Melbourne   Sydney

EDITIONS DE LA MAISON DES SCIENCES DE
L'HOMME

Paris

Published by the Press Syndicate of the University of Cambridge
The Pitt Building, Trumpington Street, Cambridge CB2 1RP
32 East 57th Street, New York, NY 10022, USA
296 Beaconsfield Parade, Middle Park, Melbourne 3206, Australia
and Editions de la Maison des Sciences de l'Homme
54 Boulevard Raspail, 75270 Paris Cedex 06

Originally published in French as *La République bourgeoise, de Thermidor à Brumaire 1794–1799*
by Editions du Seuil, Paris, 1972
and © Editions du Seuil 1972
First published in English by Editions de la Maison des Sciences de l'Homme
and Cambridge University Press 1984 as *The Thermidorean regime and the Directory 1794–1799*
English translation © Maison des Sciences de l'Homme and Cambridge
University Press 1984

Printed in Great Britain by the University Press, Cambridge

Library of Congress catalogue card number: 83–7672

British Library Cataloguing in Publication Data

Woronoff, Denis
The Thermidorean regime and the Directory,
1794–1799. – (The French Revolution; 3)
1. France – Politics and government – Revolution,
1789–1799   2. France – History – Revolution,
1794–1799
I. Title   II. Jackson, Julian
III. La République bourgeoise de Thermidore à Brumaire
(1794–1799). *English*   IV. Series
944.04′4   DC176.5
ISBN 0 521 24725 X hard covers
ISBN 0 521 28917 3 paperback

ISBN 2 7351 0036 7 hard covers (France only)
ISBN 2 7351 0037 5 paperback (France only)

Contents

Maps

Chronology

1794

ix

NIVÔSE

4 (*24 Dec.*)   Abolition of the *maximum*

1795

PLUVIÔSE

1 (*20 Jan.*)   The French occupy Amsterdam
4 (*23 Jan.*)   The Dutch fleet is captured on the Helder
15 (*3 Feb.*)   Fall of Rosas
19 (*7 Feb.*)   Arrest of Babeuf
20 (*8 Feb.*)   'Depantheonisation' of Marat
29 (*17 Feb.*)   Treaty of La Jaunaye

VENTÔSE

3 (*21 Feb.*)   Freedom of worship. Neutrality of the state
12 (*2 March*)   Arrest and indictment of Barère, Billaud-Varenne and Collot d'Herbois

GERMINAL

10 (*30 March*)   Commission of the Eleven to work out a new constitution
12 (*1 April*)   Popular uprising in Paris
13 (*2 April*)   The uprising is crushed
13–15 (*2–4 April*)   Incidents in Rouen, Amiens, Saint-Germain
16 (*5 April*)   Peace of Basle between France and Prussia
21 (*10 April*)   Law disarming the Terrorists and confining them to their homes

FLORÉAL

15 (*4 May*)   Massacre of Jacobins imprisoned in Lyons
27 (*16 May*)   Treaty of alliance between France and Holland
30 (*19 May*)   The pamphlet *L'Insurrection du Peuple* circulates in Paris

PRAIRIAL

1–4 (*20–23 May*)   *Journées* of revolt in Paris
17 (*5 June*)   Massacre of Jacobins in Marseilles
20 (*8 June*)   Announcement of the death of Louis XVII

MESSIDOR

5–9 (23–27 June)	Landing of *émigrés* at Quiberon
6 (29 June)	Verona Manifesto

THERMIDOR

3 (21 July)	Hoche's victory at Quiberon

FRUCTIDOR

5 (22 August)	The text of the constitution is adopted by the Convention
20 (6 Sept.)	Beginning of the constitutional referendum

YEAR IV VENDÉMIAIRE

1 (23 Sept.)	Proclamation of the constitution
7 (29 Sept.)	Law regulating worship
9 (1 Oct.)	Annexation of Belgium
13 (5 Oct.)	Royalist uprising against the Convention
29 (21 Oct.)	Elections to the Legislative Body

BRUMAIRE

3 (25 Oct.)	*Emigrés'* relatives excluded from public office. Daunou's law on education
4 (26 Oct.)	Amnesty except for *émigrés*
9 (31 Oct.)	Election of the executive Directory
25 (16 Nov.)	Opening of the Club du Panthéon

FRIMAIRE

14 (5 Dec.)	Babeuf in hiding
19 (10 Dec.)	Vote of forced loan

1796

PLUVIÔSE

15 (4 Feb.)	Project for a bank of issue
30 (19 Feb.)	End of the *assignats*

VENTÔSE

6 (25 Feb.)	Stofflet shot
9 (28 Feb.)	Bonaparte closes the Club du Panthéon
12 (2 March)	Bonaparte appointed General-in-Chief of the Army of Italy
28 (18 March)	Creation of the *mandats territoriaux*

GERMINAL

9 (29 March)	Charette shot
10 (30 March)	Formation of the 'Insurrectional Committee' of the Equals
23 (12 April)	Montenotte
24 (13 April)	Millesimo
26 (15 April)	Dego

FLORÉAL

2 (21 April)	Mondovi
9 (28 April)	Franco-Sardinian Armistice of Cherasco
13 (2 May)	Dismissal of the Paris Police Legion
21 (10 May)	Lodi. Arrest of Babeuf and his friends

PRAIRIAL

1 (20 May)	Bonaparte pays his soldiers half their wages in metallic currency
4 (23 May)	Anti-French uprising in the Pavia region
16 (4 June)	Kléber beats the Austrians at Altenkirchen
24 (12 June)	French troops invade the Legations

MESSIDOR

5 (23 June)	The Pope signs an armistice at Bologna
21 (9 July)	Moreau victorious at Ettlingen

THERMIDOR

18 (5 Aug.)	Castiglione

FRUCTIDOR

6 (23 Aug.)	Bernadotte beaten at Neumarkt

7 *(24 Aug.)*	Moreau beaten at Amberg
22 *(8 Sept.)*	Bassano
23 *(9 Sept.)*	Incident at the Grenelle camp

YEAR V VENDÉMIAIRE

14 *(5 Oct.)*	High court of justice at Vendôme
23 *(14 Oct.)*	Demonstration at Milan in favour of independence
25 *(16 Oct.)*	Proclamation in Bologna of the Cispadane Republic

BRUMAIRE

25–27 *(15–17 Nov.)*	Battle of Arcole

FRIMAIRE

25 *(15 Dec.)*	French fleet sets off towards Ireland

1797

NIVÔSE

25 *(14 Jan.)*	Rivoli
26 *(15 Jan.)*	First Theophilanthropic worship

PLUVIÔSE

11 *(30 Jan.)*	Arrest of Brottier
14 *(2 Feb.)*	Mantua falls
16 *(4 Feb.)*	Official return to metallic currency

VENTÔSE

1 *(19 Feb.)*	Treaty of Tolentino with the Pope

GERMINAL

1–12 *(20–31 March)*	Elections to the Legislative Body (renewal of the second third). French offensive towards the Tyrol
28 *(17 April)*	Anti-French uprising in Verona
29 *(18 April)*	Preliminaries of Treaty of Leoben

FLORÉAL

1 (20 April)   Moreau crosses the Rhine

PRAIRIAL

7 (26 May)   Barthélemy elected Director in Letourneur's
                                    place. End of the Vendôme trial
8 (27 May)   Babeuf and Darthé guillotined

MESSIDOR

28 (16 July)   Ministerial reshuffle carried out by the
                                    triumvirs

THERMIDOR

8 (26 July)   Sotin at the Ministry of Police
20 (7 Aug.)   Augereau in Paris

FRUCTIDOR

18 (4 Sept.)   Anti-royalist *coup d'état*
19 (5 Sept.)   Passing of emergency legislation
22 (8 Sept.)   Merlin de Douai and François de Neufchâteau
                                    elected Directors

YEAR VI VENDÉMIAIRE

9 (30 Sept.)   Bankruptcy of the 'Two-Thirds'
26 (17 Oct.)   Peace of Campoformio

FRIMAIRE

8 (28 Nov.)   Congress of Rastatt

1798

NIVÔSE

22 (11 Jan.)   Berthier marches on Rome

PLUVIÔSE

3 (22 Jan.)   *Coup d'état* in The Hague

9 (28 Jan.)	Mulhouse annexed to France
23 (11 Feb.)	Berthier enters Rome
27 (15 Feb.)	Roman Republic

GERMINAL

20 (9 April)	Meeting of primary assemblies

FLORÉAL

22 (11 May)	Large-scale invalidation of newly elected left-wing deputies
26 (15 May)	Treilhard elected Director
30 (19 May)	The French fleet leaves Toulon for Egypt

PRAIRIAL

29 (17 June)	François de Neufchâteau appointed Minister of the Interior

MESSIDOR

13 (1 July)	The French disembark in Alexandria

THERMIDOR

3 (21 July)	Battle of the Pyramids
14 (1 Aug.)	The French fleet destroyed at Aboukir

FRUCTIDOR

19 (5 Sept.)	Jourdan's law on conscription
23 (9 Sept.)	Law on the *décadi* and the festivals

YEAR VII VENDÉMIAIRE

21 (12 Oct.)	Beginning of the 'War of the Peasants' in Belgium
24 (15 Oct.)	First national exhibition organised by François de Neufchâteau
30 (21 Oct.)	Anti-French uprising in Cairo

FRIMAIRE

3 (23 Nov.)   Law on land tax
4 (24 Nov.)   Imposition of the tax on doors and windows

1799

PLUVIÔSE

4 (23 Jan.)   Championnet enters Naples
7 (26 Jan.)   Neapolitan Republic
27 (15 Feb.)   Battle of El'Arîsh

VENTÔSE

17 (7 March)   Capture of Jaffa
29 (19 March)   Siege of Acre

GERMINAL

1–30 (21 March–19 April)   Elections to the Legislative Body
5 (25 March)   Jourdan beaten at Stokach
16 (5 April)   Schérer defeated at Magnano
21 (10 April)   Pius VI brought to France

FLORÉAL

9 (28 April)   Assassinations of Bonnier and Roberjot on
                                  their departure from Rastatt
10 (29 April)   Suvorov in Milan
27 (16 May)   Sieyès replaces Reubell on the Directory
28 (17 May)   Bonaparte raises the siege of Acre

PRAIRIAL

16 (4 June)   First Battle of Zurich
28 (16 June)   The Councils call on the Directory to give
                                  an explanation of the situation
29 (17 June)   The election of Treilhard is annulled. Gohier
                                  is elected to the Directory
30 (18 June)   The Councils force La Révellière and Merlin
                                  to resign

MESSIDOR

1 (19 June)	Macdonald beaten at La Trebbia. Roger-Ducos on the Directory
2 (20 June)	Moulin on the Directory
18 (6 July)	Foundation of the Jacobin Club at the Manège

THERMIDOR

7 (25 July)	French victory of Aboukir over a Turkish army
18 (5 Aug.)	Royalist uprising in the south-west
28 (15 Aug.)	Joubert killed at Novi

FRUCTIDOR

6 (23 Aug.)	Bonaparte leaves Egypt
10 (27 Aug.)	English landing on the Helder
3rd Jour complémentaire (19 Sept.)	Brune victorious at Bergen

YEAR VIII VENDÉMIAIRE

3–5 (25–27 Sept.)	Battle of Zurich
17 (9 Oct.)	Bonaparte lands at Fréjus
24 (16 Oct.)	Bonaparte in Paris

BRUMAIRE

1 (23 Oct.)	Lucien President of the Five Hundred
18 (9 Nov.)	The Councils are transferred to Saint-Cloud. Sieyès, Roger-Ducos, Barras resign
19 (10 Nov.)	The Councils give in to force. They designate three provisional consuls – Bonaparte, Sieyès, Roger-Ducos – and two commissions to prepare a new constitution

Preface

Recalling 9 Thermidor in his *Mémoires*, Thibaudeau quoted the remark of an émigré: 'there are no longer men in France, there are only events'. This harsh judgement is one that many people would apply to the period which separates the fall of Robespierre from the rise of Bonaparte, a period in which history seems to have unfolded in a minor key. From these five years emerges an impression of confused mediocrity, of an interregnum lacking brilliance. And whether they have been discredited or neglected, the closing stages of the Revolution have hardly won the favour of historians.

But this drab interlude between two epic periods is crucial for an understanding of the origins of contemporary France. Behind the incoherence, the spectacle and the scandals, one can trace the extraordinary tenacity with which the republican bourgeoisie maintained its hold on power. 'Respectable' citizens searched ceaselessly for 'the means of terminating the Revolution'[1] to their own benefit. They hoped to define, in a set of institutions, in a society, in an ideology, a system which would consolidate and sum up their conquests. That this regime of '*notables*' was, in its original form, only able to survive by means of expedients in no way detracts from the interest and modernity of what was being attempted. The great figures had fallen silent. But would it be too much to claim that after the sound and the fury it becomes easier to distinguish a different form of discourse? Not the language of popular protest, which, outside moments of explosion, reaches us in an increasingly distorted and muffled form, but the language of moderate politicians – of whom Thibaudeau and La Révellière-Lépeaux could be taken as the spokesmen – whose demands, contradictions and indeed very ordinariness were representative of the new dominant classes. One must also be aware of provincial voices.

---

[1] To take up the title of the law of 5 Fructidor Year III (22 August 1795) which proposed a new constitution to the French people for their ratification.

But it remains difficult to know what these were in spite of extensive research which has perhaps concentrated too narrowly on the northern half of the country. Paris retained the initiative and the last word. But as well as similarities of attitude one ought also to pick out time-lags, even discrepancies, which varied depending on the region and the problem. For the relaxation of revolutionary constraints seems to have released powerful centrifugal forces: in many cases the right to make autonomous decisions had been achieved at the local level. As Richard Cobb has written, the country became 'communalised' in Year III; a remark generally valid for the whole of our period. More than ever, diversity was the hallmark of France. Finally, the political upheavals, the 'events' at home and abroad, must not obscure a more secret, because silent, history – that of the underlying forces in society. The Directory was perhaps a period of weakness, but it was also a period rich in political and cultural potential, in transformations, in social tensions. In short, not everything can be reduced to mere spectacle in a period which has been characterised as frivolous in order, perhaps, to evade proper assessment.

Although some uncertainties remain, there are no serious gaps in our knowledge of the political history of the years from 9 Thermidor to 18 Brumaire. On the other hand little progress has been made concerning more 'structural' problems, where areas of darkness persist. For example, the working of the Councils and the Directory is much better known than that of the ministries, let alone that of the administration of the *départements*. Yet the proliferation of bureaucracy seems to have been a characteristic of the regime. In the economic field there are a myriad unresolved questions. As to the evolution of the economic situation, regional variations have barely been examined – though such variations are all the greater because the political crisis reinforced the compartmentalisation of markets. So too variations according to sector, which would allow us to plot disparities of development. The cultural history of the Directory has long been restricted to laments about religious persecution and about the frivolity of Parisian society. Recent research has helped to produce other perspectives, but popular culture remains almost unknown. Finally, beyond the narrative of battles and the naming of military units, there is a need for an analysis of a military society: of the development of an *esprit de corps*, of the changes in hierarchical relationships, of the wealth of the generals – areas of enquiry that would illuminate the

Thermidorean Convention and the Directory. This still virgin territory has sometimes stimulated highly original work. But such research is very isolated compared to the dominant historiographical tradition which allows us to describe the origins, establishment and triumphs of the regime.

1

A difficult transition

'The people want order, peace and the Republic, and they will have them'
Benjamin Constant in a letter to Mme Nassau, 6 Prairial Year III

The end of the revolutionary government

The fall of an individual or the end of a system? From 10 Thermidor the debate had commenced. Barère presented the previous day's events as 'a slight commotion which left the government intact'. This interpretation was to be disproved as the Convention began to undermine the revolutionary system, and public opinion attacked with increasing stridency those responsible for the Terror.

On 11 Thermidor Barère, in the name of the 'Great' Committee of Public Safety, proposed three candidates for the posts vacated by the 'conspirators'. Tallien, Legendre and Thuriot imposed a more radical solution: a quarter of the membership of the committees would be renewed each month, the outgoing members becoming ineligible for a month. This put an end to the stability of the government. In the end six deputies were selected to replace the 'triumvirs', Prieur de la Marne, Jeanbon Saint-André – the pretext for their removal being that they were on mission – and Héraut de Séchelles, who had been guillotined with Danton. They were replaced on the Great Committee by Tallien, a repentant Terrorist, Thuriot and Bréard, both Dantonists, Treilhard, a member of the Constituent Assembly, and Laloy, a moderate, together with only one of Barère's candidates, Eschasseriaux. The composition of the Committee of General Security was also modified. Three Robespierrists, including the painter David, were excluded. Of its four new members, two – Legendre and Merlin de

I

Thionville – represented the Dantonist faction. Thus the ephemeral leaders of Thermidor – Barère, Collot d'Herbois – were isolated in the government by old and new softliners.

The concentration of power, another revolutionary principle, was also undermined. Cambon, who had always succeeded in protecting the autonomy of the Finance Committee and the Treasury, denounced the Committee of Public Safety's self-identification with the executive. He proposed that each of the twelve commissions (that is, ministerial departments) be attached to the twelve principal committees. But the majority, while aware of the danger of fragmentation, was even more worried by its experience of the disadvantages of a monopoly of power. The decision reached on 7 Fructidor (24 August 1794) carved up the powers of the Committee of Public Safety, restricting it to its former domain of war and diplomacy. The Committee of General Security kept its control over the police. There was now to be a total of sixteen committees with the Legislative Committee, having responsibility for internal administration and justice vested in it, being raised to the level of the two 'Great' Committees. These measures, then, increased to some extent the efficiency of the government, but not its unity.

The dismantling of the system of Year II affected, finally, the instruments of the Terror. The law of 22 Prairial, which in practice suppressed judicial guarantees, was very quickly repealed, and the Revolutionary Court, paralysed by the imprisonment of Fouquier-Tinville, was reorganised. Thanks to the introduction of the 'question of intent' (without proof of counter-revolutionary intentions defendants could not be found guilty), numerous breaches were opened in the apparatus of repression. The surveillance committees, which had been the organs of the Terror, experienced the full repercussions of these various breaches with the past. Partly in response to a violent campaign against these committees, the Convention left only one in each district in the provinces and twelve, instead of forty-eight, in Paris. Their powers were restricted, and the conditions of membership modified to make it harder for the *sans-culottes*★ to join.

These few weeks had resulted in the disbanding of the revolutionary government.

★ The term literally meant someone without (aristocratic) breeches: hence a radical Republican. [Trans.]

A new equilibrium

Ending the Terror meant opening the prisons. If the Convention failed to understand, the pressure of public opinion set about convincing it. At the end of July 1794 approaches were increasingly made to the authorities, and crowds gathered outside the prisons with growing frequency. When the first prisoners were released in August there was an explosion. All sections of the population, all political tendencies, had been represented among them; their liberation seemed a common victory for the French people. The Paris police reports evoke this moment of unanimity, exemplified by the revolutionary committee of Saint-Pol (Nord) in a phrase to the representatives on mission: 'Everyone is holding hands.'[1] Almost everyone, for these hundreds of suspects, freed because no charge against them had been proceeded with, began with their relatives to demand accountability from those who had been responsible for their arbitrary arrest, that is from the Jacobins.

The Jacobins occupied strong positions in the administration and in government, especially on the Committee of General Security. From August to October they succeeded in holding their ground. In Paris they were threatened by two forces, the moderates and the neo-Hébertists. Accounts of life in prison and various other revelations stoked the campaign against the 'blood drinkers'. The most important leaders of this campaign, the former Terrorists Fréron and Tallien, had two crucial forms of action at their disposal: the press and the street. Freedom of the press, demanded by everyone, was quickly obtained after Thermidor. Right-wing papers run by talented journalists – Dussault on *La Correspondance politique*, Richer de Sérizy on *L'Accusateur public*, Fréron himself on *L'Orateur du peuple* – incited the population to revenge, gave instructions for action and pointed out the most dangerous Jacobins. And the '*jeunesse dorée*',* which included young bourgeois, lawyers' clerks, artists, military absentees and deserters, began to stir up noisy disturbances in the Palais-Royal quarter. Led by an adventurer, the Marquis de Saint-Huruge, and the dramatist Martainville, these youths intervened in theatres, shouting down actors reputed to be Terrorists, interrupting plays and giving readings or

---

* Literally gilded youth; the groups of young aristocrats who assaulted the Jacobins. [Trans.]

[1] Quoted by G. Sangier in *Le District de Saint-Pol de Thermidor à Brumaire* (Blangermont, 1946), vol. 1, p. 8.

singing songs. Such ostentatious displays had a certain intimidatory value.

In the course of their campaigns these fops were careful not to confuse the 'bloodthirsty Jacobins' with the 'decent *sans-culottes* of the faubourgs'. Although their attitude and vocabulary betrayed condescension towards, and fear of, the people, this position also marked a convergence between the moderates and the neo-Hébertists in a common hostility to the consequences of revolutionary government. The popular society known as the Electoral Club and the Gravilliers and Museum sections served as rallying points for the leaders of the popular movement. There were demands for unrestricted press freedom, for an elected municipality, and for an application of the constitution of 1793. *L'Ami du peuple*, edited by Châles, and Babeuf's *Le Tribun du peuple* developed these themes further. Until the end of Vendémiaire the community of views between these two currents of opinion seemed perfect.

The Jacobins, the third element in this triangular confrontation, were momentarily at a loss. Everything about the new course of events seemed inauspicious to them: the emptying of the prisons, the destruction of the revolutionary government, the now free and self-confident right-wing press. When there was an explosion at the powder factory of Grenelle, probably from accidental causes, murmurings were heard in the crowd. 'This is the result of freeing the prisoners' (police report, 31 August 1794). To deal with this 'aristocratic plot' the Jacobins demanded a return of the Terror. In September they went on the offensive. Some ill-considered releases from prison and the excesses of the fops began to annoy many members of the sections. The majority on the Convention adopted a policy of continuity, as in the transfer of Marat's ashes to the Pantheon, of reconciliation, as in Lindet's economic programme of 20 September, and of caution. In addition, the Convention had also rejected Lecointre's denunciation of Barère, Collot, Billaud-Varenne and their friends.

Finally, encouragement came from the provinces where local Jacobins expressed their discontent in numerous formal addresses. The mother-society therefore had hopes of gaining the advantage in the Parisian sections. At least eight of them supported the text of the Dijon Society, which strongly set out the Jacobin viewpoint. Similarly, when the Lindet report was laid before the sections, the Jacobins replied with a speech by Audoin which was a violent declaration of war against the 'respectable citizens'. The debate turned to the advantage of one or other party depending on the sections and the composition of the assemblies. The Jacobins could only claim a small number of successes. Their victory was limited and precarious because it rested upon a minority of activists; it was dangerous because it pushed the Thermidoreans away from compromise and encouraged them to break with the policy of balance.

In the provinces the implications of Thermidor were not immediately understood, at least in certain *départements*. For example, in Brest, as in Nîmes or the Ardèche, there was no let up in the Terror, while in Besançon, an exceptional but not unique case, the Jacobins hailed the triumph of the 'true patriots', and the moderates took fright. The situation was clarified by the decree of 7 Fructidor which virtually abolished the surveillance committees. What policy should now be adopted? The conformity of the messages of support for the Convention failed to disguise the disarray of the authorities. Local reactions ultimately reflected the great disparities in local situations during the course of the Terror. In places where conflict had been acute and where the representatives on mission called for revenge – Boisset at Bourg, Goupilleau at Avignon, Auguis and Serre in Marseilles – local officials were decimated by arrests and exclusions, and a large-scale release of prisoners took place. By contrast, political stability was maintained until the winter in the Hérault, the Haute-Saône, the Nièvre and the Ardennes, etc. Indeed, some representatives played a moderating role. Bayeux was perhaps a typical case: the mayor resigned after Thermidor, the Terrorists made themselves scarce, and the most conspicuous of them were purged from the popular society.

The modification in the balance of power was more marked in the large cities. At Le Havre the municipality and the conseil général soon included only shipbuilders and businessmen. In Toulouse the Girondins made themselves visible in large numbers. The reactionaries took the Jacobins to task in the streets of Lyons and Marseilles. Thus, in different ways and at different speeds, the revenge of the defeated of Year II took shape.[2]

The resurgence of the reactionaries

At the height of the Jacobin offensive, the trial of the Nantes federalists handed the initiative over to the Thermidoreans. The defendants

---

[2] See M. Schlumberger's up-to-date assessment, 'La réaction thermidorienne à Toulouse', *Annales historiques de la Révolution française* (April–June 1971), pp. 265–83.

denounced the atrocities committed by the town's revolutionary committee. At once a newspaper campaign began to exploit these revelations about summary executions and drownings. During September feelings of revulsion and anger spread through Paris. The acquittal of the accused, on 15 September, marked out the real culprits: the Nantes Committee and, even more, Carrier. The right, spurred on by Tallien and Merlin de Thionville, could have imagined no more suitable subject for debate. In mid-October the Nantes Terrorists appeared before the revolutionary court. The indictment of Carrier posed greater problems: mooted as early as 20 October, it was not achieved until 23 November. The former Montagnards, the 'Crêtois' (the men of the Crest), had fought a lukewarm rearguard action. And many members of the Convention, whether through caution or legalism, were careful not to act too quickly. But the intrigues of the Jacobins in Paris and the provinces, especially Marseilles, were worrying enough to push Thuriot, Merlin de Douai and Cambacérès towards the most stringent action. On 16 December Carrier was condemned to death and guillotined.

It was easy to slip into a policy of ascribing guilt by association; all Jacobins were at risk. On 16 October the Convention had forbidden the mutual affiliation of popular societies, their correspondence with each other and the submission of collective petitions. This broke the Jacobin network of solidarity, which had already been considerably undermined by purges and defections. Fréron's bands and the right wing of the Convention demanded even more: the closure of the 'den of thieves' – achieved on 12 November in an atmosphere of a witch hunt and after two onslaughts by the fops.

The majority of the sections approved this measure, which raised hardly a stir. Put to the test, the Jacobins lacked leaders of stature. Duhem and Goujon, in spite of their courage, were no substitutes for Barère, Collot and Billaud-Varenne, silent since their resignation from the Committee of Public Safety on 1 September. The Jacobins were not only weakened, they were also isolated and lacking in popular support, as was shown by the success of the moderates in capturing their remaining sections. The closure of the Jacobin Club gave an important impetus to the struggle for power in the assemblies. For the opportunists and waverers this was a signal for the imminent victory of the moderates; the downcast Jacobins lost control of sections which they had previously only held because of the absence of any firm opposition. At the end of November the overwhelming success of the moderates

had overcome the last bastions: those of the north-west, the Piques
(Place Vendôme) and Butte-des-Moulins (Palais-Royal) sections, and
those of the left bank, the Université (Monnaie) and Thermes
sections – to mention only the most important.

As for the Hébertists, they were no longer able to pursue their action
in favour of direct democracy. The Electoral Club, declared subversive
by the Committee of General Security, attempted to continue to
function, and in mid-November it became the instrument of resistance
to the moderates, the irreconcilable Jacobins having taken refuge with
the friends of Babeuf. Later, in a celebrated piece of self-criticism,
Babeuf was to draw the lesson of this reversal of alliances: 'When I
was among the first to thunder vehemently in order to bring down
the monstrous structure of Robespierre's system, I far from imagined
that I was helping to build an edifice which, in a completely different
way, would be no less harmful to the people' (*Le Tribun du peuple*,
18 December 1794). Mutual suspicions were blunted; reaction forged
unity in the popular camp. But the club was constrained to silence. A
few sections, including those of Montreuil (Faubourg Saint-Antoine)
and Gravilliers, stuck to a 'Hébertist' position during the winter.

The persecution of the former personnel of the sections gathered pace
at the end of November. Extraordinary commissions carried out
purges, hounding especially the former members of the revolutionary
committees. In spite of the flood of denunciations, the government
openly checked this process. On several occasions the Committee of
General Security protected or freed public servants, as if it wanted to
contain the repression within limits compatible with the exercise of
power.

In the Convention the moderate counter-offensive took a different
form. There were demands that the seventy-five protesting deputies
excluded after 2 June 1793 should be reinstated. The Dantonists,
supported by Tallien ('in a Revolution men must not look behind
them') tried to oppose this; but, against the Jacobins and Hébertists,
how in this month of Brumaire was it possible to do without the
support of the moderates? In the struggle the Girondins became both
a stake and an ally (Mathiez). On 8 December Merlin de Douai gave
the agreement of the committees. Seventy-eight deputies ultimately
came back to take up their places.

The '*Montagne*' and the majority on the Councils had allowed this
to happen in the hope that in the process the reaction would burn itself
out. In fact, during January, there was on the contrary an intensification

of agitation in the capital. The *jeunesse dorée*, whom this first success had made all the more aggressive, adopted an attitude of provocation, imposed their new hymn 'Le Réveil du peuple' instead of 'La Marseillaise', and publicly attacked all those whose reading, whose comments, whose very dress, put them in the extremely large category of Jacobins. The police, half powerless and half sympathetic, did little to prevent such behaviour. Sometimes soldiers who were passing through Paris took it upon themselves to riposte.

The first objective of the right-wing extremists was to bring Barère, Collot and Billaud-Varenne to trial. It took them more than two months (27 December to 2 March) to overcome the resistance of the *Montagne* and of part of the '*Plaine*'. The other battle-cry of these bands was the denunciation of the cult of Marat. This meant both asking the Convention to go back on its own decisions and offending the susceptibilities of the *sans-culottes*. The fops thus turned in a distinctly counter-revolutionary direction. The Committees, even Fréron, were worried about this development. But a three-week campaign of hunting out busts in the theatres was enough to make the Convention comply by 'depantheonising' the 'Friend of the People' on 8 February 1795. 'La Marseillaise', Marat, the *bonnets rouges*,★ the '*sans-culotte* style': it was in short a certain conception of the Revolution, egalitarian and austere, which had now lost the war of symbols. On 8 March the surviving Girondins, outlawed since 2 June 1793, were called back to the Convention. The return of Isnard, Lanjuinais and their friends well and truly signalled the end of the illusions and ambiguities of Thermidor.

ECONOMIC CRISIS

The abandonment of the 'maximum'†

The destruction of the system of revolutionary government eventually brought about the end of the Economic Terror. With restrictions relaxed and 'Jacobin' measures out of favour, it seemed to peasants who avoided requisitioning and to manufacturers who delayed meeting state orders that they were but slightly anticipating an imminent abolition measure. But on 7 September the Convention extended the general

---

★ The name given to the revolutionaries after their red Phrygian caps. [Trans.]
† On 29 September 1793 the law of the *maximum* introduced general price controls. [Trans.]

maximum, as well as that on grain, for the duration of Year III. This was in fact merely an act of conservatism; the tendency was certainly towards liberalism. As Lindet had promised in his speech of 20 September, foreign trade was the first beneficiary of the government's concern. It was freed from restrictions in several stages. On 17 October and 26 November the unrestricted importation of unprohibited goods was allowed; on 15 November captains of neutral vessels were authorised to negotiate private contracts in French ports. As winter approached the committees took measures to ensure that the Republic was supplied with foreign grain. Similarly the state handed over some sectors of the economy which it had been running, such as the foundries of Toulouse and Maubeuge and the arms factories of Paris. In the latter case, considerations of public order pushed the authorities into dispersing the bulk of the workforce to the provinces. In doing this the Committee of Public Safety was innovating less than has been claimed. 'Nationa-lisation' had always seemed to it to be a makeshift solution. For example, on 8 Pluviôse Year II, Carnot and Prieur de la Côte d'Or had opposed the state take-over of Creusot in these words: 'No factory should be a burden on the Republic; all should be in the hands of private enterprise.'[3]

If Thermidor did represent a break with the past, this was above all in its order of priorities: the return to normality was to suffer no more delays or exceptions. Given this fact, could the *maximum* – the linchpin of the system of regulation – be indefinitely maintained? There was a brief attempt to appease resentment in the countryside. From 9 November the failure to fulfil levies no longer entailed more than the confiscation of the required quota. To take account of criticisms, the somewhat unrealistic national *maximum* was replaced by prices calculated at district level. The peasants deserted the markets and sold their harvests secretly for the highest prices, sometimes in exchange for metallic currency. 'As the peasants' fear vanished', wrote Georges Lefebvre in *Les Paysans du Nord*, 'so did their scruples, and their ill will became apparent.' In Paris no one – neither con-sumers nor police – any longer believed in the *maximum*. Because the black market was plentifully supplied, the idea – echoed by Babeuf and the Electoral Club – took hold among the masses that price control equalled scarcity and that free trade would bring back abundance. It was generally supposed 'that prices would rise but that

[3] Quoted by G. Bourgin, 'Régie ou Entreprise' in *Revue d'histoire économique et sociale* (1912). Many other writings expressed the same sentiment.

then they would fall as a result of competition' (police report, 7 October 1794). This autumn illusion was to be shattered in the winter. But the *maximum* had in effect already been abandoned when the Convention decided to put a formal end to it on 4 Nivôse Year III (24 December 1794). Freedom to buy, sell and transport grain was restored; once current requisitions had been delivered, only purchases were to take place. The Thermidoreans had taken a gamble, yet to be won, in both the monetary and the economic sphere.

Currency, prices, food supplies and scarcity

The collapse of the *assignat*★ was the most noticeable result of the return to free trade. Paper currency fell from 31% of its face value in August 1794 to 24% in November, 17% in February and 8% at the beginning of April. The price-rise encouraged the peasantry to slow down sales in the hope of increasing profits. This price-rise, and the accompanying currency depreciation, was accentuated by speculation in a whole variety of goods such as grain, cloth, candles and ice. Confronted with the price explosion – in Paris prices doubled during Nivôse – the government was again forced to resort to printing money, since it was unable to raise sufficient funds through taxation. The land tax for 1794 was not fixed until the end of the year. Tax revenues came in slowly and were paid in depreciated *assignats*. But this continuous note issue, raising the circulation from 7·6 thousand million *livres* in August 1794 to 11·4 thousand million in May 1795, dangerously undermined the value of the currency. The flight from the *assignat* sometimes developed into a reluctance to accept *assignats* at all, especially in the frontier *départements*. The crisis of confidence was so severe that many expected, even prepared for, demonetisation. The poorer classes were the most certain losers in this situation, because although the level of currency depreciation outstripped the note increase, the rise in the prices of essential items considerably exceeded the rate of currency depreciation: taking 1790 as the base, the price index of foodstuffs stood at 819 in April 1795 and the *assignat* at 581.

The ending of controls, the effects of speculation and the debasement of the paper currency are not in themselves enough to explain the dramatic rise in food prices during the winter of 1794–5. The decisive

---

★ Originally bonds issued upon the security of confiscated Church lands; by this period they had become simply a form of paper money. [Trans.]

factor, as always in pre-modern economies, was a crisis in the supply of food. By autumn it was clear that the harvest of Year II was rather poor, especially in the Paris basin where there were usually saleable surpluses within reach of urban markets. The devastated north was experiencing obvious difficulties, but it was worrying to note that the harvest of, for example, the Bayeux region was down by a third compared with 1793. More serious, in certain areas (around Cambrai, Semur, Auxerre, Avranches, etc.) people were reduced to consuming seed. Certainly climatic conditions had been unfavourable: hail in the spring, rain in the summer. But other factors had played a part, among them the *levée en masse*,★ which deprived agriculture of the manpower on which it was still largely dependent. A shortage of men meant less ploughing and tilling, delays in carrying out agricultural works and an extension of fallow land. The requisitions, although they had fed the armies and saved the large towns from famine, had also undoubtedly discontented the peasant sellers. The hiding of grain was their classic counter-attack, probably accompanied by a cut-back in sowing and a reduction in livestock. Finally, in the short term, two elements contributed to transform a shortage into a near-famine. Peasants who were able to wait were careful not to sell until the price reached its peak in the spring. And the terrible winter of 1794–5 considerably hampered the circulation of goods even in the Midi: rivers were iced over and roads impassable. By November it was clear that the elements of a grain crisis existed throughout France.

In such conditions the essential concern of the central and local authorities was to ensure at all costs a basic survival ration for the most volatile, if not the poorest, section of the population – the inhabitants of the towns. There were two ways of achieving this: importation and regulation. Through the agency of merchants and bankers who had retained credits abroad, the Committee of Public Safety embarked on the purchase in Hamburg of grain from the Baltic, and in Genoa of grain from the Maghreb and Thrace. But there was no hope of receiving the bulk of deliveries before the spring. In spite of the blockade the first convoys reached the coasts of Normandy and Provence in January; but they were unable to unload because of ice in the Seine estuary, as well as in the port of Marseilles and in the Rhône as far upstream as Avignon. The municipalities of some large towns also resorted to the importation of grain. The grain from Genoa enabled the population

---

★ The mobilisation of the country's full human and material resources. [Trans.]

of Grenoble to survive and contributed slightly to the provision of supplies to Lyons.[4] But this solution was too problematic and too expensive. So the authorities generally reverted to measures of control. Peasants in the Nord and the region of Le Havre were obliged to put their harvests on the market. Around Bayeux and Lille soldiers were billeted on the recalcitrant peasants. Montargis and Pithiviers resumed requisitioning in December 1794; most of the towns in the Paris region adopted an identical policy, but they suffered because they could be outbid by the agents of the supply commission who used their pre-emptive rights to the profit of the army and the capital. The Economic Terror seemed to have made its return: grain prices were fixed in Cahors; peasants were assaulted and arrested near Dieppe; in the Dijon region the authorities acted ruthlessly against hoarders. But this policy of force often came too late – since the grain had already been sold before the winter to rich individuals – or it merely exacerbated the peasants' resistance.

The crisis was partially an artificial one, since at the same time the free markets in Paris, Grenoble, Cahors, etc., were flooded by food products – but at enormous prices. A pound of meat in Paris cost 40 *sous* on 20 January, 1795 and 7 *livres* 10 *sous* on 1 April. The urban populations depended, then, entirely on the goodwill and available means of the municipality. The worst could certainly be avoided by resorting to rationing, but the situation deteriorated at the end of the winter. In Paris, which was in a favoured position, the daily bread ration – the only food in time of scarcity – fell from one and a half pounds to one pound per person between February and March 1795. In some sections not all the ration cards were honoured. Provincial towns could not even attain this level. In the same period, the poor in Le Havre could not count on more than half a pound of bread five days a week, and in Bordeaux on half a pound every other day; otherwise they had to survive on rice. In Lyons the ration was one pound of bread every three days in ten. To meet their obligations, the authorities could not raise prices above a certain threshold. Distributing these rations at a loss (in Bayeux rice was sold at a third of its cost), they inevitably ran into debt and tended to rely on merchants and contractors.

Severe hardship was experienced by most of the population during the terrible winter of 1794–5, the coldest since 1709. Olive trees were

---

[4] And also to Toulouse. Cf. M. Schlumberger, 'La réaction thermidorienne à Toulouse', *A.h.R.f.* (April–June 1971), pp. 265–83.

killed by frost in the Midi; wolves prowled at the gates of Paris. For lack of fuel, which was too scarce and too dear, many householders had neither heat nor, as in Lyons, the means to cook the rice which they were offered. Furthermore, they often ate unhealthy food: unripe corn, mouldy vegetables, rotten fish and meat. Deficiency diseases and epidemics soon added to the misery of famine. The mortality rate increased; in Rouen it seems to have doubled. But death, like hunger, affected the poorest above all. The better-off sections of the urban population and the substantial husbandmen and tenant farmers did not feel the effects of the crisis; most of them even benefited from it. Rarely had the division between 'the fat and the thin', between, as the inhabitants of Marseilles put it, the 'two tribes', been more manifest; rarely, also, had the bitterness of social antagonism aroused such hatreds on one side and such fear on the other. Without doubt the greatest sufferers were the landless and sometimes unemployed day labourers of Normandy or Picardy who could hope for no aid from the towns. In this roster of misery the inhabitants of the small and medium-size towns north of the Loire also underwent great hardship. They provided the bulk of those bands of beggars and criminals which plagued the roads from the Somme to the Beauce. They flocked to Paris, congested the hostels and fell into prostitution. In the end, apart from being in the army, the safest place to be was Paris or certain other exceptional regions (perhaps Aquitaine, because of its maize; the Mediterranean coast, thanks to international trade; and the Auvergne, where chestnuts occupied the position held elsewhere by cereals). It was, however, in Paris that social discontent was to crystallise into political protest and lead to the popular uprisings of the spring.

THE CRUSHING OF THE POPULAR MOVEMENT

Discontent

The least threatened were without doubt the most threatening. Below a certain threshold of physiological deprivation, protest often fades into resignation, or breaks out into acts of individual revolt. Collective action occurs rather on the verge of famine when energies are galvanised by the first shortages and when the necessity for mere survival has not yet extinguished all other preoccupations. Moreover, the Parisian *sans-culottes* had, during five years of struggle, acquired unparalleled political experience and awareness, while the centralisation of power in Paris transformed any subsistence crisis into a crisis for the regime. People were dying of hunger in Amiens and Gonesse, but the faubourgs of Paris held the main attention of the authorities.

Discontent increased along with the shortages. 'Opinion is becoming more and more agitated about the high cost of food' noted a police report of 7 February. In the endless queues for bread, meat and coal, individual resentments grew into a unanimous murmur of discontent against the 'aristocracy of dealers' and, already, against the powerless or conniving Convention. Could the Neo-Hébertists harness this anger? It seemed not. Babeuf was arrested on 7 February for calling for a 'peaceful insurrection'. Several clubs had to close. Moderates took control of the last patriotic sections. But the agitation continued in secret. The irreconcilable gathered together in clandestine meetings. On 12 March a poster headed 'People, awake, it is time' appeared on many walls, causing small crowds to gather. This launched a campaign of posters financed by subscription. Thus the popular movement was reborn out of a coalescence of the anger of the masses and the dynamism of the activists.

In the Convention, debate was centred on two issues: the fate of Barère, Collot, Billaud-Varenne and Vadier, and the implementation of the constitution of 1793. Desirous of finishing once and for all with the 'Four', the majority refused on 29 March to refer their trial to the future Legislative Body. As for the constitution, a commission set up in December had decided that it should be accompanied by organic laws. On 30 March a new committee was set up on this basis. In fact many Thermidoreans believed the text of the constitution of Year II to be dangerous and beyond reform. But in these highly explosive conditions caution impelled them (as La Révellière-Lépeaux (henceforth La Révellière) would later admit) to proclaim the opposite, at the same time as preparing a document more in line with their philosophy. The immediate priority was, however, to preserve order. There were constant scuffles between the fops and the *sans-culottes*. More serious was the threat uttered by the delegates of the Faubourgs Saint-Marceau and Saint-Jacques to the Convention on 17 March: 'We are on the verge of regretting all the sacrifices that we have made for the Revolution.' On 21 March it was the turn of the orators from the Faubourg Saint-Antoine. On the same day Sieyès had a police law passed which laid down the death penalty for those who used seditious words against the Convention. Rifles were distributed to the 'good citizens', the faithful nucleus of the National Guard. The trial of strength was approaching.

Germinal

An illegal meeting was held at the Gravilliers on 7 Germinal (27 March). On 10 Germinal all the sections called their general assemblies. The political geography of Paris emerged clearly from these events. While in the sections of the centre and west formal addresses called for the punishment of the 'Four' and passed over the food shortages, the sections of the east and the faubourgs demanded measures to deal with the grain crisis, the implementation of the constitution of 1793, the reopening of the popular societies and the release of imprisoned patriots. On the next day members of the section of the Quinze-Vingts presented the deputies with a petition on these lines. It ended with the following words: 'We are on our feet to uphold the Republic and liberty.' This was to say, in the already defined language of revolutionary uprisings, that the people were preparing directly to exercise their sovereignty.

On the morning of 12 Germinal (1 April) crowds gathered on the Ile de la Cité. The former commander-in-chief of the section, Van Heck, led a column of demonstrators (soon swelled by a crowd of men and women from other sections) in the direction of the Convention. Among the most determined were the numerous building workers living outside Paris whom a recent decree had excluded from receiving distributions of bread. At around 1 p.m. this crowd pushed aside the fops and palace guards and burst into the chamber where the Convention met. Amidst the uproar, Van Heck and the other spokesmen of the sections outlined the people's grievances to the assembly. The Committee of General Security, which had no restrictions placed on it, ordered the reliable battalions of the National Guard to assemble outside the national palace and kept the others in their respective sections. In spite of the slowness and disorganisation of this mobilisation, the government had won the contest by 6 p.m. At this moment the demonstrators, lacking arms and leaders, were surrounded by the battalions loyal to the Convention and were forced to withdraw. This *journée*,* which had been a mass demonstration rather than a riot, gave the right a pretext for revenge. Paris was put in a state of siege

---

* *Journée*: an important day, especially one on which events of revolutionary significance took place. [Trans.]

and Pichegru named commander-in-chief, with Barras and Merlin de Thionville to assist him. The Montagnards, although they had in fact requested the *sans-culottes* to leave the chambers, were accused of collusion. In spite of renewed incidents, Barère, Collot and Billaud-Varenne were deported from Paris on 13 Germinal. Vadier was also condemned, but could not be found. Six other 'Crêtois', including Duhem and Châles, were sent to Ham fortress. Their departure provoked a skirmish after a rumour that the Convention wanted to abandon Paris. Finally, on the night of 13 Germinal, Pichegru easily dispersed some thousand men gathered in the Quatre-Vingts section. On 21 Germinal the Convention decided to disarm the 'Terrorists'. By this new law of suspects, thousands of revolutionary activists (1,600 in Paris) were transformed into outcasts. For in republican ideology the carrying of arms could not be separated from the status of a free man. To be disarmed meant to be barred from public office, and entailed the loss of civic rights and sometimes of employment.

Other hunger riots broke out in the Paris region during the second *décade*⋆ of Germinal. This synchronisation has raised the suspicion of a plot. News, if not actual orders, from Paris probably acted as a catalyst. But more important was the fact that the capital, monopolising all the available grain in the areas which it traditionally supplied (the Seine-et-Marne, the Oise, the Eure, the Somme), was starving the towns situated on its entry roads. The nearer a town was to Paris and the smaller it was – thus lacking its own resources – the more serious its situation became. There was a corresponding disparity between the towns and their neighbouring rural communes. Thus Saint-Germain suffered more than Amiens, Sotteville than Rouen, Ingouville than Le Havre. At the end of a very harsh winter, the rise in prices, the decrease in rations (5 ounces of bread four days a week in Le Havre) and the proximity of the deadline for April rents maintained a mood of effervescence among the working class of these cities. The movement took on a different form depending on the line up of local forces and the activities of agitators. In Rouen, from 13 to 15 Germinal, and at Amiens on 14 Germinal, the rioters demanded 'bread and a king'. On the other hand, the members of the sections of Saint-Germain rose up on 17 Germinal to demand cheap food and the constitution of 1793. Ultimately both attitudes attributed a similar importance to politics and shared the same desire to find a replacement for Thermidorean power.

In Floréal the food shortage of Germinal turned into famine. The

⋆ *Décade*: the ten-day revolutionary calendar. *Décadi*: the tenth day of a *décade*. [Trans.]

Parisian authorities had no further advances of grain. The ration fluctuated between quarter and half a pound. Malnutrition and unemployment pushed the poor towards acts of desperation. *Le Messager du soir* of 27 Floréal, for example, noted that 'the number of suicides is truly frightening in this unhappy commune'. Others turned to looting. As in Rouen or Amiens, a current of popular royalism developed, although it remained very much in a minority. There were others who openly regretted the passing of 'the reign of Robespierre'. But for most people it was the constitution of 1793 – seen as literally a liberating utopia – which represented the solution to all evils.

Prairial

A new explosion was on the horizon. The Committees wanted to reinforce the National Guard and the Legion of Police by regular troops. This presence of regular armed forces in the capital broke with revolutionary tradition. It was short-lived because the *sans-culottes* began to fraternise with the detachments of troops; soldiers and gendarmes had to be quartered at the gates, away from such infectious examples.

Insurrection was being openly prepared. On 30 Floréal a pamphlet, *L'Insurrection du Peuple pour obtenir du pain et conquérir ses droits*, called for an uprising and established as its slogan 'bread and the constitution of 1793'. At 5 a.m. on 1 Prairial (20 May 1795) the tocsin sounded in the Faubourgs Saint-Antoine and Marceau. Workers, followed by bands of women, streamed down the streets calling upon the members of the sections to take up arms. While the men attempted to win over the constituted authorities, the commanders and the official committees, the women headed off towards the Convention. At around 1 p.m. the crowd occupied the public galleries and penetrated into the chamber. They were cleared out with whips. Two hours later the battalions from the Faubourg Saint-Antoine entered the Carrousel. This was the decisive struggle. In the confusion the deputy Féraud, killed by a pistol shot, had his head cut off. It was carried around on a pike before being presented to the president of the session, Boissy d'Anglas. After an hour of uproar a few rebels managed to read out *L'Insurrection du Peuple*. Chaos developed,but none of the ringleaders thought of implementing the key item of this programme: the overthrow of the government.

The Committees had feared that their offices would be occupied and a central revolutionary committee set up. They used the respite which the rioters had left them – though not without difficulty – to call in both the troops concentrated in the Sablons and the battalions from the western sections. Although these elements were in principle loyal, they could not be counted on absolutely in this fast-changing situation. The session of the Convention resumed at 9 p.m. The new president, Vernier, allowed the session to go ahead in order both to win time and to compromise the Montagnard deputies. The latter had indeed been responsible for the passage of decrees favourable to the rebels: Duroy and Romme obtained the release of the patriots; Soubrany secured approval for the abolition of the Committee of General Security, to be replaced by a provisional commission dominated by his friends. The trap had worked, and it only remained for the government to take the offensive at 11.30 p.m. Two armed columns entered the chamber and cleared out the rioters. As after the *journées* of Germinal, the liberated Convention rounded on the Crêtois. Warrants were issued for the arrest of fourteen of them. The people had lost the first round because they had not struck at the true centre of power. They then indecisively repeated the mistakes of the previous day. The Convention was protected by some regular troops and by battalions of the National Guard. The Thermidoreans ran an enormous risk when the battalions of the Faubourg Saint-Antoine, who had trained their cannons on the Convention, persuaded the gunners of several moderate sections to defect. The Committees had no option but to counter-attack by fraternising as well. A deputation went to address the *sans-culottes*, promising them speedy measures against the famine. The tactic was successful: when night fell the battalions returned to the sections. Now the government regained the initiative. On 3 Prairial it assembled troops to put down the Faubourg Saint-Antoine. This armed force consisted of several thousand troopers, chasseurs and dragoons, and National Guardsmen selected from among those 'who had a fortune to preserve' – 20,000 men in all. On the morning of 4 Prairial a column of 'young men' entered the faubourg, but surrounded by barricades, it had to negotiate a retreat. At this moment the inhabitants of the faubourg seemed inclined to resist; the Committees' summons produced no effect. But when the troops moved against the barricades at 4 p.m., the rebels allowed themselves to be disarmed. The surrender of the faubourg was complete by 9 p.m.

Uncertainty about how to react and hesitancy in action had doomed the popular movement to throw away its last chance in battle. During Prairial preparation had certainly been meticulous. Drawing the lessons of Germinal, the democrats had organised the uprising according to the plan reproduced in *L'Insurrection du Peuple*. But the lack of revolutionary leadership on the very field of conflict had partly rendered these efforts fruitless.

The repression

The military commission set up on 4 Prairial pronounced thirty-six death sentences. The murderers of Féraud, the gendarmes who had gone over to the rioters, and the deputies Romme, Duquesnoy, Goujon, Duroy, Soubrany and Bourbotte were all lumped together in the same category. The condemned deputies, wishing both to demonstrate their inviolable liberty and to challenge their accusers, attempted to kill themselves before being conducted to the scaffold. The first three were successful. Soubrany died as he reached the guillotine; the others were executed alive. This 'heroic sacrifice' put the 'martyrs of Prairial' in the pantheon of the popular movement. But it highlighted the insoluble contradiction of their position. As the prisoners of two irreconcilable obligations – to rally unconditionally to the uprising or to respect totally bourgeois legality and bourgeois solidarity – these would-be revolutionary leaders had lived in isolation since Floréal. On 1 Prairial the most lucid of them understood the trap and consciously walked into it. By their 'devotion to duty' and their stoic end they were able to ease their consciences, but not to ward off inevitable defeat.

The repression took on the appearance of a massive settling of old scores. All those who had played an active role in Year III – members of the Committees and representatives on mission – were affected, in some way. Few had the luck of Carnot, who was belatedly proclaimed 'the organiser of victory'. In the sections, moderates were seized by the same frenzy to carry out purges. In Paris, 1,200 Jacobins and *sans-culottes* were imprisoned; in the provinces, tens of thousands. The Committee of General Security, faithful to its policy of moderation, saved a certain number of them. The 'Great Fear' which gripped the propertied classes pushed them beyond these reprisals into consolidating their advantage. On 16 June the National Guard was transformed into an instrument of class from which workers were almost excluded. The reporter of the law explained this quite openly: 'There must be arms', he had declared, 'but they must be placed in pure hands.' The popular movement was, then, decimated and disarmed. It remained to discredit it, that is to undermine the values on which it was founded. Cobb has shown how below the surface Thermidorean vocabulary was charged with social hatred. Poverty became a stigma, the hungry became 'starvelings' ('*faméliques*'), the citizenesses of the people 'bitches' good only for breeding. Caricatures, in emphasising the unkemptness of the people, made the same point. Vocabulary, the reflection of the new order, was affected by a corresponding social inflation: everyone attempted to rise above their present status and gain admission to 'respectable' ranks. In this way it was believed that the people were being kept in their place. Probably the Thermidoreans' view of this mass of workers, shopkeepers and artisans was much the same as that expressed by a national commissioner about the former Dieppe Committee: 'Oppression and tyranny had dragged them out of their social insignificance. Justice and humanity have plunged them back there for ever.' 4 Prairial Year II is one of the crucial dates of the revolutionary period. The people had ceased to be a political force, participants in history. They were now no more than victims or spectators.

ROYALISTS WITHIN, ENEMIES WITHOUT

The rebels in difficulties

In the west, the process of pacification was at a standstill. The Catholic army had been destroyed at Savenay (23 December 1793), but the excesses of the young recruits had helped to give the uprising a second wind. Fleeing the 'infernal columns', the peasants rejoined the troops of Charette, Sapinaud and Stofflet. To the north of the Loire, above all in Morbihan, the Chouan bands, recently swelled by survivors from the Vendée, engaged in guerrilla warfare. Robbers and republican deserters carried out exactions on their own account, which, given the precariousness of the distinction between true and false Chouans, did not help the cause of the Royalists among an already unenthusiastic population. But Joseph Puisaye, a former federalist leader, had succeeded in uniting nominally all the Breton fighters. He had left for London at the end of August 1794 to persuade Pitt to help him; the main objective was to organise a landing of *émigrés*, supported by the Chouans.

Even before Thermidor, Carrier had been recalled, Turreau's columns dissolved, and measures taken to quarter the soldiers and forbid looting. The new policy, demanded by the urban bourgeoisie, developed this trend by gambling on appeasement. The representatives on mission (Bollet, Boursault, Ruelle) and the new military leaders (Hoche in Brittany, Canclaux in the Vendée) played the card of clemency. On 24 September and 13 October an amnesty was offered to the rebels of Ille-et-Vilaine and the Morbihan, who were to give themselves up within ten days. The decree of 2 December extended this deadline to a month. The Convention in addition ordered its representatives to negotiate with the royalist leaders.

At the same time the Republicans resumed a more active military policy. Canclaux isolated Stofflet and Charette; Hoche organised an effective anti-guerrilla campaign. Was it now possible to hope that the civil war could be brought to a conclusion? The Treaty of La Jaunaye (17 February 1795) provided for an amnesty, freedom of worship (already re-established in Morbihan) even for non-jurors, exemption from military service outside the Vendée and assistance for the reconstruction of devastated villages. Charette and Sapinaud signed this treaty, while Stofflet, who had carved out a sort of principality for himself in Anjou, persisted in refusing. But having been quickly tracked down, he had to accept a similar agreement.

If the Vendéans had been obliged to win time in order to avoid the dispersal of their troops, the Chouans were in no position to make a different choice. On 3 January Puisaye's deputy, Formartin, secured a suspension of hostilities which saved the Bretons from complete destruction. By the treaty of La Prévalaye (20 April) they obtained conditions identical to those of the Vendéans. Certainly this lifeline had provisionally saved the Chouans. But the concessions made by the Republicans fitted into a new objective: to exploit the demoralisation and lassitude of their opponents, and to secure the neutrality, if not the support, of the peasants by handing them back their priests. Besides, as Maurice Hutt has pointed out, liberalism did not preclude vigilance. The surveillance of the Breton coasts prevented the unloading of large quantities of arms. The truces were not observed for very long, but when Frotté and Cadoudal in Brittany, and Charette in the Vendée, took up arms again, the Republicans were not, whatever has been said, in too bad a position.

The Church reborn

The freedom of worship offered to the rebels of the west in the autumn of 1794 was not immediately acquired by other Catholics. The most prominent Thermidoreans favoured an anti-religious policy. In fact churches continued to be closed after Thermidor (in the Doubs, the Haute-Saône and the Côte-d'Or); returning priests were sent to the scaffold; and in many *départements* Republicans pushed priests and pastors into resignation. On 18 September 1794, in abolishing the budget of the official Church, the Convention was, without announcing it, repealing the civil constitution. But this economy showed no sign of portending a change in attitude. Grégoire attempted a breakthrough. 'Freedom of worship exists in Turkey', he declared to the Convention on 21 December, 'but it does not exist in France.' The majority, scandalised by such audacity, set aside Grégoire's motion. In the end the Bishop of the Loir-et-Cher was successful. How could loyalist Catholics be denied what had been granted to rebels? On 3 Ventôse (21 February 1795) a decree restored freedom of worship, provided that the ceremonies took place in a private place without any external manifestation. The Republic declared its neutrality as long as the law was respected. Boissy d'Anglas summed up the spirit of the decree thus: 'Keep a watch over what you cannot prevent, regularise what you cannot forbid.'

During the winter of 1794–5 Grégoire and some constitutional bishops had formed a council (the Evêques Réunis) with the aim of reconstructing the Church. An encyclical of 15 March reaffirmed Gallican doctrine and concerned itself with assisting the bishops in their tasks and with finding them replacements through the setting up of a college for *curés*, or a 'presbytery', in each diocese. To propagate their views the Evêques Réunis made use of the *Annales de la religion*. But the real beneficiaries of the Ventôse decree were the non-juring priests. In Paris at Easter large crowds flocked to the chapels where they officiated; there was a movement in favour of retraction among the clergy who had sworn. In the provinces, especially the countryside and the frontier *départements*, the non-juring priests came out of hiding to reorganise 'Roman' parishes. The Convention, wanting both to take account of this popular upsurge and to stem the flow of reconversions, decided to authorise religious services in non-alienated churches and to oblige ministers of religion to swear an act of submission to the laws. Emery, the Superior of Saint-Sulpice, held that this oath was merely an act of formal obedience to a *de facto* government. The majority of non-juring Parisian priests rallied to this point of view. But in the provinces the *émigré* bishops made their clergy refuse to swear. The Bishop of Bayeux, who had taken refuge in Jersey, went as far as to insist that children from 'swearing' parishes be rebaptised. And the local authorities did not try – or failed – to impose the application of the oath. The rebirth of religious feeling seemed irresistible.

The White Terror

The return of the non-juring priests ('they swarm like the locusts of Egypt in every *département*', protested *Les Annales de la religion*) and the influx of *émigrés* profiting from the new circumstances (for example, the law of 20 Nivôse Year III authorising *émigré* workers to return) heralded days of vengeance. Although the harassment of Jacobins increased throughout France, it was only in the south-east that it took on the character of a 'White Terror'. In this area the excesses of the repression during Year II had drawn together many sections of the population – not necessarily the wealthiest – in hostility to the local Terrorists. The proximity of the frontier made infiltration easy. The moderates, indeed even Royalists, occupied a large part of the political vacuum created by the collapse of the structures of Jacobin power and by the weakness of the new authorities, who lacked both means and allies. The first massacre of prisoners took place in Lyons on 2 February 1795. Three weeks later Jacobin prisoners at Nîmes suffered a similar fate. Two circumstances helped to make this phenomenon more wide-spread. First, the law of 21 Germinal, by disarming the Terrorists and confining them to their homes, singled them out for attack. Second, and above all, the new *journées* raised fears of an upsurge of Jacobinism. When at the end of Floréal the *sans-culottes* of Toulon rose up for the second time and marched on Marseilles to release the prisoners, the moderates were gripped by fear, and a collective psychosis comparable to that of 'September' pushed the most determined of them into carrying out a sort of preventive counter-revolution. Already on 4 May thousands of demonstrators in Lyons had converged on the prison of Roanne, massacred the prisoners and attacked two other jails. The representative, Boisset, had refused to give the order to open fire. Other killings occurred in Aix, in the vicinity of Orange and in Tarascon. The most serious of these incidents was the massacre on 5 June of some hundred Jacobins locked up in the Fort Saint-Jean at Marseilles. The representative Cadroy did all he could to delay the intervention of the National Guard. Such outright attacks were spectacular, but every day and night Jacobins were assaulted, wounded, even thrown into the Rhône. The Company of Jesus in Lyons and the Companies of the Sun in Provence, which enrolled the demonstrators and organised the Counter-Terror, recruited their henchmen from among deserters and former federalists. Thanks to lists of denunciations, they carried out a selective repression against the former agents of the administration and against the correspondents of the popular societies, against, in short, all the Montagnard personnel. These bands seem to have been fairly centralised, with Lyons forming the main centre of co-ordination. From the Haute-Loire to the Bouches-du-Rhône the killers tracked down the Republicans, who had often been marked out as victims by a justice of the peace or an innkeeper. This unleashing of frenzy against the Terrorists was mixed up with private hatreds; but religious motives predominated. A prosperous peasant from the Lozère might be victimised both as a Protestant and as a purchaser of national property. The Jacobins of the south-east who had not fled were swept aside in this 'pogrom'. In the summer the Thermidoreans,who until then had stood passively by, became worried by this resurgence of royalism and federalism. On 24 June the people of Lyons were ordered to give up their arms, to expel foreigners and to hand over *émigrés* and murderers. Kellerman was instructed to march 12,000 men on the town. The threat was sufficient: the population of Lyons submitted.

Quiberon

The death of Louis XVII, announced on 8 June, dismayed the moderate monarchists who had hoped for a long regency of a Feuillant* type. On 4 June the Comte de Provence, now Louis XVIII, announced from Verona his intention to restore absolute monarchy 'without the abuses'. Although his tone was moderate, his intransigence barred the way to a speedy solution. Mallet du Pan put this to the Pretender forcefully: 'the great majority of Frenchmen will never surrender unconditionally to the old authority and its depositaries' (letter of 3 July). There was a clear difference between the émigré Royalists, whose predominant sympathies were absolutist, and those within France, where the moderates, partisans of a conditional restoration, seemed to be very distinctly in a majority – except in the west and in the Parisian network of the Comte d'Antraigues.

Powerful but divided, the Royalists also had to take account of the attitude of the great powers, especially that of England. The cabinet

---

* The Feuillants were constitutional monarchists who wanted to re-establish the monarchy through a conservative revision of the constitution. [Trans.]

in London was kept informed by, among others, Wickham, who had been sent to Basle by the Foreign Secretary, Lord Grenville. Besides providing information, Wickham worked to increase the disturbances in the south-east and to spark off others in Franche-Comté. However, he came up against the anglophobia of most of the federalist leaders and his success on this score was disappointing.

But the trump card in the Royalists' 'Grand Design' of the spring of 1795 was a landing in Brittany, combined with the expected defection of Pichegru. From the beginning, however, the expedition was dogged by misunderstandings, disagreements and improvisation. It was misunderstanding – or weakness? – which had led Artois to promise to be present, a promise that he did not keep. There was disagreement between Puisaye and the Paris Agency: the former member of the Constituent Assembly being 'neither *un pur* nor an émigré', the absolutists would have preferred to support Charette. There were also political and strategic disagreements between Puisaye and Hervilly, who was also in command of the operation. Finally, there was improvisation in joining the *émigrés* with Republican prisoners recruited in England – of dubious loyalty since they had been forcibly enlisted – and in the poor establishment of contact with the forces within France, whose intervention was crucial. After the initial success of the landing at Quiberon (23 June 1795), Hervilly allowed himself to be trapped in the peninsula and was killed during a fateful attack. When Sombreuil's contingent joined the first wave of invaders, Hoche had had the time to gather his troops. On the night of 20 July the Republicans, taking advantage of a storm which drove the fleet away, surprised the defenders of the peninsula, routed them, and took about 9,000 prisoners. The law of 27 Brumaire Year III condemned to death every *émigré* who had returned to France armed. Hoche and his officers hesitated before such a step. Tallien carried the decision through: 754 prisoners were executed. The regime extracted considerable propaganda success from this victory. The absolutist Royalists had seen their hopes vanish on the 'inexpiable beach of Quiberon'.

The Dutch alliance

The victories of Year II had bestowed upon the Thermidoreans a favourable situation abroad. It was essential to consolidate it first militarily and then diplomatically. Carnot, who had remained a member of the Committee of Public Safety until 5 March 1795, ensured a continuity of military policy. The first task was to complete the liberation of French territory. The enemy still held Valenciennes, Le Quesnoy and Condé, which threatened the French rear. The French plan was that the Army of the North, under Pichegru, would strike the decisive blows and seize control of Holland by co-ordinating its activities with those of the Army of the Sambre and Meuse, commanded by Jourdan. Schérer's siege of the three fortresses was slow; Pichegru delayed, so that the Army of the North's offensive could not begin until the end of September. It reached Bois-le-Duc on 10 October and Nijmegen on 8 November. The winter promised to be very severe; the badly equipped troops suffered considerably. But Pichegru, previously hesitant, now wanted to exploit his success. Two reasons, one political and the other tactical, impelled him to act. The Dutch patriots of Paris, encouraged by François de Vinck, were agitating for a crusade and predicted the fall of William V. Carnot, who was kept informed by his brother-in-law Collignon, remained cautious. Most importantly, the canals and rivers were iced over. The invasion of the Netherlands was thus no longer an obstacle course and the Dutch lost their ultimate weapon – flooding.

The French crossed the Meuse on 27 December and the Waal during 8–10 January. On 17 January they reached Utrecht; on 20 January, Amsterdam. Elements of the Dutch fleet were trapped by the ice off Texel. On 23 January a few hundred cavalry, assisted by infantrymen and gunners, seized these vessels. This feat had a great effect on public opinion and helped to increase Pichegru's popularity. Zeeland and Groningen were conquered. By mid-February the French were at Ems. The Duke of York's British contingent managed to escape destruction, but the disastrous defeat of the Dutch army caused a change of regime. William V had fled. On 16 February the Estates-General proclaimed the abolition of the Stadtholderate and the sovereignty and independence of the Batavian people. They also sent emissaries to Paris, hoping that after their revolutionary action France would not impose an unequal treaty on them. But in vain. Reubell and Sieyès went to The Hague to dictate their terms as conquerors: the annexation of all the country south of the Meuse, an indemnity of 100 million florins – of which half was to be paid in ready money – and a defensive and offensive alliance between the two republics (16 May 1795).

An incomplete peace

Jourdan had not co-ordinated his action with Pichegru's. He attacked at the beginning of October. The Army of the Sambre and Meuse entered Cologne, and, on 4 November, Kléber accepted the surrender of Maastricht. In the plan of the campaign the Armies of the Moselle and of the Rhine, commanded by Moreau and Michaud respectively, took second place. The soldiers of the Army of the Moselle had the task of capturing Trèves and Luxemburg, which, thanks to its fortified site, was a formidable fortress. As for Michaud's troops, they found themselves held up outside Mainz without being able to prevent supplies reaching the fortress. The siege was very difficult. Thus at the end of December the Army of the Rhine took up its winter quarters.

It was when Warsaw was taken by Suvorov that Frederick-William II considered signing a treaty with France (October 1794). Involved in two wars, Prussia was in the process of being ousted from Poland, on the eve of the second partition, by the collusion between the Russians and the Austrians. This collusion became manifest in the Treaty of St Petersburg (8 January 1795), which determined the Prussians to devote their efforts to 'Ostpolitik'. Opinion in France was very divided on what demands Barthélemy should present to the Count of Goltz. It seems that a majority on the Committees inclined towards ensuring a safe frontier demarcated by the divide of the Meuse. To ask for more risked restarting the war. This view was shared by moderates like Barthélemy, and by disguised Royalists, out of hatred of revolutionary war. But there were those who demanded a Rhine frontier. Some, like Sieyès, saw this as a security; others, like Reubell, had their eyes on Alsace; many were motivated by patriotic fervour. Carnot himself was won over for a moment: 'It will not be said', he declared on 14 November, 'that you have allowed the enemy to keep a foot on our territory, for we now consider as such all that lies on this side of the Rhine.' In a hurry to conclude an agreement, the Prussian negotiator, Hardenberg, signed at Basle a treaty by which Prussia recognised the French occupation of the left bank of the Rhine, subject to compensation in a general peace treaty. A second agreement provided for the neutralisation of certain states of northern Germany (5 April and 17 May 1795).

Carnot's plans for the fronts of the Midi left the Army of the Alps with only a secondary role. It settled down on the Teste Pass. The winter anyway made any operation almost impossible. On the other hand, the two armies directed against Spain showed evidence of greater dynamism. That of the western Pyrenees, commanded by Moncey, seized San Sebastian on 4 August 1794 and then occupied Navarre. In the winter it was ravaged by typhus. Its advance was from now on to be much slower, not reaching Bilbao till 19 July. In the eastern Pyrenees a vigorous offensive was conducted. Carnot hoped to create a Catalan Republic which would have let France benefit from its brilliant economic expansion. Diplomatic contacts at the end of September dragged on inconclusively. Dugommier, killed before the capture of Figueras, was replaced by Pérignon. After the fall of Rosas (3 February) the hostilities continued without decisive results. The French had to deal with an uprising in Cerdagne. The fall of Bilbao decided the Spaniards to negotiate. On 22 September 1795 Barthélemy and Yriarte signed a peace treaty at Basle which ceded to France the Spanish port of Santo Domingo. This transfer was to remain purely theoretical: hostilities with the English continued on the island, and General Toussaint-Louverture, master of the rest of Santo Domingo, retained his autonomy in spite of the French alliance. Guadeloupe had been liberated in October 1794 by Victor Hughes. Guyana, Senegal, the Mascarene Islands and La Réunion remained French, but English naval supremacy prevented contact with the mother country.

Austria, fortified by English financial support, refused any peace which would have legitimised the occupation of Belgium. The capitulation of Luxemburg on 7 June scarcely altered the situation. In fact, by the summer of 1795 the French army was suffering from considerable lassitude. Growing difficulties of supply, caused largely by the disorganisation of the agencies, encouraged desertion at a time when many soldier-citizens felt relieved of any obligation to serve, now that French territory had been liberated. During the summer desertion, which had until then been endemic, became a torrent. The Army of the Alps alone lost three thousand men during Messidor.

In addition, the ambitious and pleasure-loving Pichegru, the new commander of the Army of the Rhine and Moselle, disappointed by a Republic which had so little concern for its loyal upholders, seemed to Wickham and Condé to be easy prey. Contacts made in mid-August 1795 created a certain complicity, if not actually treason. Both sides showed caution. But the Committee of Public Safety began to be irritated by the slowness of the military operations. Pichegru's delay had let Wurmser regain the initiative and lift the blockade of Mainz, The Convention, as it reached its final days, had not succeeded in ridding itself of the war.

THE NEW INSTITUTIONS

The middle way

The 'Code of Anarchy' – as the constitution of 1793 was called by its conservative opponents – had been definitely discredited for the Thermidoreans by the *journées* of Prairial. The Commission of Eleven (Daunou, Lanjuinais, Boissy d'Anglas, Thibaudeau and La Révellière were its most notable members) applied itself to drafting a text which would reflect the new balance of forces, to finding, in Thibaudeau's phrase, 'a middle way between royalty and demagogy'. Boissy d'Anglas presented the commission's report on 5 Messidor (23 June), and the text of the constitution was definitively passed on 22 August. It was preceded by a 'Declaration of Rights and Duties', duties forming the necessary antidote to rights. If the constitution of 1793 could be defined by its democratic and egalitarian aspirations, the new institutions rested upon two principles – property and liberty. In this the Thermidoreans went back to the constitution of 1791, back, that is, to the dominant ideology of the century. Equality was certainly reaffirmed, but contained within the limits of civil equality. Thus numerous rights – the right to work, to relief, to education – which the advanced revolutionaries had succeeded in imposing in the particular circumstances of Year II, were omitted from the new constitution. As for the right of insurrection, it seemed safest not to mention it. In short, the Convention wanted to give the bourgeoisie of wealth and merit a chance by simultaneously rejecting both the privileges of the old orders and social levelling. The system rested, then, on the France of the property owners.

Every man over twenty-one years old, born in France, resident there for a year and paying direct tax, was held to be a citizen. At the primary stage of voting, selection by money already formed a contrast with the system of universal suffrage envisaged in 1793. By this means the constitution went back to the distinction between active and passive citizens, obeying a principle clearly stated in the *Gazette de France* (24 September 1795): 'In all ordered associations, society is composed solely of property owners. The others are only proletarians, who, ranked in the class of supernumerary citizens, wait for the moment which allows them to acquire property.' But the electoral base was wide, wider than that of the constitution of 1791. The barrier, the real electoral qualification, occurred further ahead. Only citizens over twenty-five years old, disposing of an income equivalent to two hundred days' work, were eligible to be electors. This electoral body, which held the real power, only included 30,000 people, that is, half as many as in 1791.

The principle of liberty as applied to the institutions was supposed to protect the Republic from two dangers: the omnipotence of an assembly and dictatorship. Returning to an idea rejected by the members of the Constituent Assembly, the drafters of the constitution proposed to set up two assemblies. The Council of Five Hundred, whose members had to be at least thirty years old, had the initiative in proposing laws. The Council of the Elders, made up of 250 deputies over the age of forty, approved or rejected the texts proposed by the Five Hundred. Whether or not, as Thibaudeau remarked, this provided a mouthpiece for both the imagination and the reason of the nation, the members of the Convention believed that they were safeguarding the regime against sudden fluctuations. Executive power was to be shared between five Directors chosen by the Elders from a list, prepared by the Five Hundred, of ten candidates for each post. A fifth of the Directory was renewable very year. The outgoing members remained ineligible for five years. These precautions were intended to limit the risks of encroachment by the executive. There were in addition numerous provisions to protect the legislature against a repetition of the events of 31 May. The most significant of these forbade the Directory, without the authorisation of the Councils, to send troops within sixty kilometres of the site of their debates. These safeguards seemed inadequate to Sieyès, a great drafter of projects, who withheld his approval. But the constitution won the general support of all those who wished, for various reasons, to ensure the collective power of the bourgeoisie. This meant that even the monarchists, so influential in the capital, saw no reason to reject the text. They hoped that the existence of the five Directors would provide a stepping-stone towards the restoration of constitutional monarchy. All, then, was to be staked on the elections. Everything indicated that it was the Royalists who would obtain a majority in the Legislative Body. This threat forced the Thermidoreans to make the first move. In the decrees of 22 and 30 August they stipulated that two-thirds of the newly elected members had to come from among the members of the Convention. If this proportion should not be attained, the new representatives would fill their ranks by co-option. This effectively barred the way to the monarchists. The ratification of these texts in September sparked off severe struggles in the sections, mainly in Paris. On 23 September the results were announced: the constitution was accepted by over one million votes, with 49,000 against. The 'two-thirds' decrees obtained only 205,000 votes in favour and 107,000 against. The second vote was all the more dubious since the Convention had not taken account of the votes of those sections who were unanimously against but who failed to provide precise figures: forty-seven Parisian sections had rejected the decrees.

Vendémiaire

Faced with an imminent uprising, the committees took two steps which in fact caused the crisis to break out. Troops converged on Paris and, more importantly, former Terrorists were once more granted the right to take part in the meetings of the sections. Were they to be re-armed and a new terror started? This is certainly what some moderates believed and their leaders – Richer-Sérizy, Fiévé, Lacretelle – took the opportunity to build up a union of 'respectable people' around this fear.

The Lepeletier section became the controlling centre of the movement. When news arrived of royalist incidents at Dreux, on 10 Vendémiaire, the members of the sections considered that the moment had come. The Parisian sections were called upon to make their way on the next day, bearing arms, to the Théâtre-Français. This meeting was inconclusive, but, during the night, seven sections (including the Lepeletier, the Buttes and the Théâtre-Français) proclaimed themselves to be in a state of insurrection.

On the same evening the Convention entrusted its defence to a five-member commission which included Barras. On 12 Vendémiaire General Menou was ordered to bring the members of the Lepeletier section to heel. It was without enthusiasm that he moved against his former friends, and, on receiving from them no more than a promise to disperse, he withdrew his troops. After this climb down the Commission of Five relieved him of his command and replaced him by General Bonaparte. The latter, noticed by Barras at the siege of Toulon and known for his Jacobin views, had everything to gain on this occasion since he had burnt his boats by refusing a post in the Vendée. In theory the armed force of the sections was considerable: over 25,000 men were opposed to 5,000 regular troops and a few hundred volunteers. But this coalition of moderates and malcontents had neither a plan nor support. The Royalists of the d'Antraigues network (Brottier, Duverne de Presle) did not in any way associate themselves with this uprising of Feuillants, believing that the conflict had nothing to do with them but that it would weaken each of the two sides to the benefit of absolutism.

Barras and Bonaparte set about transforming the Tuileries into an entrenched camp. Murat brought back some pieces of artillery from the Sablons camp, thereby ensuring that the central committee of the sections could not lay hands on them. On 13 Vendémiaire, between 3 p.m. and 4 p.m., columns of confused demonstrators attacked the Convention from the right bank. Their attempts at fraternisation failed and they were greeted by a hail of bullets. The mass of the insurgents – shopkeepers, landlords, racketeers and *rentiers* – fell back in disarray leaving behind three hundred dead. The Church of Saint-Roch remained in royalist hands until the morning of 14 Vendémiaire. The rioters were dislodged from it, but not, as a far from disinterested legend would have it, by Bonaparte. The repression was limited. The gates of Paris remained open and most of the leaders were able to flee. Only thirty came before a military commission, which handed out seven death sentences, five of them in the absence of the accused. Popular opinion did not fail to contrast this discreet repression with the massive reprisals after Prairial. The most determined, because most compromised, Thermidoreans would no doubt have readily extended the circle of victims to include the deputies of the right: Boissy d'Anglas, Lanjuinais, Larivière and Lesage. But class interest militated against a vendetta of this kind; the orators of the *Plaine*, such as Thibaudeau, made this clear to Tallien.

The electoral results – which showed an upsurge of reactionary support – were more worrying than the presence in the Convention of a few deputies sympathetic to the rioters. The left-wing Thermidoreans considered quashing the elections, dividing the Convention into two chambers and electing the Directory without further ado. Faced with the hostility of the moderates, Tallien dared not put forward such a plan. On the other hand, on 3 Brumaire Year IV (25 October 1795), the members of the Convention passed a law for the safeguarding of the Revolution. *Emigrés* who had not been definitively struck off the lists, the relatives of *émigrés*, and citizens guilty of having put forward seditious motions during the elections were all barred from public office.

In addition, the laws against refractory priests were brought back into operation. After the 'two-thirds' decree the Convention thus set up another legislative barrier to salvage its settlement. On the following day it decided on a general amnesty for 'facts simply connected with the Revolution'. The Prairial deportees, the *émigrés* and the Vendémiaire rebels were not included in this. The main beneficiaries were the members of the revolutionary committees – of both the districts and the municipalities – who had been the main victims of persecution during the previous year. This magnanimous gesture by the Convention at its last meeting was not without the ulterior motive of political seduction. In a few weeks the Thermidoreans had come up against the two key problems which would dominate the Directory: to survive, the liberal regime could not do without the revolutionary constraints, but it was in principle irreconcilable with them. It also needed to find its own political and social base, otherwise it would become the prisoner of its own support. But in the immediate term the failure of the royalist *journée* had consolidated the position of those whose reason made them Republicans.

With the popular movement broken, the Royalists within and without France beaten, foreign peace partially secured and new institutions set up, the members of the Convention could consider that they had successfully carried out a difficult transition. But they bequeathed to the Directory a catastrophic economic situation, and, more importantly, the various oppositions, temporarily muzzled, remained formidable. Rather than achieving pacification the new regime, thanks to the army, had won a respite that served only to push back the moment of reckoning.

2

On two fronts

'What crime would there be in forcing two equally dangerous parties each to tread the straight path, and to bring them by the force of circumstances to merge into the constitutional party?'

La Révellière-Lépeaux, Mémoires, vol. 1, p. 406

THE STATE AND THE CITIZEN

One month after taking up office, the Directory wrote to the executive's commissioners in the *départements*: 'The Constitution is accepted; all the wheels of government have been rapidly put in place; movement and life have been given to this enormous machine; it is working.'[1] In fact the early days were less smooth than this triumphant communiqué allows one to believe. But the success of the Directory depended largely on its ability to construct a new state and make the political system function correctly. Failure would mean being swept away.

The approval of the constitution was followed by elections. In the primary assemblies which sat without a break, universal suffrage was the rule; but scarcely one million Frenchmen exercised their right to vote. In some places there was even a decline in participation between the referendum and the elections. This was no doubt partly due to the fact that country people could not spare the time to come and vote in the chief town of the canton during a busy agricultural period. And many participants must have been discouraged by the procedural complexities: the list of members of the Convention, the new third, the election of replacement deputies, the checking of the credentials of new deputies, the numerous rounds. But the disaffection which occurred in, for example, Besançon (from one poll to the next

---

[1] Quoted by J. Brelot (47), p. 44. (Books included in the bibliography are referred to by their author and entry number.)

participation decreased from 36·4% to 24·7%) or in the Meurthe undoubtedly stemmed from deeper causes: propaganda by returned priests, factional rivalries, and above all a lack of enthusiasm for political life at the national level. The Thermidoreans thus paid for having imposed the 'Hobson's choice' of the 'two-thirds'.

Meeting during Vendémiaire, the electoral assemblies were the affair of the *notables*. In accordance with the conditions of property qualification, the electors had singled out business men, well-off peasants, lawyers, journalists and administrators. In the Meurthe as in the Sarthe, in Toulouse as in Elbeuf, the 'pull' of its sociological base and the experience of six years of revolution had inclined this class towards conservatism.

This refusal to take risks did not have the same significance everywhere. The elections of Year IV thus provide us with a map of the political divisions and sensibilities of the propertied classes of France.[2] The main bastions of reaction were in the Paris basin, the middle reaches of the Loire, Normandy and Provence. Apart from the *départements* of the Nord and the Ardennes, there were a few islands of Jacobinism in the west (the Vendée, the Sarthe) and in the Massif Central (the Haute-Garonne and the Ariège). For most of the substantial electors 'anarchy' was the major threat; their votes put the seal on the defeat, if not the physical elimination, of the Jacobins. In the areas of counter-revolution – whether active (the west) or latent (the country-side of the Nord and of the Haute-Garonne) – to opt for the left indicated an attachment to the Republic of a bourgeoisie which was under assault but still in command of the vote. The Jacobinism of the Limousin or the Ariège perhaps benefited from the longstanding dechristianisation of these regions, and implanted a durable political tradition upon the conquests of the Revolution. Elsewhere the newly elected deputies were divided among different tendencies or took refuge in an indeterminate centrism. The trend was at any rate clear: the 'respectable citizens', on whom the constitution had in effect bestowed a monopoly of political expression, had backed the moderates or, to put it differently, had avenged the Girondins.

On 6 Brumaire 741 deputies were called upon to take their seats;[3] 243 of them, chosen by lot from among those over forty years old, made up the Council of the Elders, and the others formed the Council

---

[2] J. R. Suratteau (62).
[3] For detail on the post-electoral manoeuvres, the anomalies and the mistakes, see J. R. Suratteau (62).

of the Five Hundred. The members of the Convention had, thanks to the 'two-thirds' decree, avoided a débâcle, but they were clearly the losers. It was significant that only 394 of them had been elected by virtue of the 'two-thirds' decree. As had been foreseen, another 105 of them had to be 'retrieved'. Moreover the new third included only four outgoing deputies. The main losers were the survivors of the *Montagne*. There were no more than 64 'advanced' deputies including Audoin, Poultier and Marbot. The right's advance was on the other hand spectacular: 88 deputies displayed frankly counter-revolutionary views, and 73 others were moderate Royalists. As further evidence of this trend, the leaders of the reaction won the largest number of multiple elections: Lanjuinais had been elected thirty-nine times, Henry Larivière thirty-seven times, Boissy d'Anglas thirty-six times. Finally, the crushing defeat of the outgoing deputies was matched by the triumph of the ghosts from the past: former members of the Constituent Assembly such as Dupont de Nemours. Lecouteulx-Cauteleu and Tronchet, and former members of the Legislative Assembly like Laffon-Ladébat and Lacuée.

The supporters of the constitution divided into two groups. One, containing 139 deputies, represented the moderate Republicans as firmly opposed to a new Terror as to a restoration. These included Thibaudeau and Daunou. The other group consisted of 242 deputies, including Barras, Merlin de Thionville and Tallien. This was the syndicate of Thermidoreans: having succeeded in holding on to power, they intended to keep it. The regime set up in Year III was not a parliamentary one, but, without a wide base, the 'perpetual' members ultimately risked forfeiting their hegemony. The only conceivable majority combined the two wings of the 'constitutional' centre and the support of the *Plaine* (a hundred deputies of divided or indeterminate loyalty). In other words it was a political necessity for those whose reason inclined them to republicanism to rally around the leadership of a small core. The composition of the new third showed this well: in casting its votes, the country had gained only a reprieve.

The installation of the new power

The election of the executive Directory was the first test of this solidarity. Through a manoeuvre prepared by a small committee, the majority among the Five Hundred imposed its choice on the Elders. For the required list of fifty names it adopted those of Sieyès, Barras,

Reubell, La Révellière, Letourneur and forty-five undistinguished deputies.

The Elders reluctantly accepted the first five names. But Sieyès, who, out of caution or spite, was keeping himself at a distance from the Republic, refused to serve. Carnot was chosen instead by the same procedure. The five Directors, all regicides, belonged to the clique which had monopolised power for the previous year. But their different temperaments and political ambitions meant that coexistence promised to be difficult. La Révellière had obtained most votes because he was too dull to be controversial. As a former Girondin he was taken to represent a happy medium. But this moderate and vacillating figure had one obsession, sustained by personal hatreds: to prevent the revenge of the nobles and priests. Reubell, known as a jurist, was held in esteem for his energy and capacity for work. He had remained a Montagnard and an annexationist, and often behaved curtly towards his colleagues. In the final analysis he alone displayed the qualities of a statesman. Barras had many clients but few friends. But the members of the majority believed that they could not do without this feared and efficient individual, crowned with the glory of Vendémiaire. He was determined to survive, but in fighting for himself he was led to defend, at least provisionally, the interests of the coalition in power. Letourneur, a military engineer, a technician rather than a politician, had been chosen in order to avoid having to choose Carnot. When the latter was elected he faded into the background. The 'organiser of the Terror' entered the Directory with the reputation of a Terrorist. Only later did it emerge that he was at heart a conservative. In short, Reubell, with La Révellière in his wake, was the pivot of two possible majorities, either helping Carnot to contain the democrats or allying with Barras against the royalist threat.

The Directors divided up their tasks according to their wishes and their experience. Reubell took charge of foreign policy, finance and justice; Barras, the interior; Carnot, war; Letourneur, the navy; La Révellière, industry and education. According to the constitution the ministers had to apply the policies which were instigated by the Directory. Besides Merlin de Douai at the Ministry of Justice, the Five therefore chose hitherto little-known individuals. Bénézech obtained the Ministry of the Interior in spite of his reputation as a crypto-Royalist. Charles Delacroix was appointed Minister of Foreign Affairs; Aubert-Dubayet, then Petiet, Minister of War; Truguet, Minister of the Navy; and Faipoult, quickly to be replaced by Ramel-Nogaret, Minister of

Finance. Finally, on 2 January 1796, the Directory secured from the Councils the setting up of a Ministry of Police. Its aim was to provide appropriate means for the struggle against subversion. After Camus' refusal, this new office was taken by Merlin de Douai, who gave up the Ministry of Justice to Génissieu.

At the two main levels of administrative life, the *département* and the canton, the Directory was represented by a commissioner who supervised the application of the laws by the elected authorities. In choosing these agents of central power (and also the commissioners to the courts), the Directors took responsibility for the regions that they knew best: La Révellière, the west; Reubell, the east; Barras, the Midi, Carnot, the north; Letourneur, the centre. In spite of this division of labour, they were forced in practice to rely on the advice of local *notables* or of their personal correspondents, especially since the commissioners had to come from the *département* in which they were to serve. The most convenient solution seemed to be to ask the views of the deputies, or at least those of the 'two-thirds'. Thus, by becoming intermediaries, the deputies found their importance enhanced. Provided that they remained united, they now functioned (as Reinhard has shown for the Sarthe) at one and the same time as representatives of a tutelary power, as spokesmen of local interests and as employment agents. While waiting for all these officials to be appointed, the Directory asked the administrators of the *départements* to designate interim commissioners. This procedure was unavoidable but, to say the least, paradoxical. The local authorities then attempted to make these provisional appointments permanent, and often succeeded. But in spite of the difficulties and peculiarities of this process of selection, the commissioners ensured a continuity of executive authority and carried out their tasks of informing and surveillance perfectly well. The Directors, especially Barras and Carnot, had tried to fill these strategic posts with reliable men devoted to the Revolution, chosen from among the former members of the Convention or from the Jacobin administrators. They took the risk of creating opportunities for conflict between the commissioners and the elected moderates. But on the other hand they constructed a strong network for themselves.

The bureaucratic phenomenon

The efficiency of the system rested on a sizeable administration. The state apparatus of France had been modernised and enlarged during the last years of the *ancien régime*. Moreover, the war effort and the exigencies of a controlled economy in Year II had further increased the weight of the administrative departments in the body politic. And yet the Directory seems to have been a decisive period in the development of French bureaucracy.[4] The executive branch had an important staff in the Luxembourg. This included a general secretariat, offices corresponding to each of the big ministries, a topographical bureau and an archive department – in all some eighty employees, without counting the twenty or so personal secretaries of the Directors. The ministries probably had a staff of some five and a half thousand. The case of the Mont-Terrible, studied by Suratteau, suggests that the numbers were similarly inflated in local administration: the administration of the Mont-Terrible employed fifty-nine people at the beginning of Year IV.

This proliferation was no doubt attributable largely to the growth of a class of dependants (this can be seen, among other places, in the entourage of the Directory) and to the need for protection, or even for survival. At its humblest level the bureaucracy provided a refuge for victims of persecution – *sans-culottes* and Jacobins – for priests who had resigned, for notaries and lawyers without clients, etc. For obvious reasons of economy, the central authorities wanted to clear the administration of this 'tertiary parasitical' level. In the case of the Mont-Terrible, the Minister of the Interior succeeded, after a year's efforts, in reducing the staff to twenty. But there was no very serious campaign to prune the administration. Political considerations and contingent circumstances apart, the government probably considered it necessary not to weaken the administrative machinery of a country which was, overall, under administered, for the stresses and innovations of this transitional period required a strong state apparatus. An analysis of the staff of the ministries suggests that a process of amalgamation was taking place. A fusion, in the first place, between different political 'strata': *ancien régime* officials, Year II civil servants and newly recruited employees. Sometimes continuity prevailed. Thus the elder Arnould, head of the Bureau de Commerce from 1795 to 1798, had joined this section of the administration in 1771. His brother had been working at his side since 1787. And in the Mont-Terrible, Suratteau has noted the persistence of a sort of right of survival. But generally the higher civil service had felt the effects of the Revolution. There was, for example, a noticeable infusion of younger blood into the ministries.

[4] C. Church (49).

What is more, the administrative staff tended to climb a ladder of promotion which led from administration of the canton or *département* to the central ministries. In this way, at least in the upper echelons, the state achieved a unity of outlook and practice which allowed it to avoid provincialism and contradictions of policy.

On the other hand, the distinction between the heirs to wealth, power and culture (sons of the bourgeois, of deputies, of lawyers) who held positions of real authority, and the hard-working poor who carried out their orders was accentuated. This social division of labour carried over the fundamentally hierarchical nature of the new regime into the administration. The bureaucracy of the Directory suffered from an alarming contradiction. The system had deprived the citizens of part of their political duties, and in addition it had to support the consequences of a serious decline in the standards of behaviour of its elected representatives. This placed yet more obligations, especially in a period of crisis, on an administration which was badly paid, or not even paid at all. Efficiency suffered from the development of activities on the side, that is from the search by administrators for some remuneration from those whom they administered, who in extreme cases became their real employers. In addition, the two unavoidable but restrictive requirements of education and 'republicanism', when they were adhered to, narrowed the possibilities of recruitment. The Directory did not, therefore, have the effective means to carry out its ambition of building a modern state.

A reticent population

On one side the state, on the other the citizens. Reinforced by the disappearance of the district, the *départements* remained the normal setting of political confrontation. They were now run by five administrators chosen by the electors of the secondary stage. Thus there were no serious divergences between these administrators and the deputies; they all reflected the interests of the local oligarchies. At the most it is possible to discern certain nuances. The elected administrators of the *départements* were often more representative thanks to the more assiduous attendance of their electors. They were less affected by the swings of national elections: local personalities kept, or regained after the Terror, the positions they had acquired in 1790. In his study of the Meurthe, Clémendot has stressed that although their political outlooks were broadly similar, the political spectrum of the central administration of the *département* was wider than that of the deputies because in the former case the electors had taken greater account of the competence of the people they were choosing.

These local *notables* were supposed to be responsible for the execution of the law; and in particular they were to supervise the raising of taxes, the maintenance of public order and the supplying of markets. These were heavy tasks that were not made any easier by the system of by-elections, comparable to that for the Directory. Thus the central commissioners were often called upon to shore up a weak administration. Moreover, conflicts between the representatives of the Directory and the elected administrators were not infrequent, and action was paralysed until Paris stepped in to resolve the issue. In practice, then, the administrators did not fulfil the important role assigned to them by the constitution.

The communes, the basic units of administration, in most cases lost their decision-making power. In the rural conglomerations the place of the old municipal councils was taken by an *agent* and his deputy, who were both elected by the assembly of citizens. The Thermidoreans believed that, for lack of enlightened personnel, it was impossible to maintain a viable administration in towns of less than 5,000 inhabitants. But on the other hand, communes with between 5,000 and 100,000 inhabitants were provided with full municipality, and towns of over 100,000 with *arrondissement* municipal councils co-ordinated by a central bureau. These urban municipalities represented the most wealthy sections of the population: they were dominated by land-owners, business men and lawyers. Poorer elements, who had played a part in running their towns during Year II, were excluded by the property qualification and the costs of office, if not indeed by the cost of the election campaign itself. Finally, certain candidates might stand out for their individual achievements.[5] Thus at Elbeuf, in Year IV, one finds a municipality in the hands of entrepreneurs and merchants.[6] In this the Directory had, it is true, only accelerated a process perceptible since 1793, after a brief opening up towards the lower middle class and the artisans. Similarly, in the Sarthe, the municipal officers came from the ranks of the richest city dwellers: notaries, surgeons, apothecaries and barristers.

The cantonal municipalities – an intermediary level between *départ-ement* and rural commune – were composed of communal *agents* and a president elected by the primary assembly. Thus the rural communes

[5] R. Marx (56).   [6] J. Kaplow (29).

were grouped into a sort of administrative super commune under the eye of a commissioner. This bold reform, which allowed the Directory to exercise a certain control over local political life, was an almost universal failure. The rural community, the parish, retained its vitality, and the division into cantons, however rational it may have been in certain respects, merely created an artificial institution. Above all, the setting up of these municipalities was hampered, if not completely blocked, by an electoral strike. Few people wanted to take on civic responsibilities, particularly in the areas which were not at peace. In the Côtes-du-Nord, fifty cantonal municipalities out of eighty-nine were functioning in March 1796. Of these, thirty-nine were composed only of the commissioner and his deputy.

This reluctance to stand for office and the string of resignations which accompanied it did not affect only the cantons. The setting up of central administrations in the *départements* posed similar problems: it took several months to set up that of the Vienne. Even the urban municipalities suffered from this disaffection. In the Côte-d'Or, resignations multiplied during Year IV. At Elbeuf the municipal elections dragged on for nine months. There was no lack of reasons to explain this apathy on the part of public opinion: the pressure of the Chouans, the refusal to take the oath, hostility to the regime. But beyond such political divergences, many of these *notables* believed, like those of Elbeuf, 'that it is unpleasant to administer a starving population'. In a sense this evasion of political responsibility by the elites gave central power a greater freedom of action. But, although this political void allowed the agents of the executive to impose their own men in cases where the citizens' abstention from political activity threatened to result in paralysis, passive resistance considerably hindered the application of the law. In the outlying regions of France the constitution failed to function. In spite of the setting up of administrations for the *départements* and municipalities, Belgium was in fact living under military rule. The rebellious Vendée remained under martial law; attempts to nominate cantonal administrations, even puppet ones, had had little success in the autumn of 1796. In the south-east, Reverchon in Lyons and Fréron in Marseilles governed according to 'revolutionary' methods.

Political activity, both on the part of the chief towns of the *départements* and on the part of the *notables*, was doubly diminished. It was hardly a propitious omen that on this narrow base the new regime was unable, from the beginning, to obtain the consent of the majority.

THE EQUALS: A PROPHETIC MINORITY

Democratic agitation

In spite of its centrist pretensions and its policy of rallying the opposition, the Directory remained, in its first months, a prisoner of its origins, that is to say, of the victory of Vendémiaire. The real intentions of the government were revealed less in the nomination of former members of the Convention as commissioners, or in Antonelle's presence at the Luxembourg, than in the debate between the Directorials and the right wing on the Councils about how to fill vacancies in the courts. The Directory secured the exceptional right to appoint judges whom the primary assemblies had not had time to elect. It was crucially important for the Directory to be able to place its own men in a judicial apparatus which was often hostile and which in some places was even won over to the Counter-Terror. This was admitted by Barras in his *Mémoires*. Having recognised the strength of the opposing arguments, he added: 'but our minds were far from being at rest, and the body of electors which had given us the new Third...was not very reassuring; since the victory of 13 Vendémiaire had established the Directory and its rights it was necessary that it preserve itself in its very principle'. The desire to conserve the law of 3 Brumaire, to reactivate the laws against refractory priests and to confer upon the executive the right to strike *émigrés* off the lists, were all indications of the same trend.

Was the policy, then, one of no enemies on the left? Whether willingly or not, the Directors accepted Barras' tactics of conciliating the left. Thousands of patriots had been released after the amnesty of 4 Brumaire. The Jacobin press in Paris attempted to combat the dominant influence of the moderate and crypto-royalist press. The *Ami des lois* edited by Poultier, Duval's *Le Journal des hommes libres* and Louvet's *La Sentinelle* all received subsidies for this purpose from the government. But such generosity would not have had a great impact if the resurgence of the neo-Jacobins had not derived from their own vitality. Throughout the provinces the patriots joined together once more. Popular societies, with or without camouflage, came to life again in the Côte-d'Or (Dijon, Beaune, Nuits-Saint-Georges), in Angers, Nantes, Toulouse, etc. Some of them corresponded with each other; there was a renewal of the fabric of Jacobin organisation. Many of these members of clubs, or at least their leaders, were rich bourgeois who were not enthusiastic about social equality. Only royalist propaganda tried to depict them as levellers.[7]

As for the democrats in Paris, having now regained their liberty, they felt constrained to feel their way forward tentatively. Small meetings took place in cafés; some Jacobins advocated critical support of the Directory and former Robespierrists dreamed of reviving the Economic Terror, while in his newspaper – which had reappeared during Brumaire – Babeuf denounced the plutocratic nature of the regime and prepared public opinion for a confrontation. This seething atmosphere should not mislead us: it involved only a handful of activists who were trying to break the silence of the masses. Thus a tactical regrouping seemed necessary. It took the form of a new patriotic society, the Club du Panthéon.

The alliance was constructed around the position of the moderates. Those among the founding members who stood closest to Babeuf, such as Buonarroti and Darthé, were too isolated to be able to impose their views. Moreover, they wanted to build a united front poised for the offensive; this was therefore hardly the moment to make a stand. With its clientele of bourgeois patriots – the subscription was 50 *livres* – its restrained debates, its function as a mutual aid society and its 'war veteran' style, there was nothing in the club to alarm the Directors, who finally gave their agreement. For Barras, the club acted as a way of both purging and channelling discontent. Several factors transformed the nature of the club, and, consequently, the attitude of the government. Babeuf's campaign for social revolution met with an increasing response. In the midst of intellectual confusion the Equals gave renewed hope to those dissatisfied by the backward looking attitude of the Jacobins. In the Club du Panthéon, the success of Babeuf's ideas went hand in hand with an influx of new members (1,500 at the beginning of Frimaire, another 2,000 fifteen days later). Common people attended the debates in ever larger numbers without, it seems, profoundly transforming the social composition of the club. The widening audience of the 'Panthéonists' and the hardening of their tone were enough to alarm most of the Directors. It was necessary, as La Révellière explained, to reassure peace-loving citizens tempted by royalism: 'once reassured...these well-intentioned citizens would combine with us in an effective manner to uphold the Constitution of Year III'. The danger was that the fear of anarchy would drive them definitively into the arms of the opposition if the Directory appeared to act too indulgently.

[7] J. Beyssi (45).

The societies had far from obtained popular mass support, but the terrible hardship of the Parisian population in the winter of 1795–6 threatened to provide the activists with troops. In fact the crisis – which we will examine below – did not result in the expected outburst. But it did sufficiently radicalise the more advanced elements for the Directory – in spite of Barras? – to want to call a halt. On 27 February 1796 it decided to close the Club du Panthéon, one other patriotic society, and, for good measure, a few royalist meetings. Bonaparte, commander-in-chief of the Army of the Interior, carried out these measures assiduously in spite of his proclaimed Jacobinism. At the moment when his candidature for the Army of Italy was meeting certain difficulties, it was useful for him to give the Directory this guarantee of his loyalty.

Babouvism

In asserting himself as a leader and a rallying-point, Babeuf had become the government's chief target. On 5 December he had just managed to evade the police; and from this time onwards he went into hiding. During his last weeks of public activity, his ideas had not only gained in appeal but also in coherence. His small group of original followers – Germain, Antonelle, Maréchal – had been joined by 'left-wing Robespierrists' such as Buonarroti and Darthé. And in spite of these different origins and various tactical divergences, a fusion took place. This community of views was a prelude to organic unity and the emergence of a new political movement – Babouvism.

Since the work of Georges Lefebvre, all studies of Babeuf's thought have emphasised continuity.[8] While his ideas certainly did change, this occurred through a process of building on the existing foundations rather than through the addition of entirely new elements. In the beginning Babeuf's communism derived – to simplify enormously – from his reading and from his observation of a social phenomenon. His reading included, of course, Rousseau and Malby, but also, and most important of all, Morelly's *Code de la Nature* (at that time attributed to Diderot), which depicted a system entirely ordered by the principle of equality. The precision of this construction and the nature of the model proposed were to have a lasting influence on Babeuf and several of his friends. The social phenomenon which struck Babeuf was the attachment shown by the peasants of his native Picardy to their collective rights, prefiguring the social relations which would prevail

[8] J. Dautry (51).

once feudalism had been uprooted. Two moments appear to have been crucial in Babeuf's later political experience. First, as a Parisian in Year II, he was able to see how the Revolution, in its ascendant phase, provided two responses to the crisis: dictatorship and the controlled economy. Second, he experienced as a prisoner the ebbing of the tide in Year III. It was then that he became aware of the need, if the popular movement was to be successful, to provide it with a structure and with leadership. Finally, Babouvism cannot be separated from the economic circumstances of the day: food shortages and constraints on productive capacity. This was the reason for its lack of any reflection on economic development and for its vision of a future of austere egalitarianism, as if redistribution were the only economic variable. Just as certain modern ideologies can be seen as the offspring of a period of growth, so Babouvism was the ideology of stagnation and rationing.

The whole structure rested on equality. Without it, there could be no common well-being. If equality was not to be illusory, all goods had to be held in common. But this could not be achieved without abolishing the right of property, the root of all evil. Although property would remain in individual hands, the nation would become its sole owner. While in 1796 Babeuf seems to have envisaged collective farms, this idea formed no part of the Babouvism of Year IV. Indeed, the urban masses to whom he spoke would hardly have understood the concept of a collective organisation of labour at a time when small-scale production was everywhere predominant. On the other hand, the sharing out of resources was worked out in minute detail, with the state obtaining a monopoly over distribution. Labour was to be regulated: the community would allocate tasks and judge of their usefulness. Social equality would have its political counterpart: political sovereignty was to be expressed in grass-roots assemblies, power was to be divided up and vigilantly controlled. The overall structure would retain cohesion thanks to a 'national, common and equal' education which would mould citizens worthy of their city. The result would be the creation of a new breed of men, liberated from need and egotism.[9]

How would this transition to a redistributional communism occur? In the first place, by means of a provisional dictatorship of which the Equals formed the embryo. Then a 'large community' would run a sort of national domain and would gradually be joined by vestiges of the previous society. Some people have seen this as the genesis of a party. But it could be characterised more accurately as a prototype or a model.

[9] The clearest analysis of the doctrine is given by C. Mazauric (57).

The doctrine did, however, contain the fruitful notion of a transitional period in which the two forms of social organisation would coexist after the revolutionary break with the past. As contained in the articles and correspondence of Babeuf, in Maréchal's *Manifeste des Egaux* and in various texts attributed to Buonarroti, Babouvism leaves one with a sense of incompletion. It was a doctrine still in the making, which, at the moment when the conspiracy was unmasked, was no doubt far from its full development. Its fundamental weakness was to build a progressive society on a stagnant, frozen and fragmented economy. It has often been said that these were the very features of a *sans-culotte* ideology. This claim ignores the fact that the abolition of property was the keystone of the Babouvist system and differentiated it radically from the conceptions of the artisans and shopkeepers. Perhaps the distinction between national property and its exploitation by individuals was a way of bridging this gap, although this theme, common in the country-side, had little appeal in the towns. But Babouvism, linked, as we have stressed, to the particular circumstances of the day, was above all a profoundly political doctrine. In other words, it expressed a compromise between the logic of a theory concerned with the future and the need for action in the present. Only the *sans-culottes* could provide the necessary mass support to carry out this enterprise; they were however incapable of assuming the task, indeed of even understanding the doctrines. The ambiguity of Babouvism reflected this contradiction while simultaneously attempting to overcome it.

The anatomy of the conspiracy

After the closure of the Club du Panthéon, a few Panthéonists, such as Buonarroti and some friends of Babeuf, met for a time at the house of Amat, together with some former members of the Convention. Whether through caution or as a result of differences, these meetings soon ceased. In fact the time for discussion was over. Many felt the need to organise around a single centre. The response of Babeuf, Antonelle, Maréchal and Lepeletier was to found a secret Directory. On 30 March 1796 the original group was joined by Buonarroti, Darthé and Debon. They had not renounced their Robespierrist past: it was simply that the retrospective debate was over. Except for Darthé, there is no doubt that all the other conspirators had rallied to Babouvism. Each had come to communism by an individual itinerary. For Buonarroti, for instance, this had included a reading of Rousseau and

Morelly, a period in Corsica, where an archaic form of agrarian democracy functioned, and, finally, a period in Oneglia, near Menton, where he carried out an experiment in revolutionary power in an attempt to apply his egalitarian principles.

The conspiracy of the Equals was organised with minute care. At the summit, the Directory, meeting every day, dealt with correspondence and examined political proposals and plans for insurrection. In each *arrondissement* of Paris it communicated its instructions to a carefully selected revolutionary agent. These agents kept the Directory informed and recruited new followers. On their shoulders rested the success of the movement. A special effort was made with regard to the army, which had already intervened twice to save the Thermidoreans. Military agents made contact with elements of the Paris garrison and with the Police Legion, among whom Bonaparte had placed many firm patriots after 13 Vendémiaire.

In the provinces Babouvist propaganda was spread by various clubs; even the army was affected, including the troops in the Armies of Italy and the Rhine and Moselle. But the network remained fairly loose. In some regions the conspirators attempted to set up a more effective infrastructure: in the Pas-de-Calais, thanks to the personal influence of Babeuf, in the Marne, thanks to Drouet, and in Lyons where Bertrand, one of their number, had been mayor. Besides *Le Tribun du peuple*, which continued to appear, the Equals relied on *L'Eclair du peuple*, edited by Maréchal, and on Antonelle's *Journal des hommes*. This press campaign was supplemented by posters; the groups who stuck up these posters then passed commentary on them in the presence of bystanders. Babouvist slogans were popularised in pamphlets intended for soldiers and workers. The agents were instructed to instigate small meetings in attics at which these tracts would be read out. Similarly, propaganda through songs was not neglected. For instance, 'La Chanson nouvelle à l'usage des faubourgs', written by Maréchal, enjoyed great success among the *sans-culottes*.

How many people were affected by these ideas? It is difficult to make an estimate. The secret Directory had calculated that it could count on 1,700 in Paris (of whom 1,000 were provincials who would be brought into the city). This number included the grenadiers of the Legislative Body and, most important of all, the Police Legion. But although the Military Committee was certainly successful among the members of the Legion, there was a danger of attributing too much importance to café talk, of assuming all discontented soldiers to be revolutionaries.

More interesting than such fanciful and vague estimates are the lists of subscribers to *Le Tribun du peuple* and of 'patriots capable of taking command', which were seized after the uncovering of the plot.[10] The first – entirely predictable – feature to emerge was the strength of the Equals in Paris (58% of subscribers). This phenomenon is all the less surprising considering that in Year III the capital served as a refuge for the persecuted. The sample was socially heterogeneous. Most of the provincial subscribers came from among the more well-to-do classes (landlords, business men, the professions), but artisans were also represented. A cross-check of the Parisian lists reveals a 'predominance of artisans and shopkeepers' and a weak representation of the two extremes of bourgeoisie and proletariat. After correcting various distortions (the cost of subscriptions, difficulties of identification, etc.), one can conclude that the bulk of the conspiracy's potential support was to be found among small employers in Paris and bourgeois patriots in the provinces. In its most developed form, Babouvism was totally opposed to the spontaneous ideology of this social milieu, which, in its heterogeneous class structure, was only a reincarnation of the *sans-culottes*. This uneasy grafting was the main reason for the ambiguity of the political platform and for the gap between the nucleus of leaders and their followers. In Germinal of Year IV the propaganda of the Equals quickly led to the crystallisation of an important movement. Their radical and lucid analysis of the regime fulfilled the hopes of the defeated of Year III. Revealingly, Barras and Tallien wanted to exploit this new force to their own ends. But the Equals rejected these advances, thereby demonstrating the irreducible originality of their ideas.

Failure

Carnot also took an interest in this rise of 'anarchism'. As a lifelong conservative he was both frightened by the threat of social subversion and anxious to clear his name. Moderate opinion was still haunted by his 'black legend'. What is more, as a military specialist, he was very unwilling to put up with the spread of Babouvism in the armies. He was therefore – with the new Police Minister, his protégé Cochon – the main force behind the repression.

On 28 April the government decided to transfer five battalions of

---

[10] A. Saboul, 'Personnel sectionnaire et personnel babouviste', *Annales historiques de la Révolution française*, no. 4 (1960), p. 436.

the Police Legion to the frontier in order to put an end to the agitation. When two battalions refused to obey, the Directory pre-empted the conspirators who had just finalised their '*Acte Insurrecteur*': the leaders of the mutiny were arrested and the Police Legion dissolved. This prompt action by the government did not cause too much protest, and the Equals lost their main trump card. Political isolation, and perhaps lack of funds, pushed the Babouvists into changing their tactics towards the former members of the Convention. Their sectarian attitude was succeeded by an attempt at conciliation. It took three weeks to come to agreement on the composition of the assembly which would be set up after the seizure of power. What seemed to be merely tactical differences often overlaid insurmountable conflicts of principle.

The police – or rather the police forces – followed the conspiracy closely. Barras was kept informed by Poultier. But the decisive piece of information was given to Carnot by one of the conspiracy's military agents, Grisel. On the morning of 10 May the main leaders of the plot were arrested. In the provinces the repression which followed did not distinguish between Babouvist leaders, former Terrorists and other left-wing opponents. As Drouet, a member of the Five Hundred, was among the conspirators, the Directory had to get the Councils to accept his indictment – not without discussion – and to have all the conspirators tried before a High Court. This procedure was extremely cumbersome, and the trial, which took place at Vendôme, did not begin until 20 February 1797. The Directorial and moderate press took advantage of this delay to arouse opinion against the Terrorists. The defendants managed to agree on a system of defence. This involved saving those least implicated and avoiding contradictions. Since twenty-three of the forty-seven had had nothing to do with the conspiracy, they decided to deny its very existence. On 26 May the jury gave its verdict: Babeuf and Darthé were condemned to death; Buonarroti, Germain and five Babouvist activists were sentenced to deportation; and all the others were acquitted. On the next day Babeuf and Darthé attempted suicide, but they died on the scaffold.

Meanwhile an incident at the Grenelle camp had, at just the right moment, revived the fear of 'anarchists'. In the autumn of 1796 some Parisian democrats, at a loss how to react, had hoped to incite the 21st Dragoons of Colonel Malo to revolt. But the colonel, invited to join the enterprise, had warned Carnot who, seeing the capital that could be made out of this, instructed him to let it proceed. On the night of 9–10 September, a few hundred Jacobins approached the camp to fraternise with the soldiers. They were met with a hail of bullets. Many people were arrested, often far from the scene of hostilities; by the formal demand of the Directory they were brought before a military commission, although their cases in fact fell within the jurisdiction of the ordinary courts. The government thus compounded its guilt: having provoked the demonstration, it now made illegal use of the courts. Thirty-three of the demonstrators were condemned to death, of whom thirty were executed. The Court of Appeal, by no means to be suspected of Jacobinism, was later to quash this judgement and send the survivors before the civil courts.

It would be wrong to say that the demise of Babouvism was greeted with indifference. During the Vendôme trial some courageous journalists stood up for the defendants. And the aftermath of the Grenelle affair aroused a certain emotion in Paris. But the masses did not react. The price of the Equals' role as front-runners was isolation. They had felt the need not to repeat the mistakes of Prairial, the need, that is, to construct a tightly knit organisation. But they had not succeeded afterwards in renewing contact with the people. Not only was their ideology inaccessible to the *sans-culottes*, but their 'elitist' conception of how to conduct the struggle did not put them in a position to create a broad popular movement. 'Actions without ideas' were succeeded by 'ideas without actions'. But the fact remains that their doctrinal rigour and the strictness of their organisation were harbingers of the future. The Equals were, in the fullest sense of the phrase, a prophetic minority.

THE ROYALISTS BETWEEN THE MILITARY PATH AND THE PARLIAMENTARY PATH

The price of conciliation

Could the red peril form the cement of a new majority? This was certainly believed by Carnot, who became the leading advocate of a policy of overture towards the right. In fact the Directory hardly had any choice. A war to the death, which was to shake the very foundations of the social order, had broken out between it and the democrats. Moreover, the renewal of one-third of the deputies in Germinal Year V was undoubtedly going to reinforce the most moderate wing. The Feuillants, therefore, had to be rallied as quickly as possible, before the arrival of large numbers of royalist representatives created an irrevocable situation. The Republic would be conservative, or there would be no Republic at all.

The repression of the Babouvist movement provided the opportunity for a vast anti-Jacobin purge. In Floréal Year IV, mayors – like that of Périgueux – commissioners of the Directory and large numbers of public servants were all dismissed. Applying a sort of 'spoils system', Carnot and La Révellière expelled those Jacobins and members of the Convention who had found a niche in the administration after Vendémiaire, and replaced them by Girondins and other supporters of the new policy. These changes in the political personnel placated the constitutional Royalists. Thus Dupont de Nemours congratulated the Directory for 'aligning itself more and more with the honest and imposing majority of the Nation which wants the Constitution...and detests in equal measure the Counter-Revolution and a prolongation of the Revolution'.

But the right demanded more. It wanted the removal of two ministers: Merlin de Douai, as the author of the law of suspects, and Charles Delacroix, as bearing the responsibility for the failure of the Lille negotiations. The Directory was willing to sacrifice neither. Merlin had made himself indispensable in the key position of Minister of Justice and Delacroix's dismissal would have led the Directors to disavow themselves. It was they who had instructed him not to accept the evacuation of Belgium demanded by Lord Malmesbury. The first case intimated to the moderates that the purge would have its limits, and the second that peace at any price, the watchword of the right, would never be the foreign policy of the Directory. Moreover, Bonaparte's victories in Italy whetted many people's appetites; the burden represented by the army contractors and the parlous state of the public finances pushed the government, in spite of Carnot, towards intransigence.

But the prospects of a durable alliance between the Directorials and a fraction of the right involved a more serious sacrifice – the repeal of the law of 3 Brumaire Year IV. Despite the insistence of Thibaudeau and Henry Larivière, the men in power were unwilling to give way on this point, in particular to allow the relatives of *émigrés* to hold public office. Resigned to failure, the moderates accepted a compromise. Exclusion from public office was extended to those Jacobins who had been pardoned and to sixty-eight members of the Convention. Even if, as Lefebvre wrote, this measure was a severe blow to the republican camp, the right had not entirely achieved its objectives. And at the end of 1796 it had many more reasons to prepare for the elections than to encourage its electors to sanction the Directory's policy.

Armed action

In the west the royalist forces strove to overcome their defeat. The Vendée was on tenterhooks about the possible imminent landing of the Comte d'Artois, who had arrived at the Ile d'Yeu on 1 October 1795. Charette, unable to control the coastal zone, was therefore also unable to prepare to link up with him. Thrown back inland, he was at the same time deprived of a source of supply. Artois, little interested in waging guerrilla warfare, departed for England, abandoning the Vendéans to their fate (18 November). The revolt now entered its dying stages. Stofflet, who had unenthusiastically resumed combat in January 1796, was captured a month later and shot at Angers (25 February 1796). Charette's bands, upon whom the republican forces had gradually closed, were dispersing. The peasants had regained their priests and no longer came to the aid of the rebels. The pursuit came to an end on 23 March, near Montaigu. Charette, wounded, was taken to Angers, and then to Nantes, where he was executed (29 March 1796).

Chouannerie retained a certain life in its strongholds of Morbihan (below Cadoudal) and Ille-et-Vilaine. Frotté even tried to construct another royalist heartland between Avranches and Alençon. From October 1795 to March 1796 the rebel bands succeeded in maintaining an atmosphere of insecurity by systematically attacking the administrative infrastructure. But as soon as Hoche, commanding the Army of the Côtes de l'Océan, was able to introduce reinforcements into Brittany from the Vendée, the struggle became too one-sided. Lacking both money and co-ordination, and finding less and less support from the peasantry, the Chouan leaders were forced to surrender in June and July 1796. This did not automatically bring peace, since small groups of deserters and robbers kept up their depredations. But however irritating these activities may have been for the local patriots, they were no longer a threat to the central powers. Hoche proposed using his army for an expedition to Ireland. Chouannerie, as a political force, died out for the next three years.

The revolts in the west were not the essential part of the royalist strategy. Condé and Wickham staked greater hopes on Pichegru, the commander of the Army of the Rhine and the Moselle, who had

maintained contact with the Prince's envoys during the winter of
1795–6. Pichegru accepted subsidies without making firm commit-
ments, reckoning that his troops, undermined by the propaganda of
Fauche-Borel, would gradually be won over. This, at least, as a means
of stalling, is what he claimed. He also let the Austrians retake
Mannheim (23 November), and after the armistice he billeted his army
near the front in a devastated region. This defeatist behaviour began
to alarm the Directory. Thus on 13 March 1796 it transformed the
provisional leave, which it had granted Pichegru a month earlier, into
a permanent recall. In Paris the general continued his intrigues. He
considered stirring up a *coup d'état* timed to coincide with an Austrian
offensive. But this hope was dashed by the victories of Jourdan, Moreau
and Bonaparte in June. In the autumn, however, the situation was
reversed. The defeated – but not discontented? – Moreau was retreat-
ing into Alsace. A pronunciamento became possible again. In fact by
this time Pichegru no longer seemed to favour a coup. He hinted to
Moreau that achieving a restoration meant fighting the next elections.
He no doubt also understood that if the Princes stood to triumph from
a military solution, the parliamentary path gave the constitutional
monarchists the best chance of imposing their views, or at least of
swaying the intransigence of the Pretender.

The Paris Agency, reorganised by Brottier, had believed during the
summer of 1796 that a peaceful restoration was possible. Dupont de
Nemours and his friends made their conditions known: an amnesty and
a constitution. Louis XVIII refused and disowned these overtures. The
Agency thus reverted to its original objective: an armed coup against
the Directory. Ramel, commander of the guard of the Luxembourg,
and Malo, who had achieved notoriety in the Grenelle incident, seemed
to have been won over to the plot. But in fact the commander of the
21st Dragoons, perhaps suspecting that he had been uncovered by
Barras and uncertain about the outcome of the operation, revealed the
conspiracy to Carnot. A trap was set for the conspirators: Brottier and
three others were arrested on 30 January 1797. Charette, Pichegru,
Brottier: the year 1796 had been marked by the renunciation, or defeat,
of armed action by the Royalists.

The electoral battle

In Year V of the Republic royalism was less a party than a state of
mind. What common objective could have durably united the

'absolutists', favouring an almost integral restoration of the *ancien régime*, and the 'constitutionalists', supporting the idea of a monarch who would administer the new social order? Many of the latter had hopes of the Duc d'Orléans. This seems to have been a powerful faction. Carnot and Sieyès were held to have 'Orléanist' views; it is likely that historians, reacting against the anti-Orléanist obsession of certain circles of the Directory, have underestimated the importance of this current of opinion. Others still hoped to convince Louis XVIII to accept the necessity of making concessions. Finally, there were those who wanted to marry Madame Royale to a foreign prince. All were agreed, however, on the importance of the elections of Germinal Year V. These would at last provide the opportunity at least to gain control of the Councils, if not to abolish the Directory, by legal means. Dandré, the former member of the Constituent Assembly, was to be the instrument of this change in policy. Acting as an intermediary between the Clichy party and the Paris Agency, he was able to persuade the King of the merits of this tactic. The Royalists were convinced – indeed with good reason – that they could win over the majority of voters. They needed an organisation and a sensible platform. Improvisation would not be enough. Since the Directory (with varying results) was exploiting the administrative machinery for purposes of propaganda and intimidation, its opponents had to set up a well-co-ordinated network in the country. This was the role of the 'Philanthropic Institutes' created in seventy *départements*. These local associations, which corresponded with the Paris Agency, were composed of two quite distinct types. The more numerous group, the 'Friends of Order', worked exclusively for an electoral victory. The others, the 'Legitimate Sons', were secretly preparing a general insurrection if the results of the elections should be unsatisfactory. This hard core of absolutists set up in every region a military organisation under the command of the King and the Princes. In Bordeaux two organisations developed side by side – the Philanthropic Institute with its electoral objectives (but also equipped with an armed force) and the royalist committee created at the instigation of the Comte d'Artois. On the other hand, in the Sarthe, the two forms of action were united in a single institute.

The Royalists' slogans envisaged the construction of a conservative bloc. They avoided such issues as agrarian laws and the nature of the regime; instead, they spoke of anarchism. The Directory had itself orchestrated a campaign of panic by giving considerable publicity to the conspiracy of the Equals and to the Grenelle incident. The Vendôme trial kept public opinion in a state of alarm; it became one of the arguments of the electoral battle. This was ground on which the Directory was bound to lose. It was easy for reactionary propagandists to hold it responsible for the 'terrorist advance', to recall the complaisance of Barras and Tallien towards the left, and to amalgamate all the currents of the revolution into retrospective unity.

The moderate press, dominant throughout the country, propagated these themes to the point of saturation. In those *départements*, like the Sarthe, where the Philanthropic Institutes were best organised, the same ideas were taken up by tracts, pamphlets and pictures. Often the town theatre was the arena – and stake – of political debate. In Bordeaux and Besançon, for example, the battle of songs and plays gave the young Royalists a pretext to show off their strength. But the Royalists' best electoral agents were undoubtedly the refractory priests. Their influence was felt not only in the west and in the frontier zones, but also in supposedly 'reliable' *départements* like the Côte-d'Or. Finally, the funds for this royalist offensive were to a large extent provided by the English.

The Directory reacted as best it could by instructing its commissioners to 'give a lead to the electors' and by providing financial support for the republican press. This embryo of an official campaign was not sufficient to turn back the tide. The government therefore tried exploiting the Brottier plot to win over all the Republicans – and even a few of the constitutional Royalists. But the way in which the Directory revealed the affair and embarked on legal proceedings once again left an impression of scheming, of a frame-up and of various underhand dealings. Moreover, the government made strenuous efforts to summon the accused before a court martial, which passed only light sentences on them. So the Directory then decided that they should be retried when their sentences had expired. But this only further discredited it. Finally, in desperation, the Directory proposed that all electors should swear an oath of 'hatred towards royalty and anarchy'. This would have put the electors in the same category as public servants. The Five Hundred refused. The deputies would only agree to an act of submission to the constitution of Year III. The Royalists immediately made it known that this committed them to nothing.

The election results fulfilled the hopes of the Clichyens. Of the 216 outgoing members of the Convention, only eleven were re-elected, of whom six were confirmed Republicans. The new third included figures as compromised as Claret de Fleurieu, a former minister of Louis XVI, General Willot, a protector of Counter-Terrorists, Pichegru and

Imbert-Colomès, an agent of the Pretender. Even if the Jacobins had often been forcibly kept from voting, the Directory's defeat was still resounding. The most spectacular results can be explained in the west by pressure from the Chouans, in Alsace by the return of the *émigrés*, in the south-east by the Counter-Terror and in all the Belgian *départements* by a rejection of annexation. But it would be wrong to speak of a landslide. As Suratteau has written: 'April 1797 continued and completed 1795.'[11] The moment of reckoning had arrived.

Counter-Revolution

The Directory was very divided over its interpretation of the results of the elections and on what course of action to follow. Carnot believed that the electorate had voted for order and not for a king. In his view this verdict had to be accepted. At the other extreme, Reubell called for revolutionary measures – he wanted to annul the elections and re-stage them after expelling the refractory priests and *émigrés*, to censor the press and to make the electors take the 'oath of hatred'. Neither Barras nor La Revéllière would support such drastic action; and Carnot and Letourneur threatened to resign if this policy was adopted. The executive was paralysed until the potential majority – Reubell–Barras– La Révellière – could coalesce around a programme of republican defence.

For their part, the Royalists and moderate Republicans hesitated over how to exploit their victory. The split between the hardline Royalists, nicknamed 'White Jacobins' (Henry Larivière, Willot, Imbert-Colomès), and the constitutionalists (Siméon, Portalis, Mathieu-Dumas) prevented any real concerted action in spite of the façade of unity which had prevailed at the Clichy meetings. The majority, however, was able to agree on two proposals: it elected Pichegru to the Presidency of the Five Hundred, and Barthélemy, the negotiator of the Treaties of Basle, to replace Letourneur on the Directory. If this double choice was a perfect illustration of the preponderance of Royalists on the Councils, it was nevertheless of only limited significance. Pichegru, hesitating over what course to take, was not the leader the coalition required; and Barthélemy's election did not modify the balance of forces on the Directory.

The scale of its success in the end encouraged the Clichy party to bide its time. Instead of picking a quarrel with an executive still

[11] J. R. Suratteau (63).

predominantly republican, it seemed more politic to wait for the removal, in the following year, of the last third of the former Convention. Dandré and his friends believed that they would then form an overwhelming majority and would be able to impose their views without any opposition.

The parliamentary reaction fixed upon certain immediate objectives. First, to eliminate the consequences of Vendémiaire by repealing the law of 3 Brumaire Year IV which excluded relatives of *émigrés* from public office: on 27 June 1797 the law was declared invalid. The next aim was to free religious worship from the restrictive clauses of the law of 7 Vendémiaire Year IV and to end the repression against refractory priests. In this the reactionaries were less successful, because there were, besides the Directorial party, numerous centrist deputies like Thibaudeau who did not want to be associated with an unconditional abolition of all the religious legislation. The laws of 1792 and 1793 were abrogated, but on two points debate continued into Fructidor: on the necessity for priests to make a declaration of allegiance to the Republic and on the modification of the law on freedom of worship. The third element of 'Clichy policy' concerned the *émigrés*. Should the constitution be circumvented in order to authorise new categories of *émigrés* to return, or should the Royalists merely content themselves with prolonging the stay of execution granted to the Alsatian peasants? The resistance of the centre, especially on the Council of Elders, blocked the offensive of the White Jacobins, who had to resign themselves to insignificant successes.

If the Counter-Revolution advanced cautiously in the Councils, it progressed much faster, although at a varying pace, in the provinces. The by-elections in both the *départements* and the municipalities had mirrored the national results. The political and judicial officials, on whose shoulders rested the application of the laws, were won over to the reaction in large numbers. The Directory's commissioners, isolated and overworked, were left as helpless observers of this fundamental transformation. *Emigrés* and refractory priests returned in large numbers; both posed a threat to the purchasers of national property. It seems that in many places the sale of this property was suspended or at least slowed down. The reaction was particularly fierce in the west (the *département* of the Sarthe was almost in a state of secession) and in the south-east where the White Terror continued with impunity. But the counter-revolutionary upsurge occurred throughout the country. Even a quiet *département* like the Meurthe experienced, to a lesser extent, this political, social and religious revenge. The elections of Year VI did not bode well for the Republicans.

18 Fructidor

The Republicans had not remained inactive. In Paris the Directorials, Sieyès, Treilhard and Daunou, had founded the 'Constitutional Circle' as a counterbalance to Clichy. Jacobin clubs had opened in the faubourgs. In the provinces the Republicans of the Sarthe met in 'reading committees'; in Dijon, Besançon, Toulouse and many other towns the Republicans held their ground by exploiting the anxieties of the purchasers of national property or the anti-clerical feelings of part of the bourgeoisie. The attitude of the armies was more important. That of the Rhine and the Moselle, commanded by Moreau, had for a long time been subjected to royalist propaganda. The officers, recruited by Pichegru, displayed clearly anti-republican sentiments. From them the Directory could hope for no more than neutrality. On the other hand, there was a possibility of recourse to the Army of the Sambre and the Meuse, under Hoche, and even more to the Army of Italy. In the case of Bonaparte, the Councils' opposition to his person, to his past and to his plans for the future could only further link him to the policy of the Directory. And conducting in Italy an increasingly personal policy, he needed at least the approval of a majority of the Directors. There was a threat that the Councils would impose peace without annexation; for this reason alone the young general and his army sided with the executive. In two months the positions of the Directors had evolved distinctly. If Reubell had seen his fears confirmed, and if Carnot continued to favour an agreement with the Clichy party, La Révellière and Barras realised that the counter-revolutionary tide was going to carry all before it. By the end of Messidor the 'triumvirate' of Barras, Reubell and Le Révellière was in existence. Its first decision was to make sure of the loyalty of the central administration. The Councils had wanted a ministerial reshuffle which would reflect their views and the Directory seemed ready to conform to this wish, although such action was not required by the constitution. But to the surprise of the right, these changes affected only the Clichyens: Bénézech was replaced at the Ministry of the Interior by François de Neufchâteau; Cochon at the Ministry of Police by Lenoir-Laroche, and then by Sotin; Talleyrand succeeded Delacroix; and Pléville-le-Pelley succeeded Truguet. The crucial change took place at the Ministry of

War where Hoche was appointed in place of Petiet (16 July). Two days later troops moved towards La Ferté-Alais, that is, within the constitutional belt. The members of the Clichy party, whatever tendency they belonged to, were alarmed by this violation of fundamental constitutional guarantees, and Carnot, who had not been informed, clashed violently with his colleagues. The movement of troops, moreover, had been announced before it could succeed; the Directory was therefore forced into a tactical retreat. It recognised that Hoche was not of the required age to hold ministerial office and it ordered the troops to fall back outside the constitutional zone.

At this point the Royalists' lack of unity prevented them from seizing their opportunity. Moreau, who was won over to them, did not dare make a decision. Pichegru was waiting for the reorganisation of the National Guard – on the basis of a property qualification – to produce its full effects. Besides, he had been warned that the Directory was, thanks to Bonaparte, in possession of the papers of the Comte d'Antraigues, which were extremely compromising for him. His easygoing and indecisive nature did not incline him to take too many risks in a struggle whose outcome was doubtful. In fact, as Lefebvre has written, the Directory went back on the offensive as soon as it had secured its 'replacement general', Bonaparte, who sent Augereau to make himself available to the Directors. Barras settled the details of the *coup d'état* with him. Large numbers of soldiers flocked into the capital on the pretext that they were on leave. Moreau, under suspicion, was summoned to Paris, and the sections had their rifles removed.

On the evening of 17 Fructidor (3 September 1797) the triumvirs ordered the army to occupy the two palaces in which the Councils met and called in as reinforcements the troops stationed around Paris. The gates were closed and the principal Clichy leaders arrested. Carnot, forewarned by Barras, escaped, but Barthélemy, Cochon and Pichegru fell into the hands of Augereau's troops. On 19 Fructidor the terrorised Councils voted that the two Directors should be deported to Guyana, along with forty-two deputies from the Five Hundred, eleven deputies from the Elders and numerous journalists. In forty-nine *départements* (the Paris region, the north, the Loire region, Provence, etc.) all the elections were annulled. Finally, various other measures wiped out two months of parliamentary counter-revolution: *émigrés* who had not been struck off the lists had to leave France within fifteen days, under pain of death. The refractory priests again became liable to deportation. The law of

3 Brumaire Year IV was restored and the oath of 'hatred towards royalty and anarchy' was imposed on all electors.

The triumvirs thus broke with legality in the name of revolutionary legitimacy. The operation aroused hardly any emotion and numerous messages of approval were received, not only from the armies and the Jacobin societies, but also, through a natural instinct for conformity, from administrators who had until then remained uncommitted. The Directory thus provided itself with a respite. But at what cost? It had violated the constitutional pact by refusing to bow to the will of the electorate. In so doing the ruling group implicitly admitted that the constitution was unworkable, at least until peace had been restored at home and abroad. Most importantly, to a greater extent than during the *journées* of Prairial or Vendémiaire, the army had intervened in politics. The liberal regime had now lost all credibility.

3

Conquests

'The art of war is a simple art and entirely one of execution'

Bonaparte

ENDS AND MEANS

It fell to the Directory to set the objectives, assemble the means and supervise the application of foreign policy. It was not to be expected that such a weak and divided body would be able to assume these responsibilities fully. But if the Directory was not the only inspiration of, nor, in the long run, the main driving force behind, foreign policy, it nevertheless determined the broad outlines and attempted to improve the 'war machine' which it had inherited.

The aims of the war

It has been claimed that the Directory was split between two policies. Reubell, responsible for the Ministry of Foreign Affairs, wanted to annex the Rhineland. The frontiers of the Rhine, the 'key river of Europe', seemed to him the surest way of protecting Alsace. Carnot opposed this doctrine of natural frontiers with a policy of a speedy peace, a policy, that is, which would not upset the European balance of power. This permanent conflict of opinion only reached its culmination when the victories in Italy made a choice one way or the other inescapable. It grew increasingly bitter as the tension between Carnot and the triumvirs reached crisis point. Foreign policy, which had never ceased to be an issue in the general debate, became a means of resolving it. In short, the positions of each side were progressively clarified. But it would undoubtedly be wrong to reconstruct the origins of this policy exclusively in the light of Fructidor.

Beyond this latent conflict a certain consensus had been established between the Directors. No one called into question the alliances, priorities and methods. The treaties of 1795 had protected the northern and southern frontiers and brought Spain and Holland into the French orbit. They had also established Prussian neutrality. The Directory viewed this system as the basis of its policy. Continuing a tradition of *ancien régime* diplomacy, the new regime set out to weaken Austrian power and to counteract the commercial and colonial power of England. England was the enemy. Was it not England which had been at the centre of all the counter-revolutionary intrigues, and which had only recently inspired the Quiberon landing? Did she not, in the words of Reubell, desire to destroy French trade, having first stolen France's West Indian islands? Had she not, on 28 September, revived the Anglo-Austro-Russian alliance by giving Francis II financial encouragement to stand firm? Carnot considered where best to strike in order to bring England to terms. Meanwhile Austria, France's only serious adversary on the continent, had to be disheartened.

The plan of campaign incorporated these policy choices. The Army of the Sambre and the Meuse would enter Germany by the Main valley; that of the Rhine and the Moselle was to move down the valleys of the Neckar and the Danube. They would meet at Regensburg and march on Vienna. Two diversionary operations were planned: a landing in Ireland or England by the Army of the West and an advance by the Army of Italy towards the southern flank of the Empire. The original plan had given this front only a static role, that of holding down the maximum number of enemy troops. Bonaparte, who had been consulted, secured the change of policy which did not, however, modify the overall scheme: the decisive result was to be obtained in Germany.

Would public opinion support such a policy? Exhaustion and economic hardship certainly reinforced a current of hostility to the war among the masses. The *patrie* was no longer in danger; so what was the use of continuing the struggle? The hordes of deserters seemed to be voting for peace with their feet and there was no sign that morale was holding up better behind the lines than at the front. The Royalists exploited this confusion by accusing the Republic of warmongering and by demanding a return to the former frontiers. But on this question of what constituted a just outcome to the conflict — as well as on the issue of the responsibility for its outbreak — the Directory's position received considerable popular backing. Official propaganda benefited from the anglophobia of the towns by painting the picture of a pirate nation intent on the destruction of France. Three years of revolutionary war had also left their mark: no Republican, of whatever colour, would have accepted peace without compensation. From the welcome given to the bulletins from Italy one can gain an appreciation of the depth of the patriotism – a mixture of Jacobin enthusiasm and patriotic exaltation – of the 'Great Nation'. Moreover, *brissotin** expansionism had returned to the government in the person of La Révellière. Ideology could pave the way for business: it would be interesting to know the precise attitude of industrialists, who were both hindered and stimulated by the war, and who were provided with an enlarged market protected from the English. Even if one cannot estimate the exact importance of such material considerations, one should not ignore the influence exercised by the small but active groups of foreign patriots who had taken refuge in France. Reubell surrounded himself with gallicised Rhinelanders who, at least until the peace, pressed for annexation. And, as will be seen when the Italian campaign is examined below, Buonarroti and other *fuorusciti* attempted to interest the French government in the revolution in their country. But these various pressures influenced the foreign policy of the Directory less than the constraints of the war effort, or, shortly, the desires of those who were supposed to carry it out.

The war machine

Five armies remained supposedly active, although that of the North was barely so because its sector was peaceful. Moreau's troops had the additional advantage of being provided with their pay and their upkeep by the Batavian Republic, as stipulated in the terms of the Treaty of The Hague. This doubly exceptional situation made them the envy of the Armies of the Sambre and Meuse, of the Rhine and Moselle, of the Alps and of Italy, whose situations worried the Directory. Their combined strength had been reduced by desertions to 450,000 men. Some demi-brigades consisted of only 600 men; squadrons comprised only a score of cavalrymen, often badly mounted. Many officers failed to report these deserters in order to collect their pay. Those remaining at the front lacked food and equipment. One observer described the soldiers of the Army of the Rhine and Moselle as 'starving and so weak that they were hardly able to drag themselves along'.[1] Besides,

---

* *Brissotins*: the name by which the Girondins were at first generally known. [Trans.]
[1] Quoted by J. Godechot (75), p. 78.

discipline was disintegrating and the officers were unable to prevent their troops from marauding. Royalist propaganda, very active in the Army of the Rhine and Moselle, had a visibly demoralising effect. The incredible stampede which had transformed the retreat of the autumn of 1795 into a total panic was brutal confirmation of the severe collapse of morale in the armies.

Carnot revitalised the hunt for deserters, forbade false certificates of ill health and obliged officers to carry out rigorous roll-calls. These coercive measures, like the promises of amnesty and the appeals to glory, only brought a few thousand men back to the armies. It therefore became necessary to reorganise the structure of the armies to match the real levels of manpower, that is, to recast the troop units. The number of demi-brigades was reduced from 144 to 100. In spite of this reduction there were still too many officers and NCOs. Some of these were combined into auxiliary companies. Others were relieved of their posts; they left the army with only a third or a half of the wages owing to them. These embittered servicemen were fertile soil for Babouvist propaganda.

The Committee of Public Safety had, as best it could, succeeded in supplying the armies by a system of requisitioning and agencies. It seemed opportune to the Thermidoreans and the Directory to revise this system in order to adapt it to the new economic policy. It was decided to rely henceforth on private entrepreneurs, in the expectation of avoiding the waste and delays of the administrators (January 1796). For several months the armies survived with difficulty while the old system coexisted with the new. Requisitioning provided a supplementary contribution but the method was discredited and had limited results in regions which had been over-milked already. The contractors in Year IV were looked upon with a favourable eye. Hoping to obtain better control over such transactions, the government attempted unsuccessfully to group them all together. It had to resign itself to breaking up the tenders, which already represented considerable advances of cash. Only large companies could assemble sufficient capital to supply, for example, the Army of Italy with grain or to provide transport services for the Army of the Rhine and Moselle. Many of these associations of capitalists did, it is true, subcontract on a large scale. These contractors and munitions suppliers, whose history is yet to be written, were an essential cog in the war machine. Their administration came under unanimous criticism: generals, commissioners to the armies, right-wing deputies, Jacobins, inhabitants of the conquered territories were all united in denouncing their malpractices. For example, Lanchère, a contractor of artillery and transport – 'who has managed till now to starve our armies so well', wrote the commissioner to the Army of Italy in December 1795 – was accused in October 1796 of fraud in his supplying of horses. Many of his colleagues failed to fulfil their obligations and the correspondence of generals and commissioners is full of complaints about rotten food, cardboard soles and undersized clothes. Those who did carry out their obligations exacted a high price. A quintal of wheat sold to the army cost 50% more than when sold to individuals; the price of horses and boots could double. Did the risks incurred explain such a mark-up? Certainly the state paid badly and slowly. Thus in Floréal Year IV the contractors of the Army of the Sambre and Meuse were paid in *mandats** which had lost 80% of their face value. And when the Lanchère et Cerf-Ber Company came to carry out the transportation for the Army of Italy in December 1795, it gave an opportune reminder that it was owed 34 million francs in *assignats* and 330,000 francs in metallic currency.

The form of payment varied considerably, but, for lack of metallic currency, it became customary to pay the contractors either with cuttings in national forests or by taxes levied on the conquered territories (the Flachat Company in Italy, the Lamotze Company in Germany). Among other disadvantages, this latter method deprived the military and civil authorities of part of their prerogatives and ran the risk of arousing strong reactions from the local populations. Above all, the conduct of operations could come to be influenced by the decisions of the munitions suppliers; war became a business, their business. Finally, this system encouraged corruption: the awarding of contracts, the fixing of their terms and the checking up on their application all provided opportunities for profit for the government's agents in the armies or in Paris. And what measures could be taken against them when it was known, for instance, that Ouvrard was on intimate terms with Barras and that the munitions suppliers of Italy and Germany were protected by Reubell? Waste, inefficiency and corruption – defects that had been attributed to the agencies – all reappeared once the military supply corps was handed over to private enterprise. But the nature of the regime – that is, of its supporters and its policies – did not allow any solution other than a reliance on this much vilified and yet so indispensable breed of individuals.

The Directory's problem was to ensure that its orders and authority

* For a discussion of currencies see pp. 92–4 below. [Trans.]

were respected by the army commanders. The military topographical bureau, directed by Clarke, assisted Carnot to work out campaign plans and draft directives. It does not seem that the Ministry of War had any function other than the administration of the military apparatus. Among the Directors, Reubell and Barras were in favour of a strict control of the generals, less, it seems, for political reasons than because they did not want to lose out in the scramble for spoils. Carnot corresponded regularly with the generals, and this gave him less desire to keep them under surveillance. Besides, an excessively close supervision would have been too reminiscent of the representatives on mission, who were remembered with distaste. It was unrealistic for a government whose authority at home was precarious to expect to be obeyed in the armies without a murmur. But a solution had to be found. The theatre of operations was moving further afield, the administration of the conquered territories posed complex problems and the possibility of future diplomatic contacts demanded both autonomy at the local level and vigilance at the centre. The generals-in-chief could not devote as much attention to supply as to tactics. And it was anyway desirable to demonstrate the pre-eminence, or at least the presence, of civil authority. If the chief ordnance officers ensured the general administration, the other tasks fell to the commissioners to the armies. The efficiency of these representatives of the Directory depended on their own qualities, on the attitude of the generals and on the support that they received from the government in cases of conflict. Some of them – Ritter in Italy, Haussmann in Germany – were friends of Reubell. To assist Saliceti, who was the commissioner attached to Bonaparte, Carnot himself chose his own friend Garrau. Finally, Pichegru's departure and Schérer's incompetence meant that new commanders had to be found for the Army of the Rhine and Moselle and for the Army of Italy respectively. Carnot secured the appointment of his two protégés, Moreau and Bonaparte.

THE IMPOSSIBLE VICTORY

The advantages of Bonaparte's position

To replace the ageing Schérer, who was both unadventurous and sceptical, the Directors had, then, chosen for the Army of Italy a 27-year-old general. At this stage it was possible to suspect Bonaparte of having more contacts than experience, even if his appointment did crown a remarkable success as a staff officer. Having made a name for himself as a specialist in the 'Italian question', he still had to prove his qualities as a strategist and leader of men in the field. The army that he rejoined in March 1796 was in a far from brilliant condition. Schérer had left behind some forty thousand troops, a motley collection of armed and hungry men, undisciplined and all too ready to loot. There was little cavalry and poor artillery; everything rested therefore on the goodwill of the infantry. Bonaparte could at least count on their endurance; most of these men, natives of the Alps, were embarking upon their fourth campaign. He also had the intuition to turn their poverty to good account. The famous evocation of the 'rich provinces' of Italy whetted their appetites at just the right moment; and they would be given honour and glory to boot. Bonaparte transformed another weakness into an asset: by being impoverished, the army was thereby less weighed down. Its speed (except during sieges) would create a shock effect that would compensate for its lack of resources. Bonaparte's dauntless subordinates, who were often also skilful tacticians – La Harpe, Sérurier, Augereau, Masséna – were to be the auxiliaries of his success. This was especially true of the two latter, who were able to obtain all the more from their soldiers in that they resembled them so closely. Berthier was the perfect administrator that this army needed. When Bonaparte arrived in Nice on 21 March the mobilisation of energies and resources was well under way, thanks to Saliceti, the representative of the Directory, who knew the new general-in-chief very well. They were both Corsicans and had been friends since the start of the Revolution, and had fought together at Toulon, where Saliceti had called in the extra help of Bonaparte. From this time on Bonaparte owed most of his promotions to Saliceti. And in return he had perhaps arranged for him to be appointed to the post of commissioner. Saliceti's instructions required him to assist Bonaparte, in his military tasks, devoting himself especially to administration and discipline. But it was specified that in no circumstances would Bonaparte be able to sign an armistice without the commissioner's agreement. This stipulation safeguarded the rights and authority of the government. The guiding principles of the campaign were based on Bonaparte's suggestions: to force the King of Sardinia to make peace, to secure an alliance with him and then to drive the Austrians out of the country. Whether or not they were to be pursued further north would depend on the success of the first two phases of the operation.

In the Directory's strategy the Italian patriots held a secondary but useful position. They would exacerbate the internal contradictions of the Republic's opponents and back up the military action. Buonarroti had succeeded in convincing the government of the importance of supporting the efforts of the exiles. But he had certainly not won it over to the cause of Italian unity. The Directors had no desire to contribute to the birth of an overpowerful Italy, even if they did not completely rule out the still very new idea of an independent state of Naples. Even so, Buonarroti was for a time officially recognised as the leader of the revolutionaries who would form 'a great power in Italy' (25 March 1796) in the wake of Bonaparte. As far as Buonarroti was concerned, the ambiguity did not last long, since he was arrested on 10 May. But the same question of what use to make of revolutionary war faced both Bonaparte, who had met Buonarroti, and Saliceti, whose past, there being no evidence to the contrary, gave one to suppose that he would look favourably upon the Italian Jacobins.

The fifteen-day war

The Austro-Sardinians outnumbered the French two to one. Fortunately, Colli's Piedmontese, based mainly at Ceva in the valley of the Tanaro, could not join up speedily with the Austrian general, Beaulieu, whose troops had wintered to the north of the Po. Bonaparte, believing that he had the time to strike at the Piedmontese, assembled the bulk of his divisions around Savona in preparation for an attack. An Austrian manoeuvre towards Voltri forced him to delay: Saliceti, to secure the grant of a loan, had despatched a brigade to intimidate the Genoese and Beaulieu had taken this as a pretext to advance as well. The Austrians had to be kept at a distance: Beaulieu's lieutenant, Argenteau, was held up at Monte-Nagino and then driven off the field by La Harpe and Masséna at Montenotte, north of Savona (12 April). This first victory broke an incipient front between the Piedmontese and the Austrians on the Cadibone pass. Augereau beat the Piedmontese at Millesimo on 13 April and set off towards Ceva. On the next day the breach was widened. Colli's Austrian subordinate, Provera, surrendered, while Masséna drove the Austrians from Dego after a struggle which for a long time remained inconclusive. The Austrians, who in a few days had lost eight thousand men, fell back towards the north. French efforts were now entirely concentrated on Colli. Threatened with encirclement, the Piedmontese general left Ceva for

Mondovi, where he was defeated on 21 April. Three days later the French army was at Cherasco, south of Turin. The Piedmontese sought an armistice which was signed at Cherasco on 28 April. The kingdom's military situation was not hopeless but Victor Amadeus III feared a revolution. His absolutist rule, contrary to the trend of his predecessors, had created a potentially critical situation. The arrival of the French, accompanied by Piedmontese patriots, risked precipitating the crisis. Ranza and his friends had indeed stirred up Alba and Cunca to revolt and had declared a republic. The King therefore surrendered to Bonaparte the three fortresses which the French had demanded and opened the roads and passes to his army. In this bargain the patriots were abandoned to their fate – repression. Those who escaped joined the French.

Would this situation satisfy the Directory? Initially it had undoubtedly hoped for more, but at the time that it received news of the armistice it was hunting down the Babouvists. Support for Ranza would undermine the struggle against the Jacobins within France. The most reliable course was to treat with 'our future allies' in Sardinia. This strategic motive had decided Bonaparte; it was not wise to stir up trouble in one's rear. And Carnot approved the signing of the armistice by his general-in-chief.

In Milan

After this fifteen-day war, the Army of Italy immediately moved against the Austrians. Beaulieu was waiting on the left bank of the Po, as far west as Pavia. It was from this direction that he expected the French to come. In fact they came from the south, crossing the river at Piacenza. The Austrian general, breaking off after the first contact, retreated towards the Adda where a rearguard engagement took place at Lodi (10 May). Only by personal sacrifice were Bonaparte's generals able to lead their soldiers forward, decimated as the troops were by the Austrian artillery. This costly success was presented by Bonaparte as a victory. Among other gestures, he sent the names of the bravest grenadiers to their *départements* of origin. The growing political implications of the campaign were now taking shape.

The Austrian army moved away east for fear of being outflanked. The road to Milan was clear. On 16 May the Lombard capital received Bonaparte as a liberator. The 'patriots' had seized power there three days before. With the encouragement of Saliceti, a club, a patriotic society and a surveillance committee were organised. At their meetings, run by liberal nobles and members of the bourgeoisie, there was feverish discussion of social and political revolution. This time Bonaparte allowed events to run their course. Lombardy was an Austrian dependency, not a monarchy to be treated with circumspection. Perhaps, since his triumphal entry into Milan, he was also considering the part that Italy could play in his destiny. In any case, he imposed on the city a municipality chosen from among the moderate revolutionaries. Milan became the meeting place of all the patriots of the peninsula. Ranza and the Piedmontese, Romans like L'Aurora, the Neapolitan Lauberg – all came to seek asylum there. The recently founded *Termometro Politico* campaigned for a unified republic. But it was also necessary to take account of the needs of war. The government of Lombardy was entrusted to a military agency whose immediate task was to raise a tax of 20 million *livres*. The State Congress retained its administrative functions under the control of the French. By juxtaposing old and new institutions, by simultaneously calling for independence and for requisitions, Bonaparte was attempting to combine objectives that were barely compatible. Certainly care was taken to present the levies as a campaign against the rich. Saliceti claimed that the items confiscated from the pawnshops were being handed back to the people. And Augereau demanded measures against the nobles and priests, 'our natural enemies'. But in reality the burden of the taxes fell upon the peasants, who were already the victims of exactions. On 23 May incidents broke out in several places. Peasants, but also disappointed patriots, rose up against the French. The rebels were put down, the village of Binasco burnt and Pavia plundered. This *jacquerie* had shown that it was difficult to both fleece and liberate a country at one and the same time.

Dividing the spoils

On 14 May Bonaparte received new orders from Carnot. He was instructed to give up the invasion of the Tyrol. Instead, the Army of Italy was to carry out a raid against the south. Bonaparte was in agreement with both these demands. The inactivity of Jourdan and Moreau made it risky to attempt any operation in the direction of Austria. His army needed to regain its strength. Moreover, he was not displeased at the idea of subduing the states of central Italy. But Carnot added that he should entrust Kellermann with the defence of Lombardy. Bonaparte replied sharply that nothing could be achieved in Italy without a unified command. And, seeing his ambitions under threat at the very moment that they were taking shape, he offered his resignation. Faced with this resistance, the Directory had to give way. This first show of weakness was followed by another more serious instance: on 20 May Bonaparte decided to give his troops half their pay in metallic currency. In spite of Saliceti, the Directory did not protest against this unprecedented measure which bound the soldiers to the person of their leader. Bonaparte's formidable victories had turned Italy into his domain and the soldiers into his dependants. His first successes had led several Italian princes to detach themselves from the coalition. The Duke of Parma was granted an armistice on 9 May in exchange for 2 million *livres*, for supplies and for twenty pictures. On 23 May the Duke of Modena was, in his turn, taxed to the tune of 7·5 million *livres*, as well as having to provide supplies and pictures. Against Naples, whose cavalry had acted in concert with Austrians and whose fleet was assisting the English, Bonaparte, ignoring Saliceti's advice, saw fit to impose only military neutrality. The negotiations embarked upon with the Pope had run aground. Saliceti, in the name of the Directory, demanded an indemnity of 50 million *livres* and the retraction of the bulls denouncing the civil constitution of the clergy and the Republican government. The French army occupied successively Bologna, Ferrara and Longo (13–20 June). On 23 June the Pope surrendered. He handed over the port of Ancona and agreed to pay 21 million *livres* – 15·5 million *livres* in metallic currency – as well as to provide manuscripts and pictures.

The Duchy of Toscana had been neutral since 15 February 1795. Nevertheless the Directory commanded Bonaparte to occupy Leghorn. It hoped gradually to close all the Italian ports to the English. Moreover, since the decline of Genoa, Leghorn had become a major entrepôt of the western Mediterranean. It was believed that the port contained English merchandise worth 10 million *livres*; in fact goods worth only 3 million *livres* were found (27 June). In a fury, Bonaparte blamed this shortfall on the Flachat Company, which had been charged with selling the confiscated merchandise. In the meantime he had not forgotten his own interests. He undoubtedly made several million *livres* out of this campaign. His officers – for example Masséna – and the mass of soldiers all pillaged on their own account, and when Bonaparte tried to take action against the contractors it was clear that this was because he wanted above all to leave the lion's share of the spoils for his own men. Behind the epic lay a huge 'racket'.

Success in Germany

The German front, which ought to have been the principal theatre of operations, remained static. In spite of Bonaparte's entreaties, Jourdan and Moreau amassed pretexts to delay an offensive. In the face of the young Archduke Charles, the two generals seemed extremely timid, almost defeatist. The Army of the Sambre and Meuse finally crossed the Rhine on 31 May. Kléber defeated the Austrians at Altenkirchen (4 June), but Jourdan's troops, for lack of any combined action by Moreau, bore the full brunt of the combat, and fell back on Dusseldorf. On 24 June Moreau decided to move. His army quickly advanced into Wurtemberg, reached Rastatt and drove off the Archduke's forces at Ettlingen. The Austrians retreated along the Danube, and Vienna seemed within the French grasp. Giving in to Carnot's insistence, Jourdan had again crossed the Rhine at the end of June. His army reached Frankfurt on 14 July and Bamberg on 4 August. Carnot judged that the French armies would, as planned, join up between Ingolstadt and Regensburg. He instructed Joubert, commissioner to the Army of the Sambre and Meuse, to be ready to 'revolutionise' Bohemia and Hungary. All he needed to do was to urge these subject peoples to reclaim their ancient rights. Faced with the advance of the Republic's armies and threatened with internal disintegration, the Court of Vienna would capitulate like that of Turin. These plans for psychological warfare were never to be put into action since neither Jourdan nor Moreau succeeded in advancing any further. But at the beginning of August the overall results of the campaign seemed encouraging. The spoils of the conflict formed part of the plan of operations. The advance of the Army of the Sambre and Meuse along the Main had been calculated to pass through Hesse and Franconia. The French imposed tributes on Nuremberg, Bamberg and Königstein. They extracted 3 million *livres* before being forced to retreat. The capture of Frankfurt had raised hopes of considerable booty. But this, like Leghorn, proved to be another mirage. In fact 4 million *livres* were collected, but the whole of this sum was kept by the Lamotze Company as payment due for its supplies.

The Army of the Rhine and Moselle also repeated a disappointing harvest. It passed through no very prosperous areas. The Palatinate brought in little. On the other hand, the armistices concluded along the length of the military advance gave France substantial benefits. Thus Moreau negotiated with Frederick of Wurtemberg without consulting his commissioner and obtained 4 million *livres* (17 July). On 26 July the Margrave of Bade gave 2 million *livres*. On the next day the Swabian Circle[2] signed an armistice for 12 million *livres*. In addition to these payments, they all had to contribute to the upkeep of the army. These military successes of the summer were confirmed, at the diplomatic level, by a series of treaties. In exchange for territorial compensation on the right bank of the Rhine, the Duke of Wurtemberg gave up Montbéliard and his former domains in Upper Alsace, while the Margrave of Bade gave up Kehl and Hüningen (August 1796). Thus both the military and the diplomatic position of France was satisfactory in the summer of 1796. But nothing had really been achieved. The French army in Germany had extremely extended lines of communication and was therefore highly vulnerable. In Italy, Bonaparte had still not taken Mantua. On both fronts the armies, without hope of reinforcements, seemed to be exhausted by their efforts. Above all, this three-month campaign had transformed the armies and their leaders. The war was no longer concerned with national defence, but with conquest – or even merely plunder. The generals were tending to become independent of the Directory, or at least of its representatives. But the major effect of the Italian campaign had been to transform Bonaparte, a mere staff officer, into a strategist and leading political figure.

DANGERS

Archduke Charles's counter-offensive

The plan of campaign had called for the armies of Jourdan and Moreau to act separately, but they had in fact now advanced without co-ordinating their movements. This made them vulnerable to the Austrian counter-offensive which in a few weeks was to drive them back onto the Rhine. The French armies were handicapped by their extended lines of communication and their lack of any unified command. They were also undergoing a general crisis. Jourdan had only nominal authority over his subordinates, Kléber and Marceau, who openly criticised his tactics. In the Army of the Rhine and Meuse the chief-of-staff was non-existent and the major-generals were left to their own devices – or lack of them. The commissioners reported that

---

[2] At the beginning of the 18th century the Empire had been divided into ten 'circles'. These districts were only a relic of the past in 1796.

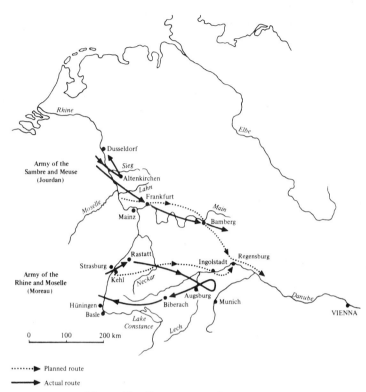

Planned route
Actual route

Map 1 The German campaign, 1796-7

the troops indulged in all forms of pillaging and brutality. Officers scarcely bothered to try and reimpose discipline within the units. The havoc wrought by the troops drove the peasantry to revolt. And French reprisals – villages burnt, summary executions – only further antagonised the population and led to yet more savagery and disobedience. Finally a deep indifference to, if not actual disagreement about, the aims of the conflict set in.

Leaving a cordon of troops facing Moreau, Archduke Charles concentrated his forces against the Army of the Sambre and Meuse. He successively defeated Bernadotte and Jourdan (23-24 August), who were forced to retreat. This first blow brought about the disintegration of the army. Everyone wanted to resign: Jourdan, who was sick and demoralised, Kléber, who was in disagreement with his general-in-chief, and numerous officers. The army abandoned its impedimenta and its spoils, and the troops scattered on marauding expeditions. Frankfurt was hurriedly evacuated. The blockade of Mainz was lifted. On 19 September Jourdan recrossed the Sieg. His rearguard was attacked near Altenkirchen on the same day, and the young General Marceau was killed in the skirmish. The replacement of Jourdan by Beurnonville could not restore dynamism to this doomed army. The former commander of the Army of the North, a mediocre and timid individual, was not the man to brave such storms. While the new commissioner, Alexandre, was attempting to restore discipline and cut down on the offensive luxury of the officers' existence, Beurnonville refused to take similar measures and even failed to defend Alexandre against the cabal of generals and contractors. In spite of Carnot, he was in no hurry to resume the offensive. October and November went by in inactivity, and he was left with no choice but to sign an armistice (8 December) and take up winter quarters.

Moreau had not tried to pursue the Archduke. He advanced south of the Danube, towards Munich. His Austrian adversary, La Tour, was beaten on the Lech near Augsburg (24 August). Was the Army of the Rhine and Moselle to continue advancing towards the Tyrol as the Directory demanded? In pushing southwards Moreau ran the risk of exposing his rear to the Archduke's forces. He chose instead to return to the Rhine. It is possible that, strategic reasons apart, he had perhaps a more secret motive. It would be wrong to say that Moreau was won over to royalism, but he was wavering. The *émigrés* fighting in La Tour's army kept up contact with the republican officers. Overtures were certainly made to Moreau himself. His inactivity on the banks of the Lech and his retreat were signs not of treason but of a certain political hesitation. The Army of the Rhine and Moselle therefore headed for Lake Constance with the Austrians at its heels. But at the edge of the Black Forest, at Biberach, it turned and inflicted a severe defeat on the pursuing Austrians (2 October). Even so the retreat still took on the appearance of a rout, the generals being unable to retain command of their own men. Some of them, such as General Tuncq who presided over the systematic destruction of Brisgau, even joined in the depredations. After several engagements, Desaix and then Moreau recrossed the Rhine (26 October). Only the fortresses of Kehl and Hüningen were still holding out. Carnot had stigmatised Jourdan's 'pitiful retreat'. But he judged that his 'dear Fabius' had extricated himself brilliantly from a difficult situation. The two armies had certainly avoided annihilation. But they were surviving with difficulty:

desertions were multiplying, and the vital defence of the two bridge-heads of Kehl and Hüningen seemed in jeopardy. The 1796 campaign in Germany marked, then, the collapse of Carnot's hopes.

Italy in question

Bonaparte's position in Italy became precarious once the Austrians again directed their efforts towards the southern front. From July to November the Army of Italy was subjected to three offensives. On 18 July Bonaparte had entrenched himself outside Mantua, the key to northern Italy and the gateway to the Tyrol. The struggle promised to be difficult because the French lacked siege equipment and the town was protected by swamps. But at the end of the month Wurmser moved down towards the plain of Lombardy with 50,000 men, intending to cut Bonaparte's lines of communication. Quasdanovitch, Wurmser's deputy, had already defeated Sauret and taken control of Brescia, cutting off the road to Milan. As for Wurmser, he drove Masséna back on to the Mincio. Bonaparte at once determined to abandon the siege and to move against the different Austrian army corps before they could join up. Bonaparte abandoned 180 cannon in the marshes, indicating that he envisaged a mobile war rather than a static, fortress-dominated campaign. He beat Quasdanovitch at Lonato (3 August) and then completed the defeat of Wurmser who had been overwhelmed by the forces of Augereau and Sérurier at Castiglione. The Austrian general judged that it would be wise to move back to the Tyrol. Carnot applauded this revival of French fortunes and requested Bonaparte to join up with Moreau. To the Prussian ambassador he gave a lucid analysis of this last passage of arms: 'Our successes are great; but they were nonetheless very close.'

No sooner had the siege of Mantua been resumed than Wurmser again prepared to relieve the town. He had recently reconstituted his army by the addition of troops made available by the victories in Germany. Bonaparte had also been reinforced by some contingents from the Vendée where the war had died out. But the French remained numerically inferior. Once again it was necessary to attack the enemy before they could combine. Bonaparte moved against Wurmser's lieutenant, Davidovitch, who was guarding the Trent region, and defeated him at Roveredo (4 September). Then he caught up again with Wurmser, who was trying to reach Mantua. Wurmser, harried by Masséna and Augereau, and defeated at Bassano, took refuge in Mantua, where he was forced to remain after an unsuccessful sortie on 15 September.

In Lombardy the agitation in favour of independence and unity had gained ground since the summer. On 26 August the military agency was replaced by a 'general administration' in which the patriots of the municipality participated. Saliceti and his colleague, Garrau, hoped in this way to improve the raising of taxes. In the process they were helping the Lombards to take over the administration of their country. For reasons of public order, the commander of the Milan fortress had, from the end of May, dissolved the clubs and societies. In July a new group was formed with the aim of arousing public consciousness and spreading enlightenment. This club, authorised by Bonaparte, very quickly became a centre of propaganda for Italian unification. It created a national militia and a Lombard legion which adopted the green, white and red flag. On 14 October 1796 it organised a large popular demonstration in favour of independence as a protest against the Directory which opposed such a solution. The Directory's position had indeed become more rigid, moving from scepticism to outright refusal. It was with apprehension that the Directors viewed the most ardent Italian patriots assume the leadership of the movement. Saliceti's name figured in Babeuf's correspondence, but he succeeded in clearing himself. Yet the impression remained that there had been a sort of international conspiracy instigated by Buonarroti. Moreover, since the majority of the Directory seemed to have come round to the policy of natural frontiers, it was vital, if this policy were to be carried through, to keep Lombardy as a bargaining counter. Bonaparte did not yet dare contradict the Directory on this essential point, and direct control of the society by Milanese or Piedmontese democrats ran counter to his views. He closed the club and replaced it with an association of an academic nature. The protector of Lombardy would definitely not allow his hand to be forced. More serious, certainly, was the decision, taken on 25 October, to confide civil and administrative authority to General Baraguey d'Hilliers, who was in command of Lombardy. This veritable coup, which left in place only the military hierarchy and the Lombard institutions, deprived the commissioners of their authority. Notified of this by Saliceti's colleague, Garrau, the Directory dared not reprimand Bonaparte. By refusing to back up its representatives, the government admitted its helplessness.

To the south of the Po Bonaparte enjoyed a greater freedom of manoeuvre because the Directory wanted to weaken the power of the

Pope and had no interest in the fate of the principality of Modena. Thus when, on 30 August, the Senate of Reggio, in revolt against the Duke, asked for the protection of France, Bonaparte, Saliceti and Garrau were not slow to intervene. The armistice was broken under the pretext that the taxes had not been paid, and the French army occupied Modena (4 October). In the Papal State of Emilia, which was in turmoil, Bologna wanted to obtain a republican constitution. From 1 July the patriots, strengthened by Bonaparte's approval, set out to achieve this. Their draft, finished by the end of September, drew closely on the French constitution. But the aspiration towards unity swept away local susceptibilities. Modena, Reggio and Ferrara wanted to unite with Bologna. Deputies from the four states set up an assembly at Modena, which proclaimed the Cispadane Republic and prepared to call a Constituent Assembly (16 October 1796). The Directory, informed after the event, made no protest, although its representatives had just formed the nucleus of the Italian Republic. Reubell and Delacroix did not let Bonaparte 'revolutionise' and occupy Genoa, which he had shown signs of wanting to do. Between Paris and the commander-in-chief there was, as Raymond Guyot has remarked, a race to negotiate the fastest.[1] In this contest the Genoese obtained fairly favourable terms from the Directory. They retained their institutions and neutrality in return for an indemnity and the closure of their ports to the English (9 October 1796).

Arcole

All Reubell's diplomatic activity was directed towards isolating Austria, towards consolidating France's gains without upsetting the political configuration of Italy. The Directory therefore signed a treaty with Naples without requiring either the surrender of any territory or even the imposition of an anti-English blockade (10 October 1796). With the Pope, on the other hand, there was no question of compromise. The French negotiators – the discussions which had begun in Paris continued in Florence between Mgr Caleppi and the commissioners to the armies – insisted relentlessly on the revocation of the counter-revolutionary bulls and edicts. The result was a breaking off of negotiations, which Bonaparte, who had been kept at a distance, blamed on Saliceti and Garrau.

The new Austrian offensive combined three movements: the

[3] R. Guyot (76), p. 254.

Hungarian general Alvinczy would advance on Verona, while Davido-vitch attacked Trent and Wurmser sallied forth from Mantua. The Army of Italy was weak and morale was low. The provision of supplies was hit by the inefficiency of the contractors. The Flachat Company was in no hurry to carry out the deliveries for which it had been paid through the taxes levied upon the Pope. To Garrau's protest against this, the Directory replied with disillusioned resignation. Bonaparte demanded fresh troops. 'The Army of Italy,' he wrote to Carnot on 13 November, 'reduced to a handful of men, is exhausted'; and on the same day Garrau went even further: 'there is no longer the same spirit, the same energy. The men are fighting apathetically, almost with re-pugnance.' From 1 to 15 November the French were unable to contain the enemy. In desperation Bonaparte moved against Alvinczy's rear, at the confluence of the Adige and the Alpone, and decided to join battle in this constricted and marshy zone. Was everything to be risked on this gamble? The Austrians held the bridge at Arcole and the French soldiers began to be seized by panic; at this point Bonaparte took the head of the column, flag in hand. He was unable to cross the bridge, but after seventy-two hours of confused fighting the Austrians fell back. With Carnot's complicity Bonaparte presented the victory at Arcole as a brilliant feat of arms. But, while displaying Bonaparte's own timely if foolhardy bravery, it had in reality served to reveal the exhaustion of an army which had been driven to its limits. Besides, nothing had been settled; Bonaparte had won a battle, but not the war.

Carnot was ready to accept the implications for French foreign policy of the French military difficulties. He was more than ever in favour of a rapid peace settlement and secretly sent an emissary to Vienna to discover the Emperor's terms. After this personal sounding out of opinion, he got his colleagues to agree that Clarke, head of the topographical bureau, should be sent on an exploratory mission. La Révellière, who was irritated by Bonaparte's behaviour, also assigned him the task of discreetly investigating the state of the Army of Italy and the conduct of its commander-in-chief. Bonaparte expressed his dissatisfaction to the Directory's envoy; France, in his view, could not trade Lombardy for Belgium and for the Rhine frontier. The balance of forces had to be modified in France's favour and negotiations begun on a fresh basis. The Austrians, in the euphoria of their offensive, fulfilled all Bonaparte's hopes: they refused Clarke his passports.

The Irish expedition

The domestic situation in England – an economic crisis, revolutionary agitation, troubles in Ireland – prompted Pitt to try his luck at negotiation. He would perhaps even have resigned himself to the occupation of Belgium in return for some colonial compensation. But by the time his envoy, Lord Malmesbury, left for Paris on 16 October, the victories of Archduke Charles had strengthened the resolve of the coalition: France was to return to her 1792 frontiers and there was to be no question of abandoning the Low Countries to her. Delacroix declared that the abandonment of Belgium would be a violation of the constitution, and the Directory, convinced that England wanted to destroy the Republic, broke off negotiations (19 December 1796).

The French government became all the more concerned to carry the war into the enemy camp. In the summer the old scheme of a landing in Ireland took shape. The leader of the United Irish, Wolfe Tone, recently returned from America, came to confer with Carnot, and helped Hoche, who had been appointed leader of the expedition, to finalise the invasion plans. The Directory's ambition was to co-ordinate the Irish landing with a raid into Wales. Contacts were also to be made with the Scots and with the English revolutionaries. This was to pay England back in kind for Quiberon. But Hoche came up against various forms of sabotage. All the right-wing Royalists and the anglophile opposition strove in the Councils to discredit the plan. The Treasury, constitutionally independent of the Directory, refused to provide the funds. From Brest, Villaret-Joyeuse expressed his preference for an expedition into the Indian Ocean. The fleet finally departed from Brest on 15 December. As soon as it had set out the flagship in which Hoche was travelling was separated from the rest of the fleet by a storm. As a result of bad weather and navigation errors, only some of the ships reached Ireland. Grouchy, who was second-in-command, dared not disembark and gave the order to retreat. Hoche, who arrived later with the other ships, could only turn back. The adventure ended in derision. Nevertheless the reasons for the invasion remained. The revolt of the Irish Catholics and the mutiny of the British fleet would give the project a new relevance later. But for the moment there was only another setback to add to the defeats in Germany, the problems in Italy and the diplomatic deadlock. The war promised to be long and hard. 1796 had been a year of missed opportunities.

Rivoli

The Army of the Rhine and Moselle was holding the two bridgeheads of Kehl and Hüningen. Their fall was ascribed to the incompetence, even treason, of Moreau. Carnot was to be a victim of the same accusation after 18 Fructidor. That Moreau, attempting neither a sortie nor a disengagement, may not have acted with the necessary determination to save Kehl does not detract from the merit due to Desaix. He resisted the siege until 9 January 1797 and almost razed the fort to the ground before capitulating. As for Hüningen, it held out until 5 February. This resistance had held down important enemy units whose absence alleviated the pressure on the Army of Italy.

Bonaparte had profited from the pause in December to reorganise his army. He had above all applied himself to improving the command and restoring discipline. In January Alvinczy moved down the Adige with 50,000 men. His objective was unchanged: to relieve Mantua. Joubert, the new divisional commander, took the initial brunt of the attack and had to retreat to the plateau of Rivoli. On the morning of 14 January Masséna arrived in support. The attackers were repulsed and hunted down by Joubert's troops. Alvinczy's defeat was resounding. On the evening of the Battle of Rivoli Bonaparte and Masséna headed towards Mantua. Since 13 January Augereau had been trying to prevent General Provera from breaking through the blockade of the fortress. On 16 January the arrival of Masséna's division ensured victory and Provera surrendered in the outskirts of Mantua. Joubert drove back the Austrians at Trent. Without reinforcements, and soon without supplies, Mantua could hold out no longer. On 2 February Wurmser surrendered to Sérurier. The fall of Mantua brought to an end a brilliant campaign in which a remarkable use of terrain, as at Rivoli, and the mobility of the troops (Masséna's division covered 110 kilometres in four days), had finally ensured decisive success. With Mantua taken, the road to the Tyrol was open.

On 3 February Barras, Reubell and La Révellière ordered Bonaparte to destroy 'the centre of unity of the Roman religion, the irreconcilable enemy of the Republic'. It is clear from this language that Barras and Reubell had taken up La Révellière's concerns the better to cement the triumvirate. The negotiations with the Pope had come to nothing since

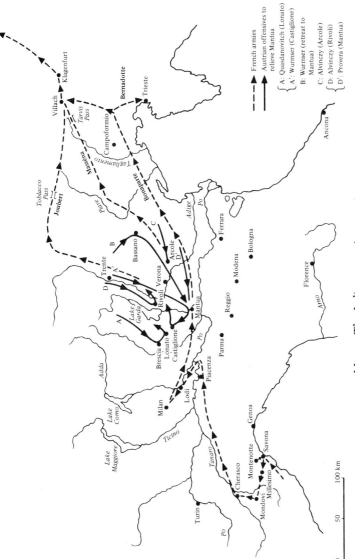

Map 2 The Italian campaign, 1796–7

French armies

Austrian offensives to relieve Mantua

A: Quasdanovitch (Lonato)
A': Wurmser (Castiglione)
B: Wurmser (retreat to Mantua)
C: Alvinczy (Arcole)
D: Alvinczy (Rivoli)
D': Provera (Mantua)

Leoben

Klagenfurt

Villach

Tarvis Pass

Campoformio

Bernadotte

Trieste

Toblacco Pass

Joubert

Piave

Tagliamento

Massena

Bonaparte

Ancona

Trente

Bassano

Verona

Arcole

Adige

Po

Ferrara

Bologna

Modena

Reggio

Mantua

Florence

Arno

Rivoli

Lake Garda

Brescia

Lonato

Castiglione

Po

Parma

Piacenza

Adda

Lake Como

Lake Maggiore

Ticino

Milan

Lodi

Genoa

Savona

Montenotte

Millesimo

Mondovi

Cherasco

Tanaro

Turin

Po

0   50   100 km

Pius VI was banking on a victory by Alvinczy to save him from the need to make concessions. After Rivoli the Pope's prevarication had to cease. Bonaparte immediately occupied Ancona (9 February) without taking the risk of advancing as far as Rome. He was in a hurry to conclude peace and resume the offensive in the Tyrol since Clarke's indiscretions had revealed that, however successful the Italian campaign might be, the Directory still considered the Italian conquests as a bargaining counter. Lombardy was definitely worth '*une messe*'. Thus Bonaparte rushed through a treaty which repeated the terms of the Armistice of Bologna. The Pope also gave up the Legations and committed himself to paying an extra 15 million *livres*.

The decisive campaign

The plan of campaign for spring 1797 drew upon the lessons of the previous year. This time the main role fell to the Army of Italy, while the Armies of Germany had to hold down the maximum number of enemy forces. Carnot sent reinforcements to Bonaparte taken mostly from the Army of the Rhine and Moselle. Thus the political composition of the Bernadotte division created acute tensions. But for the first time Bonaparte enjoyed numerical superiority. He was able to muster 60,000 men, while Archduke Charles, Austria's new hope, commanded only 40,000. This explains Bonaparte's haste to take the offensive. Joubert was to invade the Tyrol, Masséna was in command of the centre and Bonaparte and Bernadotte were in charge of the right wing. On 16 March, on the Tagliamento, they drove the bulk of the Austrian forces from the field. Archduke Charles fell back on Gradisca and then into Carinthia. Trieste was occupied on 23 March. Masséna was supposed to prevent the Austrian army in the Tyrol from making any contact with the Archduke's right wing. He defeated Lusignan's corps which held this central position and took control of the Tarvis Pass. Jourdan had advanced on the Brenner Pass, but, faced with the double threat of a counter-offensive and a peasant uprising, he had been forced to withdraw. On receiving news of the French victories, he resumed his advance, reaching the Toblacco Pass and then Villach on the banks of the Drave (8 April). On 31 March Bonaparte was already at Klagenfurt. At this point he wrote to the Archduke suggesting an end to the carnage: 'we have killed enough people and inflicted enough evils on suffering humanity'. The precariousness of his own situation worried him more than such humanitarian feelings. The French troops had ventured into the Alps without sufficient resources and without having secured their rear. The Armies of Germany had not yet moved. Beurnonville's successor, Hoche, was waiting for a move from Moreau, who had in fact made secret contact with the Austrians. A renewed offensive by the Archduke, who was gathering troops, or by the Tyrol army would probably lead to a French defeat. To hasten Vienna's answer, the French vanguard advanced as far as Leoben (7 April) where two Austrian envoys joined Bonaparte. He presented them with a choice: to give up Belgium and the left bank of the Rhine in exchange for Mantua, Istria, Dalmatia and the Terra Firma as far as the Tagliamento, or to cede Belgium, keep the Rhineland and keep the Terra Firma as far as the Adda. There was no doubt about the reply. Austria in the end cared less about Belgium than did England, and the cession of Venice was an unhoped-for bonus. Preliminaries for peace were signed at Leoben on 18 April. According to this treaty, Austria gave up Belgium and Lombardy. The problem of the left bank of the Rhine was to be a matter for negotiation at Rastatt between France and the Imperial Diet. Bonaparte thus rode roughshod over the Directory's instructions, passed on by Clarke, which envisaged sacrificing everything for the Rhine frontier. By secret clauses, Austria obtained Istria, Dalmatia and Venetia as far as the Oglio. France took the Ionian Islands; Venice was to remain independent and to receive the former Legations in compensation. Finally, Lombardy and Modena would form a single republic. All that remained was to force the Directory to accept this exorbitant act of personal diplomacy. Clarke, who alone had the power to sign an armistice, arrived at Leoben in time only to ratify the preliminaries. Bonaparte's most important priority was to prevent the campaign in Germany from modifying the balance of forces and undermining his peace settlement. He sent Leclerc to ask Hoche and Moreau to suspend their offensive. The first reaction of the two generals was not to consider themselves bound by a separate armistice, but they desisted on hearing the announcement of the Preliminaries of Leoben. To secure his position in Paris, Bonaparte arranged for rumours of peace to be spread before the Directory was in possession of the Leoben documents. Public rejoicing at news of peace would be his best support. Bonaparte also stressed that the preliminaries were not a peace settlement and that France could improve her position in the final negotiations. Only Carnot defended him. The other Directors, especially La Révellière, protested at being presented with a *fait accompli* and at the abandonment of natural frontiers. The growth of the royalist threat, an overwhelming desire for peace and, above all, the necessity to conciliate Bonaparte led them to back down.

Venice sacrificed

The neutrality of the Venetian Republic had been violated several times since Lodi. And as the campaign had shifted along the Po, it became increasingly fictitious. The Directory and Bonaparte wanted, on the other hand, to prevent Venice joining the Austrian side. This would have jeopardised any incursion into the Tyrol. Proposals for an alliance were offered, but these were rejected by the patricians who were concerned not to commit themselves for the future and who were also worried about the contagion of revolution. From this moment on, the French set about undermining the power of the aristocracy. Opportunities were not lacking. The economy of the Venetian Republic was in a critical state; Fiume and Trieste were outstripping the city of the Doges. The industrial activity of the towns of the Terra Firma, especially of Brescia and Bergamo, was much more thriving than that of Venice. This made them all the less willing to put up with the arbitrary taxation and with the conservatism of the ruling caste which hunted out the reformers. With the connivance of the French, a revolution was sparked off by patriots in Bergamo (11 March), Brescia (17 March) and Crema (28 March). These three towns set up their own governments and asked to be joined to the Cispadane Republic. By attempting in this casual way to spread the revolution, the French forces created the opposite effect among the mass of peasants. In the region of Salo armed peasants attacked the 'Jacobin missionaries'. On 17 April the inhabitants of Verona, weary of French occupation, although in this particular case possibly incited by an act of provocation, massacred 400 Frenchmen. Bonaparte had his *casus belli*. He therefore rejected the apologies of the Senate and declared war on Venice (2 May). On 15 May the French troops entered the city without meeting resistance. The democrats took power, or at least enjoyed the illusion of doing so, while the former governor signed his deposition in Milan (16 May). In their ignorance of the secret clauses of Leoben, the Venetian patriots believed that their territory was going to be reunited with Lombardy. A flowering of newspapers and clubs worked for the cause of unification and debated the reforms that should be introduced. This was the brief springtime of the Venetian intelligentsia during which the names of Foscolo and Lauberg, among others, shone forth. In fact, Bonaparte was preparing the dismemberment of their republic, and without further delay he secured the Ionian Islands. In accordance with the agreement, the Austrians, for their part, installed themselves in Istria and Dalmatia.

For the sumptuous monarch of the Château of Montbello, near Milan, what mattered above all was the fate of Lombardy, the nucleus of the new Italy. The Cisalpine Republic was proclaimed on 29 June. Bonaparte provided the nascent republic with a constitution modelled on that of France. He took the precaution of provisionally according himself the right to name the members of the government and the Legislative Body, thus placing the Cisalpine Republic under probationary liberty. He wanted to provide it with access to the sea; for this he had set his sights on Genoa. The Genoese democrats, in league with the representatives of the Directory, wanted to avert annexation, but their uprising miscarried (22 May). The Genoese aristocracy submitted to an ultimatum from Bonaparte. They allowed him to appoint a government of democrats and to impose a constitution, thus salvaging the independence of the state.

Lille and Campoformio

The negotiations between Bonaparte and Gallo, the Austrian envoy, seemed at first to be proceeding favourably. At the end of May Austria agreed to decide the German question without holding a Congress. Would she resign herself to a Rhine frontier in exchange for advantages in Italy? The Directory believed she would, but, whether as a ruse or whether as one of the peripeteias of this subtle contest, Vienna in effect disowned its representative. The discussions were deadlocked. Their outcome depended on the evolution of the crisis in France.

Within the Directory, the divide became clearer both on domestic and on foreign policy. Carnot pleaded tirelessly for a speedy peace on the basis of Leoben. The recently elected Barthélemy supported him to the full. On the other hand, the triumvirate demanded the formal recognition of the Rhine frontier. The new majority on the Councils launched a headlong attack on the whole of Reubell's foreign policy. They demanded peace without annexation and condemned the illegality of Bonaparte's conduct. Dumolard's speech on 23 June 1797 marked the culmination of this campaign. Besides this condemnation of revolutionary expansionism, the Councils hounded Bonaparte and Hoche with unrelenting hatred about the more dubious aspects of their financial administration. They were, in short, condemning and attempting to destroy the very basis of the generals' emancipation. The head of Austrian diplomacy, Thugut, hoped to exploit these rivalries and dispatched to Paris an emissary who made contact with Carnot and Barthélemy. But he arrived in the capital on 9 August, that is, the day after Augereau's appointment to the head of the garrison. There was nothing he could do; the crisis was about to come to a head. The same uncertainty hovered over the negotiations between France and England which opened at Lille (7 July). England's diplomatic isolation and the mutinies of her fleet inclined the English government towards conciliation. The Directory gave firm instructions to its negotiators. They were to demand the return of all the colonies. In fact their behaviour quickly became suspect, especially that of Maret, who, in liaison with Talleyrand (recently appointed Foreign Minister), rallied to the English cause. He provided information about the movements of the Dutch fleet and passed on the content of the treaty between Portugal and France. Barras offered his services; indeed, there were anglophile informers everywhere. 'In Lille and London', wrote Raymond Guyot, 'Frenchmen now came to offer England more than she had demanded, almost more than she had hoped for.' Pitt therefore had no interest in speeding up the negotiations.

Throughout the summer Bonaparte had observed the struggle for influence on the Directory and the struggle between the triumvirate and the Councils. For a long time he had maintained contact with Carnot, who defended him against Reubell and La Révellière. But the change in the majority's attitude, and in particular the deputies' attacks against him, forced Bonaparte to choose his camp. It was clear that a victory by the Councils would lead to a complete reversal of foreign policy and to the end of his Mediterranean plans. In these circumstances, he offered his help to the triumvirs, first in the form of messages of support from the army and then in the person of Augereau. The success of the *coup d'état* gave a new impetus to the diplomatic activity.

The logical consequence of this change of course was a breaking off of the negotiations at Lille. With regard to Austria, the Directory's demands became clearer. The Rhine frontier was no longer the main issue at stake; under the influence of the Italian democrats and of the Jacobin revival, the Directory intended at all costs to defend the Venetian revolutionaries. Bonaparte was unwilling to give in to this mood of bellicose exaltation. He was worried by the prospect of a resumption of hostilities, which was the corollary of the new policy. And he feared that the names of Hoche or Augereau might come to

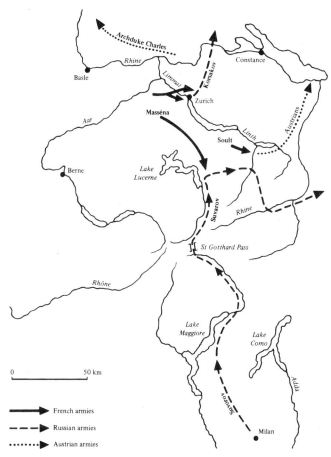

Map 3 Italy after the Treaty of Campoformio

overshadow the memory of the Italian victories. Above all, he was
gambling on peace. Having made his name as a conqueror, Bonaparte
wanted to become, in the eyes of the masses, the peacemaker. He
therefore conducted his own negotiations with Cobenzl, the Austrian
representative. By the Treaty of Campoformio, Austria recognised
France's possession of Belgium and obtained the territory of the
Venetian Republic, except for the Ionian Islands (18 October 1797).
The provinces of Bergamo and Brescia were incorporated into the
Cisalpine Republic. The cession of the left bank of the Rhine (except

the Cologne region), provided for by a secret clause, was only to occur with the consent of the Diet. The stunned Directory was in no position to oppose its saviour. The Venetians had, in the words of the most celebrated of their number, been sold like a flock of sheep. But what, confronted with the irresistible rise of Napoleon Bonaparte, was the anger of La Révellière or the bitterness of Foscolo?

4

Economic activity

'Agriculture and industry are going to expand rapidly and at last undergo new developments'

François de Neufchâteau, Circular of 9 Fructidor Year V

A debilitated economy and a society run mad: the generally accepted image of France under the Directory leaves little room for nuances. And the discredit which attaches to this period has persisted. The fact is that, between the economic controls of Year II and the stabilisation of the Consulate, between austerity and conformity, the period has rarely been studied in its own right but more often treated as a point of comparison. It is certainly true that wolves prowled at the gates of Paris in Year IV, as did the *chauffeurs** in Year VIII, and that the poor survived with difficulty while a band of parvenus squandered in conspicuous consumption the fortunes they had built on speculation. The case for the prosecution, then, does not lack arguments. But rather than judge, one should try to understand, to fit these facts into the social and economic totality which explains them. Similarly, if there was stagnation, it was made up both of technical breakthroughs which did not outweigh the continued use of old-fashioned methods, and of the setting up of new businesses which did not replace all those which had collapsed. Even if the story is finally one of failure, it is not one of total immobility. Most importantly, the overall trend should not obscure the wealth of contrasts. In the France of the Directory there were sheltered sectors, moments of respite, regions less buffeted than others.

ECONOMY AND POLICY

From Year IV to Year VII, from one forced loan to another, the government's freedom of manoeuvre in economic policy was restricted

---

* The *chauffeurs* were robbers who burned the feet of their victims in order to make them reveal where their money was hidden. [Trans.]

by the desperate exigencies of the rapidly changing situation. Inflation, deflation, racketeering, the plundering of the conquered territories and other expedients: these were the successive shocks which made up the daily economic realities of the regime. But if the immediate situation was dominated by a monetary and financial crisis which hindered production and trade and exacerbated social disparities, the government's reforming activity, at first tentative, and then coherent, nevertheless laid the foundations of a new expansion.

From inflation to deflation

When the Directory took up office, the days of the *assignat* were numbered. It took four months to disappear. Under the effects of speculation and inflation, the paper currency depreciated precipitously in the autumn of 1795: the *louis*, quoted at 2,000 *livres* at the beginning of Brumaire Year IV, was worth 5,500 *livres* in Frimaire. In the space of a month, eight thousand million *assignats* were put into circulation. The survival of the state depended on the speed and goodwill of the workers who printed the money; the threat of a strike, in Brumaire, terrified the Directory. Scorned in Paris, the *assignat* was refused in the provinces. Peasants and traders now dealt only in silver. It became necessary to protect those who were obliged to accept paper money. The law of 25 Thermidor Year III covered creditors against premature repayments. On 2 Thermidor landowners had at last obtained the right to receive half their rents in kind. Urban rents continued to be paid in *assignats* at par but landlords tended to revise contracts in order to profit from the flood of applicants.

On 28 November 1795 the state for its part adjusted the pay of its employees, raising it to thirty times the level of 1790. This was a doubly derisory gesture, both because the fall in the value of paper money had been much greater and because the payments were often not even carried out. As for the *rentiers*, they did not benefit from a similar provision until February 1796. Conversely the government was also concerned both to maintain some confidence in the currency and to ensure that its revenues should not be reduced to nothing. Thus the law of 2 Thermidor Year III compelled taxpayers to discharge half their obligations in grain or its monetary equivalent. This only made it more difficult to bring the taxes in. On the other hand, sales of national property were occurring in conditions which were disastrous for public finances. It was decided on 30 Brumaire Year IV to suspend sales until

1 Prairial. But all these rearguard actions were no substitute for more positive measures.

The government believed it had found a way out by the vote, on 19 Frimaire Year IV, of a forced loan of 600 million *livres*, payable in metal currency, in grain or in *assignats* at 1% of their face value. The richest quarter of taxpayers, divided into sixteen classes, were to contribute to this loan according to the level of their income. It was hoped that this measure would meet the most pressing obligations, absorb most of the paper money and prepare for a return to a metal currency. The loan was also seen as a revenge on profiteers. For all these reasons public opinion was from the outset very favourable to it. But the drawing up of the tax rolls raised strong protests, the administrators being accused of arbitrariness and favouritism. Some of them practised passive resistance, if, that is, they did not shirk their task completely. In the *départements* of the west the collection of the loan proceeded slowly, except in the Sarthe where the authorities had threatened the recalcitrant with military force. The reputedly calm regions, such as the east and the north-east, paid up no more speedily. The loan was supposed to have been closed in February 1796; by the summer a quarter of the total had been collected. This relative failure forced the Directory to resort to other palliatives such as a rise in customs duties, postal tariffs and registration fees, and the making of payments in anticipation of the results of the loan. But these were only provisional, not to say illusory, remedies. In any case the *assignats*, of which there were forty-five million in circulation, could survive no longer: they were worth no more than what it cost to produce them. The plates from which they were printed were publicly broken in Paris on 19 February 1796.

Given the real or artificial dearth of specie, everyone feared a sudden return to a metallic currency. Might not a national bank be able to bridge the gap? Various influential bankers – among others Laffon-Ladébat, Perrégaux and Lecouteulx-Canteleu – drafted a plan for one. In return for the acquisition of national property worth 1,200 million *livres*, they undertook to provide the state each month with banknotes to the value of 25 million *livres*. The bank would also rediscount bills presented by its shareholders, thus helping both the state treasury and large-scale commerce. The former directors of the Caisse d'Escompte resumed once again the debate over their institution which had started in the last years of the *ancien régime*. In spite of the Directory's support, the plan was rejected by the Councils. Many deputies, not just Lindet and the left-wing faction, were loath to give such a weapon to a syndicate of bankers.

The government therefore turned to the idea of issuing a new paper currency itself, and, through it, of mobilising the national property still pending sale. The law of 28 Ventôse Year IV (18 March 1796) created 'mandats territoriaux' worth 2,400 million *livres*. Holders of the new currency could obtain on request, without auction, national property valued at twenty-two times (eighteen times for houses and factories) its annual yield in 1790. The rate of exchange between the *assignat* and the *mandat* was fixed at 30:1. This was certain to result in a depreciation of the new currency since the *assignat* was worth only one four-hundredth of its face value. By linking the two currencies in order to rid itself of the former, the state deprived the operation of any credibility. The collapse of the *mandat* was rapid. On 31 July 1796 the government had to recognise this formally and halt the squandering of national property: it would no longer accept the *mandats* at par. The payment of taxes was modified as a consequence, and on 21 November the handing over of national property in exchange for metal currency was authorised. Now that the battle was lost, it was necessary to get rid of the *mandat* quickly and cheaply. A group of merchants, the Dijon Company, were entrusted with the task of speculating for a fall by using the *mandats* available in the state coffers. The state was depreciating its paper money through the intermediacy of speculators! The government's opponents denounced this operation as a scandal. And the Dijon Company did indeed emerge with sizeable profits. At least the objective had been achieved. The *mandat* was demonetised on 4 February 1797. This brutal deflation left the way clear for a metallic currency.

Financial recovery

If the return to monetary stability removed a major obstacle to economic recovery, it nonetheless remained to restore the country's finances to a secure footing. This was to be the achievement of Ramel-Nogaret (henceforth Ramel), a man of talent and energy, who had succeeded the lacklustre Faipoult at the end of January 1796. His efforts were directed towards two areas: the reduction of the National Debt and the reorganisation and efficient running of the tax system. The first objective was attained by the law of 30 September 1797. The *coup d'état* of Fructidor having put an end to parliamentary obstruction, the Directory was authorised by the Councils to repay two-thirds of the debt in 'bonds' which were valid for the purchase of national property. The remaining third was 'consolidated', that is inscribed on the National Debt register and thus only transferable with difficulty. This disguised bankruptcy saved the budget 160 million *livres* per annum. The new paper money, which was issued with perhaps not unintentional slowness, lost ground in the face of competition from other government paper. The final blow came in October 1798 with the decision that national property should be paid for exclusively in metallic currency; it fell from 37% to 1% of its face value in a year. Certainly the smallest *rentiers* had been to some extent taken care of. But overall they suffered a veritable spoliation. This act of financial arbitrariness generated bitterness and hardship. The debt had not been eliminated, it had been displaced; it became political.

At the advent of the Directory, the tax system had suffered from grave defects. The assessments of liability and the distribution of taxes owed more, at the local level, to the balance of forces or the resourcefulness of the administrators than to the real ownership of wealth. Owing to the lack both of any cadastral survey and of a competent staff, the drawing up of tax rolls for the land tax (*contribution foncière*) made only painful progress. At the beginning of Year V Ramel had only received reports of the situation in thirteen *départements*. In the Haute-Loire the municipalities indulged in a sort of sabotage, in spite of pressure from the commissioners. The registers of tax assessment, already contested in the Council of the Five Hundred, gave rise at every stage to petitions of protest. Demands for tax relief sprang up everywhere. The *contribution personnelle et mobilière* was less heavy, but just as arbitrary in the way it was drawn up. On 14 Thermidor Year V it had been divided into three categories – *mobilière* (moveable property), *somptuaire* (luxuries) and *personnelle* (a sort of poll-tax) – and it raised numerous complaints since the criteria for calculating liability varied so much from one canton to another. The Directory, hoping to correct these injustices, had set up 'equity boards'. In fact these bodies either paralysed the system or displayed favouritism. As in the past, those who were least protected subsidised the rest. Schnerb has noted, for example, that the mountainous cantons of the Puy-de-Dôme were taxed relatively more heavily than those of the rich Limagne.[1] Finally, the drawing up of the *patente* (tax on trade licences) was based on very rough estimates of the numbers liable. The collection of these taxes came up against a lack of co-operation from taxpayers, as well as against

---

[1] R. Schnerb (106).

the corruption and inefficiency of the tax collectors, assessors and other appointed officials. By 1 Frimaire Year V taxes in arrears – some owing since 1790! – had generally been paid up to Year III. It is true that those in arrears had the advantage of being able to pay half the amount in *mandats* at par or at thirty *assignats* per *mandat*. From 1 Germinal Year V payments had to be made in metal currency. Sometimes recourse was had to billeting soldiers on the recalcitrant, in spite of the protests and political risks of such a procedure.

The measures adopted after Fructidor significantly modified the situation. The amount of the *contribution foncière et personnelle* was reduced at the beginning of Year VI. In Year VII the rate of the *contribution personnelle* was fixed at the equivalent of three days' work; the rate of the *contribution mobilière* was established according to the level of the rent and a tax rate of one-twentieth was imposed on the pay of public servants. The tax system gained from this both in justice and in clarity. At the same time, on 22 Brumaire Year IV, Ramel secured an agreement for the setting up in the *départements* of Agencies of Direct Taxation. These agencies were composed of commissioners, appointed by the Directory, tax collectors and an inspector. They were supposed to assist – that is to say, in effect, to supervise – the municipalities in drawing up tax rolls, and to speed up the collection of taxes. But the already overworked staff of these agencies were not always able to cope with these new obligations. Above all, the relations between government officials and municipalities remained in flux. The Directory must nonetheless be given the credit for indicating a possible solution to the fiscal problem: the establishment of an administration which would compensate for the deficiencies of the elected representatives. The government's final innovation in this area was the creation on 24 November 1798 of the tax on doors and windows which, although successfully established in the end, was at first resented as oppressive.

From Year VI to Year VIII the yield of direct taxes improved continuously. In the *département* of the Meurthe two-thirds of the annual land and personal taxes had been paid by Fructidor Year VI. All arrears disappeared during the next year, even if there were still delays in payment. The collection of the *patente*, of which the organisation had been modified in September 1798, also became more efficient. Marcel Reinhard has uncovered the same trend in the Sarthe. Under pressure, and as much through lassitude as patriotism, taxpayers resigned themselves to paying up. In Year V – a period when order was being restored and money was scarce – taxes still came in only with difficulty but in Years VI and VII the Directory's overall achievements in the field of taxation compared favourably with those of the *ancien régime*.

Ramel had been able to reduce direct taxation because he had simultaneously increased indirect taxes. The old duties were clarified (registration fees, for example) or raised (customs, tobacco, etc.). Other taxes were created, affecting especially fishing and hunting. By instituting a toll on 10 September 1797 the government hoped to obtain the resources necessary to repair and maintain the road network. These numerous toll barriers seemed to threaten the freedom of movement. In places – Le Mans, Toul, etc. – discontent turned into rioting. Fraud developed on a grand scale and the costs of the operation in some areas (the *département* of the Mont-Terrible, for example) even exceeded the income it brought in. The tax also hampered inter-regional trade; ironmasters, for example, complained forcibly about this.

Overall the various taxes did not cover the state's expenditure. In spite of the undoubted financial recovery, the Directory continued to make use of extraordinary sources of revenue. The taxes extorted from the conquered territories brought in 158 million *livres* from Year VI to Year VIII (16 million *livres* provided by Switzerland, 40 by the Cisalpine Republic, 72 by the Roman Republic, 30 by Naples), that is, about a quarter of the annual budget. Similarly, the government remained a prisoner of the contractors and bankers who provided it with specie and paper currency. When the last forced loan was instituted to finance the resumption of hostilities (27 June 1799), the contractors had to be asked to give up part of what was owed to them in return for claims on this loan. A meeting of Parisian bankers made an advance of 30 million *livres* with the same security. Thus the restoration of the financial affairs of the country came up against the constraints of the war.

François de Neufchâteau

In the absence of French economic expansion, the financial recovery rested on shaky foundations. The rulers of France were convinced in the summer of 1797 that it was now possible to remedy this situation. In this area also the intention was to 'terminate the Revolution'. The cessation of hostilities and the strengthening of the executive at last provided the respite needed for grand schemes; 'reconstruction' became a priority. This undertaking is linked to the name of François de Neufchâteau. As Minister of the Interior from Thermidor to

Fructidor Year V, and then, after a period as a Director, from Floréal Year VI to Thermidor Year VII, it was he who provided the stimulus and who co-ordinated the various initiatives. The most urgent task, if it was hoped to escape from a situation of improvisation and uncertainty, was to draw up a balance sheet. Neufchâteau's predecessors, from Orry to Bénézech, had launched numerous surveys; but he was the first to consider using statistics as a method of government. Hardly had he assumed office than he tried to make the central administrations of the *départements* draw up charts of industrial activity (9 Fructidor Year V).[1] Only six *départements* replied positively. It was clear that the mistrust displayed by business men and the inexperience or lack of interest of the government's servants weighed more heavily than the enthusiasm of a minister. But the layout of the proposed questionnaire for the survey reveals the desire for reform. Besides the traditional questions, it asked, for example, the local authorities to single out dynamic business men, to report progress in mechanisation, to compare the current level of production with that attained in 1789, to compare French products with foreign ones, to forecast new market outlets and any possible upturn resulting from the peace. More ambitiously, the circular of 27 Fructidor Year VI requested the Directory's commissioners to undertake a statistical description of their *départements*. Other government servants, as well as societies and teachers, were later supposed to collaborate in this task. Eight *départements* sent their 'description'; this was certainly an indifferent success but it did not diminish its value as an example for the future. Chaptal and his successors were to carry on the effort, using other means. Here again François de Neufchâteau deserves the title of founder.

Faithful to his liberal philosophy, the minister believed that it was disastrous to intervene directly in economic activity. He applied himself essentially to encouraging, inspiring and spreading news of innovations. In agriculture, ably backed up by Vilmorin and Parmentier, he assisted the revival, and creation, of agricultural societies. A semi-official newspaper, *La Feuille du cultivateur*, encouraged enlightened farmers to revive the physiocratic tradition, while competitions were devised to stimulate a spirit of rivalry. He applied the same policy to industry. The department responsible for the arts and for manufactures and the Conseil des Mines distributed technical brochures to manufacturers and backed their demands from the relevant ministries, whether it was a

[2] C. Schmidt (105).

matter of payments in arrears, of protection against foreign competition or of police measures against the workers. Finally, to reinfuse industrialists with a spirit of competition and enterprise, he organised a national exhibition in Paris between 18 and 21 September 1798. The press judged it a success and the principle of an annual exhibition was adopted. Advertising and subsidies were not in themselves sufficient to end the industrial depression. But they at least helped to overcome isolation and defeatism.

AGRICULTURE: TRANSFORMATION OR INERTIA?

The consolidation of property

Between Thermidor Year II and Brumaire Year VIII the transfer of property was not the main development in the French countryside. For knowledge of the overall trend one would need to have figures for the sale of inherited property and to be able to trace how often national property changed hands. Such statistics are lacking, but those for national property alone show a marked slump in sales. The stock had been considerably depleted in the previous period. Thus, in the Haute-Loire, only one-seventeenth of the total remained to be sold at the start of Year IV; one finds the same decline in, for example, the districts of Rouen and Epinal. Yet these transactions were in themselves far from negligible. Moreover they influenced economic development, and, by the conditions in which they occurred and the individuals whom they profited, they throw light on the nature of the post-Thermidorean regime.

Legislation followed the same ups and downs as the currency and was continuously unfavourable to small purchasers. The first measure, enacted on 12 Prairial Year III, ended sale by auction and fixed the price at seventy-five times the income of the property in 1790; payment had to be made within a year. The effect of this was both to ruin the state – depreciation had reached a much greater level – and to benefit urban purchasers, large numbers of whom tendered for the lots before people in the countryside could be informed that the sales were taking place. Faced with such an avalanche of prospective purchasers, the Convention reconsidered and restored sale by auction on 27 Prairial. Although the reserve price remained fairly low, competition pushed the prices up, and the districts, responsible for the sales, were not keen to break up the lots. Only the bourgeoisie or peasants with monetary reserves were in a position to make such large-scale purchases. The episode of the *mandat* led to another upsurge of sales. Auctions were again stopped and the administration of the *département* was made responsible for both valuing and handing over the property. All these conditions favoured the bourgeoisie: the fact that sales took place in the *chef-lieu* discouraged many peasants (though the better-off did, it is true, send someone to stand in for them); the experts were often indulgent towards big buyers and the administrators could on occasion be helpful, if not partial. More than ever these transactions took place between *notables* alone. This quickly developed into a scramble for spoils, which, with the help of the *mandat*, became an extremely profitable operation for its beneficiaries. Most of the remaining property disappeared in a few weeks, often at prices below its rental value. This pillage was belatedly checked by insisting on payment by *mandats* at market prices (13 Thermidor Year IV) and then by abolishing sale by tender (20 Fructidor Year IV). Auctions were re-established by the law of 16 Brumaire Year V. Payment was to be made half in paper and half in metallic currency which had to be delivered within four and a half years. On 26 Vendémiaire Year VII the Councils, at the demand of the government, tightened these conditions: in future, purchasers of landed property were required to pay exclusively in metallic currency and within three years. Although this law had lowered the initial outlay to eight times the level of 1790, it reinforced the highly selective nature of the system: in a period of deflation only those privileged to possess wealth were in a position to make purchases.

It was the merchants, industrialists, solicitors and lawyers who emerged victorious from this contest, with the not-disinterested help of the administrators of the *départements*. They divided among themselves the bulk, in amount and above all in value, of the available property. It is known that they took two-thirds of the property in the Meurthe and in the district of Rouen; the same proportion was reached in the Nord, and in many other areas it was probably exceeded. After the splitting up of lots and the acquisition of property by part of the poorer peasantry in Year II, the fact that the last purchases of national property were monopolised by the bourgeoisie strikingly underlines – even if the quantities involved were small – the class nature of the new regime. Besides the urban *notables*, large tenant farmers also seem, in areas of large-scale cultivation, to have profited from these final sales. Inflation had enabled them to accumulate capital quickly. With some exceptions the various buyers limited their purchases to their immediate region. They were acting on their own account without intending to resell. On the other hand, the period of the Directory saw a proliferation at tenders and auctions of individual speculators and above all of companies of contractors who were quick to rid themselves of their paper money. With the return of a metallic currency these companies were well placed to dominate the auctions and rapidly mobilised their specie.

Some Parisian companies particularly distinguished themselves in this way: for example Bodin – responsible for equipping the Army of Italy – Chevallier and Rochfort. They were rife above all in the Nord, as far as Belgium and Normandy. But if, as Georges Lefebvre has claimed, the Paris region was the favoured hunting ground of these speculators, they or others similar to them (suppliers of beds, heating contractors, contractors for the shipbuilding industry, etc.) were also to be found in Brittany as well in the Haute-Garonne. More generally, this was a period in which the 'black bands', not unknown during the previous phase, thrived. The officials of the *département* acted as agents, even advisers, in many of these schemes.

The nobles, for their part, attempted to reconstitute their patrimonies. The political circumstances helped the returning *émigrés* or their families (at any rate until 18 Fructidor) to take back their property, through intimidation or by mutual agreement. This phenomenon was most evident in the west of France, but one finds traces of it elsewhere.

The peasantry were not entirely excluded from land purchases during this period even if they participated in only a minority of them. In the Meurthe they bought almost 20% of the property. Wherever little parcels of land remained, there continued to be openings for small purchasers, at least for those who had a negotiable surplus at their disposal in Year III and Year IV. A consolidation of small property took place. The speculators generally resold their purchases in small lots in order to extract greater profit from them; in this way the peasants obtained new land. But as monetary deflation gathered pace their share was reduced. In short, during the Directory, the peasantry digested its acquisitions.

Agricultural progress?

There was no lack of incitements to progress. We have described the efforts of the administration in this area. Similarly the agricultural societies took their role seriously and preached the gospel of modern agriculture both by their example and by their publications. There were about forty in existence at the end of the Directory but many only really functioned under the Consulate. Besides, composed as they were of large landowners, officials and scientists, they could only be understood and followed by that tiny elite of farmers who had the necessary intellectual and financial means. But limited sectors of the agricultural world did embark on improvements. Thus there was a spread in the employment of irrigation techniques and the propaganda in favour of agricultural progress did meet with some success (marling in the Sarthe for example). The gazettes were taken up with the improvement of ploughing implements and the search for more rational equipment (front-wheel ploughs, seeders, chaff-cutters), but without very notable results. On the other hand people do seem to have been won over from the meridional swing plough, though it is true that this occurred in the Cher, a *département* which lay on the outer limits of the Midi.

There was also progress in the choice of crops. The government stepped up the campaign in favour of potatoes. These became established in the south-east from Year III, and also spread into the north. Once agronomists had overcome the reluctance of consumers to accept this food 'good only for pigs', they studied, from Year IV, technical improvements and which varieties were most suited to which soil and climate. Thus the Directory completed the efforts of the previous thirty years to ensure food in times of grain scarcity. It did at least succeed in cushioning the effects of crises, if one is to believe the journalist who, in Year VII, celebrated 'this plant to which we partly owe the fact that we have not died from hunger'. Finally, partial improvements were achieved in the crucial area of livestock. The extension of artificial grasslands, which was of course a long-term process, can be detected in only a few areas. The struggle against epizooty gathered force. Some breeders attempted to improve the stock of cattle and sheep by cross-breeding. These initiatives were too isolated to have an immediate effect even if they were harbingers of the future. One could apply to the new agriculture the words that Clémendot used about the raising of livestock in the Meurthe: 'There was the beginning of a change but not yet a profound transformation.'

Obstacles to change

At the other end of the spectrum, traditional agriculture, based on collective rights, fallow land and extensive cultivation, put up a massive resistance to change. The dividing up of common land, decided on 10 June 1793, had not made much progress. In Year III the small peasants were still generally opposed to a division which would have deprived them of fuel for heating, even of grazing land, at least in those regions where the communal lands were too tiny and too dry to be used as arable land. In areas such as the Nord and the Allier, where landless peasants exerted pressure in favour of partition, the leading landowners contrived to block the process, perhaps through fear that it would create a labour shortage. In a decree of 21 Prairial the Directory ended these conflicts by abrogating the law of 1793. As for customary rights, they persisted regardless of laws (the *Code rural*) and exhortations. Farmers who wanted to enclose found it difficult to go against the will of the peasant community; rights of way and common grazing rights remained sacrosanct in spite of the recognised harm they caused. 'Habits which so closely affect the poorest inhabitants of the countryside could not be destroyed without dangerous disturbance' commented a correspondent of Bénézech in 1796. And it should be added that the large owners of livestock in the Midi and the mountainous regions, who, in the absence of artificial meadows, needed vast pastures, displayed solidarity with the poorer peasants on this point.

Recent developments in the forms of land tenure moved in the same direction. The onset of inflation had so harmed the interests of landowners who leased out their property that in Year III and Year IV they had adopted the habit of transforming rents into share cropping leases, which did not help promote a spirit of enterprise. Also, landowners were not prepared, despite the protests of the physiocrats, to lengthen the period of leases. Rather they considered how to defend themselves, by frequent renewals of leases, against the consequences of the monetary crisis. Finally, those peasants without sufficient financial means who had become property owners could not be expected to carry out significant improvements to their land. Thus the traditional forms of crop rotation continued under the Directory. In some places the areas under cultivation increased at the expense of moorland: owing to the lack of manure and fertilisers the appropriate response to a rise in grain prices in a pre-modern agricultural society was to extend the area under cereal crops. It does not unquestionably follow from this fact that farmers were able to 'treat' their land many times over as agronomists advised, since there was a continued shortage of manpower. Similarly, the lack of ploughing instruments – a result of the war economy and the difficulties of the rural iron and steel industry – was still causing considerable handicaps. But undoubtedly the most serious problem of all was the devastation of the forests. This phenomenon, endemic under the *ancien régime* and accentuated at the beginning of the Revolution by the 'nationalisation' of the royal and ecclesiastical forests or of those belonging to the *émigrés*, took on alarming proportions under the Directory. Small thefts, grazing in all seasons and, in the mountains, clearing for cultivation all endangered French forests and even the balance of the soil. Administrators, enlightened farmers and ironmasters were aware of this, but, except perhaps in the east, they were powerless to stem the catastrophe.

PROBLEMS AND PROSPECTS OF INDUSTRY

For the brief span of our period, it is hardly possible to discuss industry except in terms of factory production. This leaves out, of course, the mass of industrial activity, that is to say, artisanal production, about which our information is too scanty to make any overall conclusions possible. Over such a short chronological span we perceive the artisans as citizens and consumers, not as producers. Even narrowing down the area of analysis there are manifest disparities between rurally localised industries such as steel, and urban, or mixed, industries such as textiles. Besides, in each sector, factories employing several hundred workers were to be found side by side with very small units of production. Did French industry under the Directory, then, share no more than a common background of economic circumstances? If these circumstances did serve as a unifying force (but we will see that the resistance of different industries to the crisis was not uniform), there were also other factors which gave an undeniable unity to the world of industry: the transfers of property and the fluctuations in the number of businesses, the problems of labour, the attempts at technical innovation and the drying up of markets.

Business men and businesses

The Church's iron and steel interests had been almost completely sold in 1791 and 1792. But most of the industrial property which had belonged to *émigrés* was still nationally owned. The law of 28 Ventôse Year IV stimulated many makers of iron and steel to buy these forges from the government. Dozens of these properties were thus 'handed over to private enterprise' in Champagne, Burgundy, Lorraine, the Dordogne, the Ariège, etc., during the Directory.[3] In this way the lessees of forges often acquired property. The other purchasers were iron merchants. Even at auction there was hardly any competition to buy this kind of property. The acquisition of these factories was in theory a good bargain but many of them were in a state of neglect, lacking a source of supply and with their labour force dispersed. The mining industry suffered from analogous problems. The state had become a majority shareholder in the Anzin Company after the emigration of several joint owners. Two shareholders who had remained in France were authorised on 11 June 1795 to buy the confiscated portions. Here again the transaction worked to the benefit of the buyers thanks to the depreciation of the *assignat*. In addition the state freed itself of an expensive state sector, difficult to run in such times of crisis. At the same time, it abdicated its methods and principles of administration, in spite of the protests of a minority which wanted the nation to maintain its ownership of these businesses.

While in the old industries the period 1795–9 was characterised by transfers of property, in the pioneering cotton industry it was marked by the creation of factories. Moreover, in some cases this process was helped by the renting or sale of national property. Liévin-Bauwens, for example, set up his mills on the land of the Carthusians of Gand and the Minimes of Passy; Richard and Lenoir did the same in Paris. Every year workshops sprang up in Paris, in Normandy, in the Nord, as well as in the south-west. In spite of the crisis there was a body of enterprising employers either with fortunes of long standing (such as Oberkampf) or with fortunes recently acquired (such as Richard and Lenoir who had enriched themselves through speculation in national property). But the dynamism of such individuals went against the tide. Numerous forges had closed down or been destroyed (especially, but not only, in frontier regions); some mines had been flooded (among others, those in the Haute-Loire) and could therefore no longer be operated without major work being undertaken on them. The manufacture of woollen cloth in the Isère and the Nord, the weaving of flax in Brittany or of silk in Lyons had all collapsed – irrevocably it seemed – in Year II and Year III. As a result, the productive capacity of traditional French industry had diminished overall.

[3] Among the most important the following could be mentioned: Hayange, Audincourt, Clavières (Indre), Ecot (Haute-Marne).

Labour problems

It is difficult to appraise the conditions for industrial workers because on most problems – the level of employment, the intensity of work, the nature and amount of pay, industrial conflict – only sporadic information is available to us. But if the industrialists are to be believed, industry suffered from a chronic labour shortage caused by requisitioning, by competition from agricultural work and by the scarcity of food. This claim seems justified for the skilled workers of the iron and steel industry and, no doubt, for some specialised areas of the textile industry, such as coloured materials. In other cases the employment of women and children (for example in Boyer-Fonfrède's spinning mills in Toulouse) or the presence of a mass of unemployed day-labourers (in the Littry mines in Normandy) gave employers the means to resist demands for wage increases, for which the pressure was indeed intense. The old trade guilds survived and organised the workers' struggle, especially in trades with strong traditions such as carpentry or paper-making. Strikes broke out throughout the period of the Directory and the agitation came to a head in Year VII. While *Compagnons du devoir* were gathering in Tours and a violent conflict was setting workers against employers in the paper industry of the Isère, the smiths of the Aude, the Ariège and the Pyrénées-Orientales were co-ordinating action against their masters. Besides such incidents, industrialists complained ceaselessly of the 'carefree attitude', the 'absenteeism' and the 'disrespect' of their workers, which they attributed to the political disorders of the previous years. They demanded an 'Industrial Code' and, on occasion, the use of armed force. But the authorities were unable or unwilling to give them satisfaction. This failure was largely responsible for the disaffection of many of them from the regime.

Progress and obstruction

'Labour being very scarce and expensive, it is very important to insti-gate and encourage the invention of all machines which tend to take over from men', wrote a society from the Lot in 1798. Certainly England, the centre from which advanced methods spread, was almost inaccessible (although Liévin-Bauwens ventured there at the end of the Directory), but the central innovations – spinning mules, steam engines, coal smelting – were known to the French. Despite at least verbal support from the government, progress was halting. Only the cotton industry welcomed modern equipment into its new factories. Around 1797 the use of the spinning mule began to be standard in the factories of Paris, Alsace, Amiens and Louviers, after it had already been adopted in Orléans and Toulouse in the previous period. At the very end of our period, under the stimulus of Liévin-Bauwens, Gand became an important textile centre. The use of steam engines remained limited. They were employed at Anzin to pump water from the mines, and the appointment of the Périers as the company's bankers held out the hope of a guaranteed market. Plans were made to mechanise the bringing up of coal by the same means: only under the Consulate did they come to fruition, at Anzin and Littry. Similarly, the use of steam engines was envisaged in spinning mills, at least in Rouen, but nothing came of this.

From Year II the need for armaments had stimulated research. The government and certain ironmasters had embarked upon a programme of constructing steelworks, which continued under the Directory. But the stumbling empiricism of entrepreneurs prevented any important progress in this field. There was a similar failure to make use of coal. Even the most convinced manufacturers of steel did not consider it opportune, in the immediate term, to introduce such an upheaval in the running of their factories.

The most serious obstacle was undoubtedly a shortage of capital. The government was more forthcoming with verbal encouragement than with subsidies. Industrialists could not find sufficient resources to finance possible future investment themselves, and such capital as was available went into more remunerative investment. And anyway many factories were working appreciably below capacity owing to a lack of raw materials and labour. Inertia, then, decidedly prevailed over change. The spinning of wool, flax and sometimes cotton was still done by the spinning wheel. There was no advance in techniques of iron smelting. In short, in spite of all the various encouragements and symbolic breakthroughs, French industry was fundamentally resistant to technical innovation.

The balance sheet of industry under the Directory is ambiguous. Starting from the appalling levels of Year IV, production reached perhaps two-thirds of its pre-revolutionary level. The successes were uneven. The old textile industries (flax, wool) held up all the less well since the regions in which they were situated were oriented towards the colonial market (the west) or were geographically isolated

(Quercy). On the other hand, there were important markets for textiles in the armies and east of the Rhine. The cotton industry gave the impression of being an expanding sector. Its backwardness was quite blatant and entrepreneurs were stimulated by the elimination of English competition. But the prohibition of English cotton fabrics hampered industrialists by significantly raising production costs. The iron industry more or less conserved its position, except in the areas where it produced mainly for the foreign market. Two undeniable successes stand out from this uninspiring story. First a success in Belgium: the moving back of the frontier and the influx of French capital helped the mines of Hainaut, which under the Directory came to surpass their French competitors. The textile industry also benefited from access to the French market and hurried to mechanise its production in order to acquire a position of dominance which might survive the return of peace – and of the English. This phase was too brief for any certainty of success but the rapid expansion of Verviers for wool and Gand for cotton date from the last years of the Revolution. The other success was the iron industry of the Sarre and Luxemburg after these two territories had been integrated into the Republic. Technical advances in some factories and ready supplies of wood in others gave this industry formidable advantages. The effects of this were felt most by the Moselle iron industry, which had been disorganised by the Revolution and damaged by the war.

BUSINESS

Obstacles to trade

Trade was inhibited, though not completely stifled, by monetary uncertainties and shortages of goods. Within France the circulation of goods was disrupted by the tightness of credit, the deterioration of transport and a general insecurity. Moreover the continental and maritime war impeded traditional trading links with the outside world. But the needs of the economy and the prospect of large profits kept various forms of trade going, even if the result was to modify the nature and destination of the merchandise.

The lack of credit hindered the revival of business. In the absence of specialised channels for discount, money remained dear. Following the tradition of the *ancien régime*, trading houses provided banking services for some of their customers, but at rates often reaching 2% and

3 % a month. The law of 26 Germinal Year II prohibiting financial companies had been repealed on 21 November 1795. Besides, in the winter of 1795–6, Ramel had solicited the advice of various merchants 'on the need for some laws and some institutions favouring trade'. Although the idea of a bank was adopted, the conference ended without being able to agree on details. On 29 June 1796 a group of bankers and industrialists (Perrégaux, Fulchiron, Gros-Davillier, Van Robais, etc.) had founded a 'Current Accounts Bank' (Caisse des comptes courants) which discounted paper at three months' date. The 'Trade Discount Bank' (Caisse d'escompte du commerce) set up on 24 November 1797 had at first only discounted for its associates. Its promoters started to offer 'mortgage debentures' (*actions hypothécaires*) backed by the real estate of the shareholders. This system widened the possibilities of discount by using landed wealth as a security. A similar concern was shown by the 'Commercial Bank' (Comptoir commercial) which functioned at the same time as the 'Trade Discount Bank'. But whatever their innovations, these institutions, like their predecessors, reserved their discount facilities for a narrow privileged circle. In the provinces the situation was worse. A handful of old banks – or new ones (in the spring of 1798 some merchants founded the Société générale du Commerce de Rouen) – were unable to meet the needs of business. Most traders had to either attempt to get a foothold on the Paris market or turn to isolated lenders who did not charge too exorbitant a rate.

The dilapidation of the roads was another source of worry. In fact this damage had not occurred suddenly: the Directory was paying for almost ten years of neglect. According to the Conseils Généraux, in Year VIII France consisted only of 'bumpy streets or muddy ditches, smashed up vehicles, bruised passengers'. In some mountainous regions (the Isère, the Ariège) the situation was catastrophic; the collapse of bridges imposed numerous detours, but similar difficulties were reported in the Sarthe and in Alsace, where even main roads became impassable during rain. The tolls were supposed to improve this state of affairs. But besides the discontent they aroused, their most noticeable effect was to raise transport costs, since merchants and carriers incorporated them in their prices. The administration pondered various projects to build canals – in the Berry, and from the Moselle to the Saône, for example. It was clearly seen how advantageous these waterways would have been to the regional economies (for example the construction of a navigable route from Montluçon to Saint-Amand would have opened up the Commentry basin); but the money to carry them out was lacking.

Banditry was the third bane of trade. This perennial phenomenon of pre-modern societies was reinforced by the prevailing conditions, which added all kinds of deserters and outcasts to the professional brigands and to those others always on the fringes of society. It would be fruitless to disentangle poverty from political choice among the motives of the fleeing soldiers, non-juring priests, minor nobles, 'royalists of the high roads' and unemployed day-labourers who made up these bands. The weakness of the regime ensured the robbers enduring success: they held people up to ransom or killed them with impunity. The National Guard was non-existent; the gendarmerie, small in numbers and badly equipped, avoided trouble. Whether through fear or through a hatred of central authority many courts displayed startling leniency. It was not only traditionally unsafe areas (such as the Velay) or recently troubled areas (Provence, the Rhône corridor) which were affected, but also the north of the Loire where the best organised and toughest bands operated: Salembrier between Normandy and Flanders, the 'bande d'Orgères' around Chartres. In the autumn of 1797 coaches were obstructed at Villejuif, Fontainebleau and Montargis; a transport of funds for the Army of Italy was intercepted in the Auvergne.

Vigorous measures – repressive laws against compliant jailors, a reorganisation of the criminal courts and of the gendarmerie – for a time checked this wave of banditry. But the cumulative effects of the economic crisis and the conscription law were soon to cause it to redouble in intensity. As a spectacular challenge to the authority of the Directory, banditry was a symptom of decay rather than a real hindrance. But it created an atmosphere of insecurity which, in addition to other obstacles, made trade more difficult.

International trade

The new economic policy, the return of peace and the territorial conquests were all boons for international trade in 1795. Among counterbalancing disadvantages were the loss of the colonies and, more generally, the breakdown of maritime links. The leading sector of the French economy under the *ancien régime* was threatened with paralysis. On the Atlantic coast Bordeaux was able, under the Directory, to maintain 'a mediocre but respectable level of trade' thanks to the

United States.[4] American ships re-exported the sugar and coffee of the French colonies and loaded up with wine in return. This trade developed strongly between Year IV and Year VI. Other neutral ships – from the Hanseatic towns, from Prussia, from Denmark – transported wine to their respective countries (but also to the French colonies via England) in return for wheat. The large colonial entrepôt converted itself into a regional port more successfully, it seems, than Nantes, which did not benefit from an equally rich agricultural hinterland. Unfortunately the Directory's aggressive policy towards neutral countries led to an almost total rupture of relations with the United States in Year VII. The possibilities of providing arms for the colonies had disappeared; another source of profits took its place: the arming of privateers. Between 1797 and 1799 the inhabitants of Bordeaux armed 114 corsairs and searched for arms from other ports. Nor did Nantes remain inactive: privateering, wrote *Le Moniteur* on 19 September 1798, had restored to it 'an air of life and abundance'. Parisian capitalists took part in these undertakings. By these various routes colonial produce reached France. Despite the law of 30 October 1796 which had banned English goods, or those reputed to be so, cotton, coffee, sugar and tobacco continued to be supplied openly or to be smuggled in. But after the occupation of Holland the axis of European trade shifted eastwards, towards Hamburg.

Gradually a new map of French trade emerged, in which pride of place was held by northern Europe – the markets of Brussels, Amsterdam, Hamburg, Copenhagen – and central Europe, thanks to the restoration of relations with Berlin. Within French territory the importance of Belgium grew correspondingly, to the detriment of Lille, Dunkirk, Boulogne and Calais. The Lille administration's answer to the survey of Year V perhaps overestimated this competition but there is no doubt that the Belgians had monopolised part of the trade which went from Germany and Holland to the large towns of France, and even to Italy via Marseilles or to Spain via Bayonne. Similarly Strasburg suffered from the dynamism of Basle. The brokerage, banking and haulage profits which stemmed from the transportation of goods between Switzerland and Holland passed into new hands as the convoys began to take the right bank of the Rhine, preferring Cologne, Koblentz and Mainz to Strasburg.

Political and economic centralisation helped Paris under the Directory to tap an increasing proportion of this trade. Parisian establishments

[4] F. Crouzet (90).

monopolised the trade in woollen fabrics, formerly the prerogative of Rouen and Orléans. The redistribution of cotton produced in Upper Alsace and the Nord was also carried out by business men from the capital. Finally, textiles from Belgium, the Rhineland and Switzerland were most likely to find their way to the Paris market.[5]

Speculators

The world of business, however, was less interested in the acquisition of industrial or commercial profits than in carrying out speculative 'killings'. The most lucrative transactions took place with the state. We have seen the position held in the war machine by the army contractors. But they were only a particular instance – the most important, it is true – of a general phenomenon: financial chaos and the needs of the government encouraged all holders of capital (the smallest sometimes grouping their funds together) to offer their services or credit. In this the Directory was not innovatory; it was resuming a tradition of the *ancien régime*, abandoned in Year II in favour of the commissions and state-run administrations. But the extent of the phenomenon under the Directory was unprecedented. For example, Belgian national property, valued at three thousand million *livres*, was only selling with difficulty, as a result of people's religious scruples. Since rents from it came in badly, the government leased out the general responsibility for collecting them to a company formed by Liévin-Bauwens and Beths. When the toll was created it was at once decided to hand over responsibility for its collection in the same way. The state contractors likewise intervened in the conduct of public affairs, by granting themselves sources of national revenue by way of payment: delegations on direct taxes, the proceeds from the sale of cuttings in national forests, etc. There were startling success stories, but also numerous bankruptcies since the Treasury sometimes failed to pay what it owed. From this stemmed the highly speculative nature of these operations: as they were risky they had to be lucrative. All in all this capital was diverted from productive employment and went either into high profit-making areas or into absolutely safe investments (land); a part was also wasted in expenditure on prestige items. Neither agriculture nor industry succeeded in attracting this mass of capital for investment in economic development. Most of it was swallowed up by the money markets or used in commercial transactions. This phenomenon, whatever moral judge-

[5] L. Bergeron (86).

ments it might invite, provides a clear indication of the fundamentally unhealthy nature of the economy under the Directory.

Fluctuations

Considered overall the economic history of the Directory is a history of crisis. But this period of depression included moments of respite, even of recovery; in addition, the crisis had socially differentiated effects: it did not only produce victims. Thus it is necessary both to establish the rhythm of fluctuations in economic activity between 1795 and 1799 and to describe those social differences which they exacerbated.

Year IV was in all respects a terrible year. The harvest, as we have seen, had not been very good in the summer of 1794 and in many regions peasants lacked seed. Most importantly, the countryside was afflicted after the autumn by a series of climatic disasters: rain in October, frost during the winter, rain again in the summer of 1795, which delayed the harvest and damaged the grain. When the harvest was over it became clear that it was insufficient. But the scarcity which resulted was as much the consequence of an economic choice as of bad weather: the peasants, no longer fearing requisitions, did not supply the markets and kept their grain to sell in exchange for metal currency or other commodities; ironmasters bartered their iron to obtain grain. The significance of the very high official market prices was therefore difficult to evaluate; they only represented a negligible proportion of the available stocks.

The whole economy suffered from the grain crisis. Industry, already handicapped by inflation, sold less to urban consumers and found it difficult to resist repeated demands for wage rises. Some businesses seem to have held up as a result of their favourable geographical location: thus the metallurgical industry of the Roussillon provisionally kept up a respectable level of activity by providing for the replacement of the forges of Catalonia destroyed by the war. Others escaped bankruptcy by disinvestment.

With the abolition of paper money the economy moved into a period of depression characterised by a lasting fall in agricultural and industrial prices, a decline in profits and relatively resistant wage levels which were, however, affected by the scale of unemployment. This classic analysis by R. Schnerb deserves further specification and qualification.[6] First, can one measure how important agriculture was among the causes of the crisis? The 1796 harvest was good everywhere. Grain returned to the market but the prices which slumped as usual after the harvest showed stability in Year V. In Elbeuf they stayed around 11 *livres* per quintal, in the Sarthe they fell from 11 *livres* in June to 9 *livres* in December and remained at this level. In the Meurthe the annual variation was not above 10%. Finally, in the Haute-Loire a bale of wheat, quoted at 7 *livres* 10 *sous* in Thermidor Year V, had fallen to 4 *livres* 18 *sous* a month later. This was an appreciable fall due to the excessively long interval between the exhaustion of the previous harvest and the arrival of the new one – and it brought prices back down to their threshold of 1788. Prices did not really collapse until after the harvest of 1797. This time all the indicators converge; the fall in prices spread all the more rapidly as peasants had to pay their taxes in metal currency. They rushed to sell at any price.

During these two years the signs of an industrial slump multiplied, but in some regions and sectors there were also indications of a revival; the diagnosis of the situation is not therefore obvious. P. Léon has emphasized the gravity of the crisis in the Isère: a fall in prices (of 25% for iron in two years) and a drop in production, most glaring in metal and textiles (production levels were at this time half those of 1789). The Maine flax industry would provide another illustration of the crisis. Finally, the industrial survey of Year V also reveals the extent of the economic stagnation. But for certain industries Year VI was also 'a time of hope', to take up the phrase P. Clémendot has applied to the Meurthe. The disappearance of paper currency had acted as a purge. The French market was protected from an invasion of English goods while simultaneously coming to include the whole continent. The prospects of new markets and of help from the government were deciding factors in the setting up of businesses and in the search for mechanised equipment. In Year VI manufacturing in Elbeuf regained some of its dynamism. The mining companies achieved brilliant results in the extraction and even prospecting of coal. The mines of the Gard produced 5,746 tonnes of coal in 1792, 1,500 in Year III, 739 in year IV. They recovered their former levels of production in Year V and approached 9,000 tonnes in Year VI. Anzin, where production had bordered on 300,000 tonnes before the Revolution, reached 248,000

[6] R. Schnerb (107).

tonnes at the end of the Directory, after having achieved a remarkable recovery (65,000 tonnes in 1794, 138,000 in 1796, 213,000 in 1798). In the Haute-Marne the index of iron prices (its importance extended beyond its regional limits since it depended to a large extent on the Paris market) increased sharply during our period until the spring of 1799.

In short, the crisis had acted like a filter. Those entrepreneurs who were best equipped for competition and those regions which benefited most from the new situation achieved stability, even if they did not actually expand. The final crisis of the Directory was to dash their hopes. Its origins are complex. The 1799 harvest was poor everywhere except in Alsace. Spring frosts had destroyed part of the wheat; summer drought had ruined the fodder. Although the overall level was not disastrous, a slight shortfall was sufficient to endanger supplies in this pre-modern economy with its faltering transport system. This was all the more true since the return of war led, at least in the frontier provinces, to a resumption of requisitioning. Prices rose steeply in the autumn. The difficulties of agriculture partly explain the turnabout in the industrial situation. But war and the political decline of the regime exacerbated the credit crisis. Trade slackened; money went into hiding; even those sectors which had done relatively well in the previous phase were in their turn affected by the débâcle. More than the deflation, the crisis of the summer of 1799 fits into the traditional framework of an agrarian economy.

The 'nouveaux riches'

Those who came out top in this period were to be found among the ranks of the richest landowners and those tenant farmers who had profited from the years of price increases and inflation to accumulate capital and who had not been really weakened by the depression. Even more certain of success were the racketeers, or at least those who had enough flair or backing for their speculations to come off. Around these parvenus – Ouvrard, Hamelin, Flachat and so many others – clustered politicians, men like Laporte and Delaunay who were no more than 'business deputies' organising for themselves or their friends what Mathiez called the pillage of the Republic. This collusion between business and politics could be illustrated by celebrated examples: the attitude of Barras' entourage scandalised the honest La Révellière. This heterogeneous social stratum did not exist only in Paris. On a smaller scale the provincial bourgeoisie followed in the wake of the

Parisian profiteers, leading like them a life of ostentatious display and riotous parties. In Bordeaux an American traveller was shocked by the amount spent on balls, suppers and gambling by some of his hosts. As a result of this 'inflationary' mentality, money, quickly lost and quickly gained, circulated without benefiting the economy.

The losers

Popular poverty formed a contrast calculated to strike contemporaries. The crises of Year IV completed the pauperisation of the urban masses, who had already been hit in Year III. Without bread, often without work, the poor lived on public assistance and piled into hostels. The terrible winter of 1795–6 and successive epidemics struck down those who had resisted so far. The mortality rate reached record levels for the century, more than doubling in Rouen and Dieppe, and also increasing, though to a lesser degree, in Nancy and Paris. Indicative of the despair of the workers was the fact that the number of suicides in Paris increased to such a point that the Minister of Police forbade the publication of the weekly figures. Prostitution and criminality followed the same pattern. It is understandable, given this extreme poverty, that Babeuf's conspiracy did not meet with a significant response among the most deprived sections of society. After so many defeats, the poor were too concerned merely with survival to plunge into an enterprise whose outcome was doubtful. All indications are that during the second phase of the Directory this poverty was alleviated. Bread became plentiful and cheap again, except in the short final period, and wages seem overall to have held up better than prices. The balance sheet was, then, positive. But although one can observe an undoubted alleviation in the situation, the extent of unemployment would not justify the conclusion that the mood had changed to one of euphoria. The crisis in industrial and probably artisanal activity hit workers in the buildings, textile and luxury-goods (for example, cabinet making) industries. Employers preferred to lay off workers rather than to run at a loss and only kept on those very specialised workers who would be difficult to find again. Year VII, then, was not a happy year, but one of social tensions exacerbated by religious divisions. The picture in the countryside could be painted in yet blacker terms. Small landowners were victims of the fall in the prices of grain and wine. To deal with these conditions of economic depression farmers tended to get rid of part of their labour force, even though this meant reducing the amount of work done and, therefore, the size of the harvest. These unemployed workers swelled the proletariat of the towns in search of employment or assistance, but they had even greater difficulty than the urban poor in obtaining either. Hence those migratory movements of population, which, depending on the seasons, on needs and on rumour, drove the starving masses either out of the towns or towards them.

The constraints of the economic situation left only a short respite for attempts to promote economic development. Overall the period of the Directory combined a stagnation of productive capacity, a pauperisation of the masses with the brazen enrichment of a handful of speculators. But all the attempts which had been embarked on and which had half-succeeded, the plans which had been considered, all these had painfully paved the way for the consolidation of the Consulate. To emphasise this debt to the past is not, however, to underestimate the achievement of Bonaparte.

5

Beliefs, rituals and language

'What are the means most suitable to establish the morality of a people?'

A question put in a competition by the Institute in 1798

In the realm of culture the Directory strove passionately to succeed in its programme of stabilisation. The regime could not indeed achieve equilibrium so long as it had not won the battle for men's minds. The structure would only be as strong as the cement which held it together. To contest the hegemony exerted by religious ideology, to set up a new system of values and to transmit it through collective practices, education, entertainment and images – this was the implicit objective of the Thermidoreans and the avowed objective of the Fructidoreans. The ups and downs of this enterprise are relatively well known, at least to the extent that the projects and schemes of the government and the resistance encountered from traditional beliefs ultimately fall under the rubric of political history. But what was happening at a more profound level is much less obvious. Thus the types of religiosity, the spread of fashions and the forms of cultural stagnation have not attracted sufficient attention. Similarly, the problem of folklore and, more generally, of the artistic expression of the people deserve detailed study. Historians tend to behave as if the dominant models had spread without difficulty, as if there were no need to distinguish different levels of culture. But, to cite only two examples, it is clear that the provincial bourgeoisie continued to appreciate old style furniture long after interior decoration in Paris had been transformed. And, secondly, the destruction of regional cultures was not complete. During a debate on the teaching of living languages a distracted deputy declared that it was necessary to 'remove from the soil of the Republic all particular jargons so as to retain only the national language'. One notes the slip, or the confession. The most important aspects of this cultural history perhaps remain submerged.

RELIGIOUS REVIVAL

The return of the 'good priests'

The Thermidoreans were worried that a Catholic restoration might accompany the resurgence of royalism. The Convention had attempted to avoid this danger. The laws of 20 Fructidor Year III and 3 Brumaire Year IV re-activated the repressive measures against refractory priests; that of 7 Vendémiaire Year IV obliged the clergy to recognise the sovereignty of the people and promise obedience to the laws. It also restricted freedom of worship, or at least its exercise. It would be wrong to assume that this legislation represented merely a stream of paper. Insecurity remained the lot of the 'returned' priests; and harassment and police measures limited the propagation of the faith. But in spite of such obstacles the religious renaissance took on the air of a *reconquista*.

In the Sarthe, as in the Meurthe or even Paris, the search for non-jurors was pursued without much energy. Almost the only priests to be arrested were too old or too infirm to be deported. The colluding local authorities, supported by the majority of the population, not only allowed non-jurors to evade pursuit but also to officiate almost freely. In the west and in the frontier *départements* there was hardly any let up in the return of 'good priests'. As in Year III, religious revival and political reaction went hand in hand; the right wing of the Councils succeeded on 14 Frimaire Year V in neutralising the law of 3 Brumaire, and then, drawing confidence from their electoral success, in revoking the legislation against refractory priests (24 August 1797).

The Roman clergy was no longer united by success as it had been by persecution. The declaration demanded by the law of 7 Vendémiaire aroused passionate argument. The *émigré* bishops considered that it was not right to submit to an authority and to a body of legislation which had been condemned. Conversely, for many priests pastoral concerns prevailed over doctrine. They were tempted to accept the declaration as a way of retaining contact with the faithful. In Paris the cause of submission was again defended by Emery who could not 'become accustomed to the idea of a country without worship'. Thanks to his moral authority and to the support of the *Annales Catholiques* the majority of Parisian priests rallied to his point of view. In the provinces, those who submitted to the declaration (*soumissionaires*) formed a not insignificant minority. Internal tensions increased; the *intransigeants* set the faithful against the *soumissionaires* by contesting that they could validly administer the sacraments. The refractory clergy was strengthened by the uninterrupted stream of retractions. Many of the jurors began to question themselves: why remain faithful to an obsolete institution? After the wave of dechristianisation and the drama of the resigning priests, the *de facto* repeal of the civil constitution worsened the malaise. Outside the urban centres and the community of a group many jurors only put up with their isolation with difficulty. In their quest for security it is impossible to disentangle spiritual concerns from material privation. Unpaid and unprotected, the constitutional clergy felt the need for a haven. Those who took the plunge and returned to the ministry had first to undergo a penance which varied in length from diocese to diocese. The refractories and those who had retracted (the *rempaillés* as they were known in the Sarthe) were not numerous enough for the evangelical task. The missionaries provided them with vital support and, what is more, formed a link between the refractories and the *émigré* bishops. Missions were organised in the Lyonnais by the Abbé Linsolas – who concerned himself with both the pastoral care of the faithful and the theological training of clerics – but the system existed in many regions. The Abbé Plongeron has shown the conflicts of jurisdiction and of method to which this duality of ecclesiastical personnel could give rise – the complex interplay of influence between apostolic administrators and diocesan councils, between the heads of the missions and the *émigré* suffragans – as well as the enrichment of theology which so many new problems stimulated.[1]

This diverse and active clergy fought over the places of worship with the constitutional priests. In Paris twelve or fifteen public oratories were in the hands of the jurors at the end of 1795. But the refractories held services in the convents, chapels and private oratories of the capital. In August 1796 the police estimated that there were seventy-six oratories. During 1797 they reached two hundred, not counting the private mansions which secretly opened their doors to the priests.[2] In the provinces refractories who had made the declaration recovered the use of churches, even if this meant sharing them according to the agreement with the other clergy. There were also cases, for example in the Nord, where priests whose position was not regularised installed themselves in churches. The authorities, not daring to confront the population, turned a blind eye. In the first months of 1797 political developments obviously accentuated this trend. After the elections of Germinal the

[1] B. Plongeron (128).   [2] J. Boussoulade (13).

émigré priests returned by the thousand and many municipalities no longer bothered to enforce observance of the law. Similarly the restrictive clauses of 7 Vendémiaire fell into disuse. It seemed incomprehensible to the faithful, especially in the countryside, to authorise worship at the same time as forbidding the services to occur in public. On the contrary, rural communities which had regained a 'true pastor', sometimes having chased out the 'intruder', bestowed great solemnity on this reconciliation. So the banning of the various external signs of Christianity was rarely successful. The quarrel over bells went beyond the petty and futile battle to which people have tried to reduce it. The bell was the symbol of the reconquest; its restitution abolished the 'Church of Silence'. It was a manifestation of the presence of the sacred in daily life, calling people to the angelus, to the mass, to the traditional festivals. Ecclesiastical time triumphed over republican time. Similarly, the object of forbidding the restoration of the crosses on church towers, in cemeteries and on calvaries had been to secularise the landscape; but space was once again appropriated by the sacred. The law was no longer respected.

The Fructidorean persecution

The *coup d'état* of 18 Fructidor abruptly interrupted this process of rechristianisation. By the terms of the law of 19 Fructidor, the restrictions on worship were retained, but the declaration was replaced by an oath of 'hatred towards royalty and anarchy' (already required from public servants). Moreover, with the restoration of the laws of 1792 and 1793, refractories became liable to the death penalty. Priests who disturbed public order, even those who had submitted to the declaration, could be deported by order of the Directory. The Roman church was divided over the oath. The majority of the Parisian clergy submitted to it as a purely political act. The friends of Emery were frightened that by an intransigent attitude they would waste all the fruits of their efforts. A small fraction of the provincial clergy also adopted a conciliatory interpretation (defended among others by the Bishop of Marseilles) of the oath and put the welfare of the faithful before anything else. In the Sarthe 90 out of 200 'Romans' took the oath. The law also applied to Belgium. The clergy, disoriented by the departure of the bishops (except for the Bishop of Malines), was divided. The Walloon priests submitted; their Flemish colleagues opted for refusal. Within the former limits of France about one-fifth of the refractories bowed to the demands of the Fructidoreans, a fact which added a new motive for dissensions and debarments. From 11 January 1798 the refractories were declared unfit to take the oath, even if they had been *soumissionaires*. The Directory launched into a war of extermination against the Roman Church: 1,800 priests were sentenced to deportation. The convoys headed for Niort and Bordeaux, from where the refractories were to be sent to Cayenne. Only two frigates succeeded in running the English blockade. The prisoners were interned on the islands of Ré and Oléron. There were 1,300 of them, to be joined by 500 priests of Belgian origin. Not all the central administrations had demonstrated the same zeal as the authorities of Mayenne, who arrested over eighty priests, executed three of them (as *émigrés*) and deported two; or those of the Sarthe who had captured forty-five refractories and carried out one execution and nineteen deportations. In the east the moderation of the Meurthe contrasted with the harshness of the Vosges. The Roman Church seemed to have been swept away by the repression. In fact the survivors went back underground and resumed nocturnal masses (in the Lot). They once again became those 'priests of the bush' (in the Sarthe), those 'suitcase *curés*' (in the Nord) of the days of persecution.

The Gallicans isolated

The religious revival also meant a reconstruction of the Gallican Church. Its survival represented a considerable achievement amidst the successive disasters of dechristianisation and retraction. On 20 February 1796 the *Annales de la religion* published the second encyclical of the Evêques Réunis. This text developed the usual argument of the Gallicans, affirming the rights of national churches and denying the Pope the title of 'Universal Bishop'. The Evêques Réunis did not give in to the current of presbyterianism prevalent among their *curés*. But they recognised the priests' right to be 'associated in some way' with the government of the dioceses. The encyclical requested their correspondents to prepare a national council. This meeting in Notre-Dame, preceded by synods, did not open until 15 August 1797. It seems that the reason for such a long delay lay as much in the government's reluctance to authorise the gathering as in procedural slowness. The *curés* were in a majority (sixty-eight delegates against thirty-three bishops) and formed a united party imbued with 'Richerism'.[3] For this reason

---

[3] J. Boussoulade (117).

the discussion centred on two themes: the election of bishops and the distribution of power within the Church. The council decided that, as in the ancient Church, the bishops would be elected by the clergy and the people deliberating separately. The sovereignty of the people was safeguarded, but the clergy – which drew up the list of candidates – ensured that it had a dominant role. On the other hand, the episcopalian party prevented the priests from being recognised as having jurisdiction with them over the Church. Indeed, to settle, for example, questions of discipline, the bishops tended to meet as a separate group, away from the presence of the priest delegates. When the council broke up three months after opening, it seemed that Grégoire had avoided a schism, at the cost of a few concessions. But the gap between the two orders remained worrying.

Beyond this insoluble conflict – which restarted all over again the debate which had begun in 1789 – the attitude of the Gallicans could be defined as a desire for rigour and for a return to the sources of Christianity. Grégoire's friends were indeed haunted by the model of the primitive Church. This return to the institutions of the first Christians was expressed both in the creation of presbyteries and in the mode of election of bishops. In the same spirit, the clergy was urged to live its enforced poverty as an evangelical virtue. The intention was to break with the easy life of the established Church at the same time as with the formulae of Tridentine Catholicism. These precepts were applied with the utmost rigour to priests who had resigned or to other 'fallen' priests. Certainly the Paris presbytery was forced to make a distinction between excusable lapses and more scandalous cases, because the drain on numbers had been so great as to make it inconceivable to bar the return of all those who had subsequently repented. But generally it showed a greater intransigence than the 'Romans'. Without underestimating tactical considerations – it was necessary to enhance the status of a much-discredited Church – one can see here the dominant influence of Jansenist morality. This severe and austere form of religion which was held by many of the constitutional clergy helped to alienate some believers from them. Thus in Paris Catholics repelled by 'the unbending severity of these confessors' (Boussoulade) preferred priests who demanded less heroism and offered greater consolation. But if the constitutional clergy had lost followers, the reasons for this were more fundamental. The mass of believers still considered them as 'intruders' guilty of having organised the schism within the Church.

The Republicans were at the outset well disposed to the Gallicans.

All the constitutionalists had made the declaration prescribed on 7 Vendémiaire and then sworn the oath of hatred against royalty. In *Les Annales de la religion*, in sermons and in encyclicals they attested their loyalty towards the civil power and denounced the collusion of the refractories with the Royalists in terms which could not but be pleasing to the Republicans. In fact the jurors rarely found the support they needed. If they managed to escape being assimilated with the Counter-Revolution, they almost came to be suspect in its eyes. For the pronounced anti-clericals on the Directory (Reubell, La Révellière) and for many of the government's commissioners, their submission was a gesture containing 'much more hypocrisy than sincerity'. It is for this reason that after Fructidor relations did not improve in spite of the enthusiastic approval which the national council had shown for the *coup d'état*. The jurors had also wanted to be reconciled with the Pope; they refused to abandon Sunday in favour of the *décadi*. Such factors stimulated the authorities to keep a close watch. Reinhard has shown how, in the Sarthe, the Republicans' hostility to the jurors was tempered only by their fear of the refractories. To break up the Church's infrastructure, the government even decided to hand over some of the places of worship to speculators who demolished the buildings and recovered the materials. Nowhere, it seems, did this movement occur on a greater scale than in the Nord where 400 parish churches were sold off at knock-down prices. The church of Cluny suffered the same fate, and the cathedrals of Orléans and Paris only escaped because of a lack of solvent purchasers. The contemptuous neutrality of Year III was dead; it was succeeded by militant anti-clericalism.

Worship and religion

The balance sheet of the rechristianisation accomplished by the Roman Church and the Gallican Church shows striking successes. Despite harassment from the authorities, Christians flocked to services, and, in some country areas, even went back to the solemn ritual of processions and dedications. The Fructidorean legislation restricted the public expression of this faith but did not really succeed in calling into question religious practice. Yet this undoubted revival was not without its black spots. First, the most lucid observers noted that a huge attendance at church ceremonies did not imply that the sacraments were taken on a similar scale. Should this be attributed to the long absence of the clergy from many regions which had been reduced to 'white masses'? Or was it rather the case, as Plongeron suggests, that the quarrels over oaths and submission had introduced 'the poison of sacramental relativism'? There was a danger that religion without worship had been replaced by worship without religion. Moreover, the Revolution had speeded up a process of individual liberation which denied the very bases of the faith. If it is difficult, in the short span of our period, to pinpoint the effect of a weakening of the prescriptions of religion upon birth-rates, it is at least possible to note the frequency of divorces, in spite of the restrictive legislation of Year III, and to recall the wave of suicides in Paris in Year IV. Even if such attitudes were held only by a minority, the break with the past which they implied was an indication of a profound questioning of the values of Christianity. Finally, if many famous intellectuals like La Harpe and Fontanes were brought back to the Church through social fear or through following their own personal spiritual paths, the religious revival which affected the *notables* in the last years of the century was not confined within the structures of the Church. On the contrary, the example of Lyons shows that many different mystical currents could draw strength from the vicissitudes of reason.[4] The influence of Mesmer, of Swedenborg or Saint-Martin attracted restless spirits towards the experiences of occultism and illuminism. Under the Directory, anti-religious scepticism or vague deism seemed to remain the common denominator of the elites. A country parson from Rheims wrote to Grégoire in April 1795 that the municipality of the town had not yet honoured the Church with its presence. 'They still say publicly that they have replaced the nobles and that to go to mass is to merge with the dregs of the populace.'[5] And two years later it was not clear that Catholicism had guaranteed itself a decisive place among the new ruling classes. Yet it was over these classes that the ideological battle was waged.

REPUBLICAN DOCTRINES AND PRACTICES

Idéologie or the discourse of reason

Faced with the encroachments of Catholicism, what conception of the world could the new regime claim as its own? 'Idéologie' seemed to be the keystone of the Directorial system in that it gave coherence to

---

[4] L. Trenard (129).   [5] B. Plongeron (128).

the intentions of the Thermidoreans. It was not properly speaking the official philosophy of the Directory, but its 'Discourse on Method'. The Idéologues invoked the inspiration of a double inheritance: the rationalism of the Enlightenment – Volney and Cabanis had known the Encyclopédistes – and political liberalism – such as had been defended in the Constituent Assembly by Volney, Garat and Destutt de Tracy. Their scientific concerns embraced varied fields. Volney, known before the Revolution for his *Voyage en Egypte et en Syrie* (1787), which was a model of rigorous geographical writing, had established himself as a political philosopher with *Ruines ou Méditations sur les révolutions des Empires* (1790). Cabanis wanted to turn medical practice into a science. He applied himself particularly to the systematic presentation of observations, to analysis as the basis of knowledge and, finally, to the relations between the physical and the moral, to take the title of his book published in 1802 but which he had been preparing since 1796. This search for a psychophysiology brought him close to Destutt de Tracy's reflection on the genesis of knowledge. Following, then, diverse paths, these thinkers encountered the same problem: that of a general methodology of the sciences which would ground fragmented researches upon reason. The work of Condillac provided them with one of the keys. Ideas come through sensations; representations are condensed into signs that have to be decoded by analysis. Among the systems of signs, language holds a privileged position; it is the 'concrete link between representation and reflection'.[6] Hence the importance of grammar, the theory of discourse. Idéologie (the term was invented by Destutt de Tracy) offered itself, then, as the universal science which would reconstitute the genesis of all possible knowledge and allow the categorisation of particular forms of knowledge. It followed that metaphysics and revealed religion were discredited by this experimental rationalism, this principle of agnosticism. Philosophies of finitude and disillusion no longer had a *raison d'être*. Man was perfectible, and the universe, for whoever knew how to interpret it, was transparent. This rigorous and optimistic philosophy in which the intellectual trends of the century were summed up inspired considerable fervour and much research. Its hold was such that few contemporaries, from amongst the elites, succeeded in abstracting themselves from its conceptual frameworks. Daunou, Sieyès, Talleyrand, Chénier, Dupont de Nemours, François de Neufchâteau, Benjamin Constant, and many others, were influenced by it. The Idéologues naturally came to the fore wherever the new culture was being developed. The Institute, created

---

[6] M. Foucault, *Les Mots et les Choses* (Paris, 1966), p. 98.

on 25 October 1795 as a mainspring of scientific research, included a section on 'the analysis of sensations and ideas', the preserve of the Idéologues, and all its classes were peopled with friends of Volney. When teachers had to be chosen for the Ecole Normale, which was to train the core of the French teaching profession, an appeal was made, as we will see, to thinkers who, with the exception of La Harpe, all claimed allegiance to Idéologie. Moreover the influential newspaper *La Décade philosophique* developed ideas close to Idéologie while retaining, however, an attitude of independence.[7] The Idéologues could justly claim the responsibility for scientific progress. At the very least contemporary research adopted an outlook identical to their own. Pinel, Bichat and Roussel, who were all doctors, identified the bases of a science of man which could be verified by findings in psycho-pathology. In his *Traité de mécanique céleste* (1799), Laplace expounded a theory of the formation of the universe which came within the methodological framework of the Idéologues. The researches of Berthellot, Fourcroy and Vauquelin in chemistry, and of Geoffrey Saint-Hilaire in zoology, were derived from the same postulates. But this was not an unmitigated triumph. While Destutt de Tracy and Cabanis were giving classical philosophy its ultimate expression, rationalism was already coming up against its limitations. Lamarck was preparing to call into question the explanatory principles of natural history, to define new concepts of the organic and the inorganic which would allow the creation of a science of the living. More generally, Idéologie was challenged for its optimism and its pretension to exhaustiveness. The political and moral uncertainty, the spiritual renewal, led the elites down new paths. Idéologie marked the grandiose culmination of the philosophy of the Enlightenment. It is for this reason that the Directory believed that it had at last found in it the expression of its own ambitions. But the order that Idéologie established in the intellectual realm, since it took no account of tension and change, was as fragile as the other forms of order. Its modernity was illusory: it proposed the certainties of the past at a time when European society was, in the phrase of Michel Foucault, constructing for itself new levels of understanding.

Theophilanthropy

The failure of Robespierre's religious plans did not discredit the principle of spiritual regeneration. It continued to be believed that without virtuous citizens the Republic would not be viable. Among

[7] J. Kitchin (122).

the necessary forms of stabilisation, was this one not fundamental? The new regime had to give birth to a new race of men. If the state tried to impose its system without preparation, the result was bound to be unsuccessful, and in any case, to proceed in this way would ruin the spirit of the enterprise. The initiative of individuals would be the best guarantee of success. A masonic bookseller, Chemin, attempted, like so many others, to establish a 'civic and rational plan of worship'.[8] He wanted to establish, with simple ceremonies, both a natural religion, founded upon the existence of God and the immortality of the soul, and a morality of social utility. Valentin Haüy and three other enthusiastic readers of the *Manuel des théoanthropophiles* joined with Chemin to form the management committee for the worship of natural religion, soon called Theophilanthropy. The first ceremony took place on 15 January 1797 in the church of St Catherine. Sermons on moral themes, invocations of the divinity and examinations of conscience alternated with readings and hymns. The austerity of this inoffensive religion open to all quickly gained it the support of Dupont de Nemours, Creuze-Latouche and Bernardin de Saint-Pierre. Former dechristianisers like Rossignol or David also rallied to it. From this point there was to be no end to the ambiguity of Theophilanthropy: was it a religion of social harmony or a weapon of anti-Catholicism? Political conflict provided it with a more precise orientation; the Directorials flocked to the three temples of Theophilanthropy. La Révellière gave his blessing to the movement. In a speech of 12 Floréal, delivered at the Institute, on the subject of national religion, national ceremonies and national festivals, he acclaimed the new religion without naming it: 'when a religion has been cast down, however irrational and anti-social it may have been, it has always been necessary to replace it by others, or it has, so to speak, replaced itself by being reborn out of its own ruins'. La Révellière's colleagues were either hostile, like Carnot, or sceptical. Only Reubell saw the advantage to be derived from the politicisation of the religion. After 18 Fructidor the protector of the Theophilanthropists was able to impose his views. This was the heyday of the national religion, encouraged and subsidised by the public authorities. It was said that even the victor of Campo-formio had been won over to it. The promoters of the religion considered they had a right to demand access to other Parisian churches. They obtained the use of fifteen of them, which brought them into conflict with the constitutional clergy. But Theophilanthropy developed

[8] A. Mathiez (125).

considerably. First, there was a pronounced ritualisation of the ceremonial, and a priesthood of reader–supervisors grew up. The Idéologues and *La Décade philosophique* unanimously deplored this shift towards clericalism. Second, at the instigation of the Jacobins, Theophilanthropy hardened its anti-Catholic posture and became a gathering together of the most advanced Republicans. In Year VI the Directors began to suspect the zealots of this religion. La Révellière himself, divided between his leanings towards Theophilanthropy and his hatred of Jacobins, ended up by detaching himself from his new friends. By the end of the Directory Theophilanthropy had lost the advantage of being a semi-official religion. Attacked by the Catholics and by the *philosophes* and divided over what course to follow, Theophilanthropy no longer formed more than a sect on the decline. At the height of its strength the religion had burgeoned in the Paris region, the centre, the east, and above all in the Yonne where Sens constituted a veritable stronghold. In some of these areas the success of Theophilanthropy survived its overall decline in influence. But the Theophilanthropists' hope of substituting themselves for Catholicism as the dominant religion was destroyed. Theophilanthropy had ultimately only brushed the surface of the culturally unstable layers of the middle and lower-middle classes. It undoubtedly fulfilled some of their hopes, but its success was the result of a fashion or, more precisely, of a particular set of circumstances. Once the favourable moment had passed, this *mystique* which had become *politique* could not avoid the ebbing of the tide.

Festivals

In its final phase Theophilanthropy had been transformed into civic and moral preaching. In this it competed with the official festivals whose object was to bind the people to the Republic. The idea of a political ceremony as a rite of unanimity was certainly not new in revolutionary France. The laws of 19 Floréal Year II and 3 Brumaire Year IV had established and systematised the national festivals, and the Republican calendar formally instituted the rhythm of the ten-day week. Nevertheless, the Fructidorean Directory attached enormous political importance to these republican celebrations, and, through the determination of Merlin de Douai and the imagination of François de Neufchâteau, they became the great achievement of the government. It was not, indeed, enough to have declared war on Catholicism. It was also necessary to create new collective entertainments, to arouse a consensus. The decree of 14 Germinal Year IV (3 April 1798) enforced observance of the *décadi* by the state administration and state concerns. All notarial deeds, posters and gazettes had to use the revolutionary calendar exclusively. The 'old style' was outlawed. The laws of 17 Thermidor and 23 Fructidor Year VI tightened these measures. That of 13 Fructidor organised the decadal cult: every *décadi*, municipal administrators had to proceed 'in costume' to special premises; reading would take place from the texts of recent laws and from the *Bulletin décadaire*, which would contain 'bravura elements' and tales of 'deeds likely to inspire public spiritedness and virtue'. Marriages would be celebrated on this day alone; homilies and games were also planned. Primary school teachers were to be punctilious in conducting their children to these festivals. In this way it was hoped to break the domination of the Christian calendar and build up a new communal life.

Particular solemnity was attached to the national festivals which would be integrated into this overall structure. The trilogy of moral festivals – festivals of Youth (10 Germinal), Marriage (10 Floréal) and Old Age (10 Fructidor) – exalted the union of the family unit and the social organism, of private virtues and civic morality. On 10 Messidor agriculture held pride of place. To these festivals devoted to particular themes were added commemorative festivals. That of 10 Prairial, dedicated to French victories and expressing gratitude for them, had first of all celebrated the successes of the Army of Italy. On 10 August and 9 Thermidor the French were invited to rejoice in the defeat of tyranny and the restoration of liberty. On 1 Vendémiaire they celebrated the foundation of the Republic, and on 2 Pluviôse (21 January) 'the just punishment of the last king of the French'. The newest but least well accepted of these festivals was the celebration of 18 Fructidor: 'To celebrate', writes Mona Ozouf, 'is to remember and repeat.'[9] The government wanted to inculcate a collective memory, or rather a selective memory, in which the emphasis could be shifted at will. Thus Mona Ozouf shows that 18 Fructidor elevated the importance of 13 Vendémiaire – a premonitory confrontation – and minimised that of 9 Thermidor, because it had introduced a dangerous rift into the republican camp. The national festivals were rituals of both solidarity and division between the 'Great Nation' and its foreign adversaries, between the Republicans and their enemies within France. One can understand how emotions could reach a climax when, in

---

[9] M. Ozouf (126).

Augers, a victory over the Chouans was announced in the middle of a festival, and how, while commemorating the assassinations of Bonnier and Roberjot in Rastatt, the patriots of the same town had to ward off the threat of a 'general blood bath'.[10]

Did the government succeed, following Daunou's hope, in 'making patriotism the common religion of all Frenchmen'? The results were, overall, disappointing. But a detailed study shows interesting disparities. In the first place, success depended largely on administrative pressure and was therefore more certain in the towns than in the countryside, in the chief town of the canton than in the larger villages. From accounts of these festivals a geography of civic virtue emerges in which the reliable areas were, among others, Paris, the east, the Nièvre and pockets of the west, and the particularly recalcitrant zones were Lyons and, with the exception of the Isère, the south-east.

Chronology provided another variable. Attendance at the festivals, and enthusiasm, fluctuated in step with political debate, with elections and with events abroad. Thus in Year VI the threat of invasion seems to have welded many of those participating at the festivals into a patriotic communion. The decadal cult, anti-Catholic in principle and monotonous in practice, quickly wearied even those most favourably disposed towards it. The moral festivals were greeted with irony rather than approval. On the other hand, the great votive festivals could on occasion be lived with intensity. Two of them seem to have aroused popular enthusiasm: 14 July and 1 Vendémiaire. This was no doubt because in these the crowds could wallow in nostalgia for the early days of the Revolution and for a lost unanimity.

It was a utopian dream to decree obligatory civic virtue and to believe in the resolution of political problems by theatrical sleights of hand. If the masses did not join in the rituals, it was because they did not feel themselves to be integrated into them. Despite appearances the liturgy of these festivals became increasingly alienating. Precedence and distance were observed with fanatical precision. The allegories and mythological allusions and the flowery language of the orators did not encourage communication. An increasingly strict codification of ceremonial did not allow *ad hoc* adjustments; at the most local level the authorities might, if they pleased, add a few variations. This ritual, which quickly became ossified and almost incomprehensible, transformed the festival into a mere spectacle whose success varied but from which, however, all popular participation was excluded.

[10] B. Bois (116), p. 218.

Sometimes a festival could slip out of control, or, rather, one festival could grow up within another. The scandalised authorities on occasion reported that a ceremony had degenerated into debauchery, that it had ended in dancing, singing and drinking. This emphasis of the serious over the comic, of the decent over the improper, distorts the reality of these sad festivals, which was in fact one of repression. The popular worship which surrounded, for example, the person of Marat was forbidden, buried away. After the last two of them had been crushed, the *journées* were now transfigured. The Revolution ended by benefiting those who henceforth held the exclusive rights to power and to speech.

THE TEACHING OF LIBERTY

Every society has a plan for its schools and defines – or betrays – itself in its education system. In this respect the post-Thermidorean period had the advantage over the previous era of being able to put its teaching programme into practice.

On 24 September 1794 an Ecole Centrale des Travaux Publics (subsequently known as the Ecole Polytechnique) had been set up. Pupils selected through an examination in mathematics were instructed by the best teachers in the 'principles common to all engineering professions'. After three years of study they had to follow courses at a vocational Ecole (artillery, engineering, mining, etc.). The closing of the faculties of medicine was a salutary measure for everyone, and it was therefore especially important not to allow a deterioration of medical education. It was for this reason that three Ecoles de Santé were set up in Paris, Strasburg and Montpellier (4 December 1794). Besides these sporadic measures, the Thermidoreans' schools policy was applied to the problems of non-specialised education.

Instructing the people

Three months after the fall of Robespierre there had already been a clear breach with the past. Following a report by Lakanal, the Convention, on 27 Brumaire Year III, passed a law ending compulsory education. It stipulated that there had to be a primary school for every 1,000 inhabitants. Primary school teachers, whose pay was slightly increased, would be examined by education panels (*jurys d'instruction*). These arrangements embodied a compromise on principles, even if the lack of primary school teachers and the difficulties of public finance

did partially justify them. A start on applying the law was made in
the Sarthe, and in the Maine-et-Loire, where an attempt was made to
draw up a map showing areas in need. Elsewhere, investigations
confirm that the law passed almost unnoticed. On the other hand, the
bill presented by Daunou on 3 Brumaire Year IV did leave lasting
traces. According to the clauses of this bill which concerned primary
education, teachers would no longer be paid by the state. They would
be lodged and would receive remuneration from their pupils. Having
dropped compulsory education, the members of the Convention now
abandoned free education. Finally, the number of public educational
establishments was reduced; a rule of one school per canton was
adopted. This retrograde law was a considerable blow to the maintenance of elementary education in many *départements*. The distribution
of the schools sparked off confusion and quarrels between the
communes, each trying to conserve its own school. The educational
map of the Directory displayed innumerable anomalies. The most
obvious was the total lack of public schools in many *départements*: in
1798, fourteen cantons in the Jura contained no school; the same was
true of two-thirds of the cantons of the lower Rhine. And the
catchment area of a school hardly extended outside the commune in
which it was situated: given the state of the roads and general insecurity,
there was no question of imposing long journeys on children. Payment
was another obstacle. But it was too little and too uncertain (how could
teachers be sure of a regular income, linked as it was to the attendance
of their pupils?) to tempt qualified teachers. It is for this reason that
in the Meurthe the panels ended up by accepting all candidates. In the
Nord there were only thirty applicants for seventy-six places. In some
areas, notably in the west, former primary school teachers had resumed
their old employment, and among the other candidates ex-*curés* were
in a majority. But alongside these privileged schools, there were many,
like those in Lyons, where the teachers were unable even to sign their
names! This disaster derived partly from the educational failure of the
Ecole Normale. According to the terms of a decree of 9 Brumaire Year
III, 1,400 pupils over twenty years old, chosen by district, had come
to Paris to receive a speeded-up course of training. The government
aimed to transform them into qualified teachers who would in their
turn instruct candidates as primary school teachers. Eminent thinkers –
Monge, Volney, Berthollet, Laplace, etc. – gave lectures of a high level
to these heterogeneous but clearly cultivated audiences. The high
standard demanded discouraged some of the pupils and the lectures

finished after four months, on 19 May 1795, without achieving any concrete results.

The authorities noted with irritation that the state primary school teachers still used the catechism and 'books of hours' as reading manuals. The government made an effort to procure others for them. In Year IV, and even more in Year VI, it sent many copies of new republican manuals into the provinces. But they were not always welcomed. To the remonstrations of the public authorities against the works of piety, the teachers generally replied that the parents, who were paying, did not want any others. Thus the religious question impinged upon schools. For the promoters of public education the schools' function was to mould Republicans. The compulsory attendance of school children at the decadal festivals did not only reflect a concern, as has been unimaginatively suggested, to fill out the audiences. Certainly the private schools were numerous and thriving. From Year IV to Year VI religious education gained ground. In 1799 the *département* of the Doubs had 90 public and 336 private schools. The refractory clergy, constitutional priests and lay Catholics provided an education whose 'reprehensible success' saddened the minister Letourneux. The *coup d'état* of 18 Fructidor had been the occasion of a rude awakening. The republican bourgeoisie's lack of interest in elementary education had had grave consequences. In this connection, the Directory's commissioner in the *département* of the Meurthe noted that: 'The aristocracy profits from the government's neglect of this important area; it pays for and directs education as it pleases.'[11] On 17 Pluviôse Year VI the government decided to reinforce its control. In order to purge all those suspected of anti-republicanism, it introduced the inspection of private establishments and of masters who taught at home. Numerous schools were closed down after these visitations: thirty-six in the *département* of the Gers alone. But these measures, unequally applied, did not resolve the basic problem. In Year VII the Council of the Five Hundred rejected a bill for the payment of primary school teachers by the state. Even *La Décade philosophique* did not protest. The *notables* had the means to pass on culture to their children. They saw no point in making sacrifices for the education of the children of the poorer classes.

[11] P. Clémendot (6), p. 411.

The principle of the Ecoles Centrales

The linchpin of the educational system was the organisation of secondary education. On 25 February 1795 the Convention had accepted the principle of an Ecole Centrale for every 300,000 people. The spirit of the education to be provided was yet to be defined. This is what the law of 3 Brumaire Year IV set out to do. The Ecoles Centrales, one of which had already been created in each *département*, achieved a synthesis between the most modern educational concerns and the thought of the Idéologues. The schools were divided into three sections corresponding to the age groups 12–14, 14–16, 16–18. The predominance of ancient languages, which stemmed from the model of humanist culture, was replaced by an entirely new syllabus. If ideas came from the senses it was necessary to begin by mastering observation, that is, knowing how to describe and reproduce sensible objects. Instruction in drawing provided the logical starting point and natural history the first illustration. On the other hand, the Idéologues held that it was essential, in order to grasp properly the mechanisms of language, to begin studying them when young. Initiation into ancient and possibly foreign languages was thus reserved for the first section. The second section allowed children to ascend the scale of knowledge as far as those partial, but already abstract and methodical, forms of discourse, mathematics, physics and chemistry. From the age of sixteen onwards the children were judged to be ready for speculation. They were therefore given an education which concentrated on moral and political sciences (history and legislation), on belles-lettres, considered as a variation of language, and on the very logic of discourse, that is, general grammar. This ambitious and coherent progression re-enacted, in the process of education, the development of knowledge in the real world.

In response to the educational demand of the century the authors of this programme took the gamble of providing freedom: freedom for the pupils, who were not required to attend all the lectures of their section, nor all the sections of the cycle (they could choose the courses which interested them most according to their initial knowledge and their aspirations); freedom for the professors to organise courses at their convenience and without restriction of curriculum, to carry out their own pedagogic experiments and to run the schools themselves; freedom, finally, for the administration of the *départements*, whose panels had the right to select competent teachers according to whatever criteria they chose.

Training the elites

The Directory set about implementing this plan with singlemindedness. By the end of the period, the hundred or so schools planned had been created. The number of pupils attending them bears comparison with those attending the *collèges* of the *ancien régime*: 200 pupils in Angers, 250 in Rodez, 200 in Poitiers, 150 in Le Mans and 500 in Besançon, the star school. They came essentially from bourgeois circles: in Lyons, the sons of manufacturers and public servants; in Le Mans, the sons of public servants and magistrates; elsewhere there was a predominance of sons of well-off property owners. The requirement to pay a fee (25 *livres* per pupil) certainly constituted a handicap. But even more important in predetermining the nature of the school population was the level and function of the education provided. According to our present-day categories this was not secondary, but rather higher education. There was, then, a gulf, for those who had only come armed with an elementary state education, between the *petites écoles* (primary schools) and the Ecole Centrale. This cultural and social barrier was clearly admitted by the editors of *La Décade philosophique*. As one of them wrote in Year X: 'The study of ancient languages...of the sciences, of fine arts is only suitable for a child who possesses at least a decent fortune.'[12] But selection was not carried out in a rigorous way. Each Ecole Centrale received a quota of grant holders. Besides, professors often agreed to do without their fee. Thus children from modest backgrounds were enabled to go to the Ecoles Centrales. For example, in the *département* of the Mont-Terrible some sons of artisans, and even of workers, attended the Ecole Centrale. As a result of both their presence and that of adults who attended the courses (either as enrolled pupils or as unregistered students), the content of the education shifted in a more practical direction than its promoters had envisaged. The huge success of the drawing lessons derived from this pressure of demand. Similarly mathematics were often taught with a special military bias. A. Leon, examining the role of the Ecoles Centrales in technical education, has observed that some of them combined chemistry with the study of colourings, and linked natural history with the Ecoles de Santé, with pharmacy or with agronomy.[13] The 'philosophical' disciplines had little success. On this point the Idéologues' programme foundered. As for foreign languages, only the border regions seemed to show any interest. Many perhaps shared the

[12] J. Kitchin (122), p. 199.   [13] A. Leon (124).

linguistic chauvinism which made Mercier declare: 'Foreign languages! I thought there was now only one language in Europe – that of the French Republicans.' Most pupils attended only one course, or at the most two, and that for a year. None of them, it seems, went through the three sections.

The education panels, selected carefully by the *départements*, were able to recruit good candidates. Indeed, many former *collège* professors sat the aptitude tests which usually preceded selection. They came to the Ecoles Centrales with considerable experience but sometimes found it difficult to adapt to the new methods and the new framework. Besides their fee, they also earned a salary as administrators of a *département* and were held in great moral esteem, which derived from their role as orators at civic festivals and from the importance which the regime ascribed to education. All in all, if one is to believe Stendhal, who was a pupil at the Grenoble school, the Ecoles Centrales had staff of great quality. But the flexibility with which these institutions were run was too innovative. They took little account of religious feelings and humanist traditions; and one can understand how *collèges* which were still thriving – or other private schools – provided them with tough competition. In Year VI the Directory obliged candidates for government service to enrol in an Ecole Centrale. But this defensive measure did not check the upper bourgeoisie's disaffection from the state schools. And for this regime of property owners, it was a matter for serious concern to see the future *notables* escape in this way from the educational channels it had set up for them. The plans debated in Year VIII for the reform of the Ecoles Centrales did not modify this state of affairs. The conflict was political, as is shown by the violent attacks against the schools by the deputies of the right. One is reminded of the remark by a primary school teacher from the Maine-et-Loire in 1799: 'I am a Republican, pupils desert me.'[14]

ARTISTIC EXPRESSION

The audience and the function of art

Neither Directorial society nor the government's attempt to 'found the morality of a people' sought expression solely in worship and education, in the discourse of religion and reason: this dual task was

[14] B. Bois (115), p. 324.

also performed by various forms of artistic expression. But circumstances were not propitious. The economic crisis stifled artistic expression by restricting the demand for cultural artefacts. Thus private architecture – which had benefited thirty years earlier from the reinvestment of commercial profits and landed income – was no longer a living art. As for the state, if it still provided aid, it could hardly be said to supply any orders. Politically the Revolution had had contradictory consequences. On the one hand, the arts were freed from monopolies, from supervision and control. On the other, the disappearance of royal and noble patronage was a blow from which the 'artistic trades' had not recovered. Furthermore, the abolition of the corporative framework had in many cases damaged the quality of the work and hindered the handing down of techniques. The Revolution had seen the emergence of other political constraints which, depending on the circumstances of the moment, pulled the arts in different directions. The theatre – with its 'topical' plays, censorship, interventions by the public and the tribulations of its actors – provides a prime example of these pressures. On the cultural plane important changes also resulted from the nature of the new audience, which was made up of the regime's parvenus and notable figures from the worlds of money, politics and fashion. It would certainly be too simplistic to follow the standard historical judgement and contrast the philistinism and lack of taste of these *nouveaux riches* with the refinement of the former elites. The previous period had had its Turcarets, and extravagance or affectation can denote the search for a style on the part of the creator and a new attitude on the part of the 'consumer'. Thus the provocative costumes of the *Merveilleuses*, the exuberance and almost the delirium of certain interiors, were all journeys to the limits of a new freedom, experiments, as it were, in breaking with the past. And in any case, cultural continuities certainly did prevail. If, for example, we had precise knowledge of the repertories of provincial theatres and of the décor of provincial salons, the unrepresentativeness of the Parisian public would be even more obvious.

Was it possible to 'republicanise' art? The members of the Convention had thought so, and their successors nurtured the same hope. After Fructidor the question became more acute. François de Neufchâteau insisted on the importance of the arts in the formation of a public consciousness. The Institute submitted to a competition a question discussing 'the influence of painting on the morals and government of a free people'.[15] The blossoming of civic worship led

---

[15] J. A. Leith (123).

to a flood of projects for monuments, temples and triumphal arches. A journalist on *La Décade philosophique* proclaimed to sculptors: 'The Nation will make use of your chisels.' The social function of art was an assumption held by most people. Mercier had sparked off a very lively controversy by claiming to have established a hierarchy of utility in which literature was held to be the most 'expressive' while painting and sculpture were judged 'luxuries'. The prevailing view, then, rejected all forms of art for art's sake. It was not enough to 'republicanise' themes. The mode of expression also had to be 'revolutionised'. Unfortunately the criteria remained nebulous. Was it a matter of introducing republican values into art? Critics agreed in advocating austerity and sincerity. But to transpose these principles into artistic techniques posed difficulties: genres seemed unalterable and methods of composition hardly susceptible to change. New wine was needed for old bottles.

Painting

Painting did not fit the conception of a committed art form. It of course remained an elitist art to the extent that no one had taken up the novel and prophetic idea (put forward by one of the candidates in the Institute's competition) of painting 'republican frescos' on public buildings. We do not know about the market in painting – its organisation, its patrons, its prices. It seems, however, that connoisseurs relied both on the salons, which resumed regularly in Year IV, and on other exhibitions to form an opinion. Neo-classicism was aspiring to a greater starkness. Roman influences receded in favour of the Greek, and even the Egyptian and the Etruscan.

David, momentarily disquieted, was able, by developing his style to reassert himself as the leader of a school. His *Sabines* (1796–9) was received as the consummate expression of the new political and aesthetic trends. Similarly, at the end of the period of the Directory, Guérin felicitously exploited classicism for the cause of the *émigrés* in his *Le Retour de Marcus Sextus*. There was acclaim for the rare appearance of patriotic canvases: *La Mort du général Marceau* by Le Barbier the elder, *La Fidélité des hussards français* by Vernet or *Augereau au pont d'Arcole* by Thévenin. But taken as a whole, the output of pictures was moving in other directions. Instead of civic themes, painters preferred the peaceful evocation of ancient mythology. Paintings of Orpheus, Paris and Venus cluttered innumerable walls, and every salon contained a flood of landscapes and, above all, portraits. Indeed, portraits were the genre which corresponded exactly to the aspirations of the new patrons who hoped to eternalise their rise to fortune. For each Boilly, a delicate painter of bourgeois families, there were numerous merely industrious artists who achieved undeserved success as a result of this new craze. But portraiture also allowed David to affirm the variety of his genius. His two *Sérizat* rediscovered the fluidity of line and freshness of colour of the eighteenth-century masters. They express, so to speak, the other side of the coin, the moment of relaxation after the hieratic pose, a fanciful and no longer heroic world. The melancholy of Prud'hon's *Anthony* pictures fore-shadows a less serene art in which one can already detect the inspiration of Romanticism.

Entertainment

The theatre under the Directory was the favourite battleground of political confrontation. The pitched battles of 1795 were only rarely re-enacted but the pressures and political passions remained intense. The authorities stood vigilant. The section on theatres was one of the fullest in the police reports, not only because of the incidents which could break out, but also because of the very content of the plays. Thus in the spring of 1796 the Théâtre des Jeunes-Artistes in Paris had to take off a play by Martainville which violently attacked the Directory. Sometimes spectators intervened during performances to contradict the actors. Theatre became public debate. There was scarcely any place in the repertoire for the classics, apart from some tragedies by Racine. Rather favour was bestowed on works of the eighteenth century, in particular on those of Marivaux. Among new plays there were many which tried to exploit current events by evoking *L'Attaque de Grenelle*, *La Descente en Angleterre*, *La Mort du général Duphot* or *Le Héros au retour d'Egypte*. But these plays of the moment were shortlived, even when they did not sink after the first performances. Besides, authors tried to please both the government and the public, thereby condemning themselves to reassuring banalities about union and fraternity. It was for this reason that theatre directors wanted to tap another vein, that of daily life, of the depiction of manners freed from all political allusions. Sentimental plays flourished, and also tear-jerking tragedies which often displayed spectacular mechanical effects. Such works, inspired by Florian, which celebrated edifying domestic virtues, did not hold the public's attention for long. But the enormous success of *Madame Angot ou la Poissarde parvenue* (by Antoine-François Eve) indicated one of the possible forms of renewal in the theatre: satire on the new social relations. Similarly, the public seemed fond of both reading and watching melodramas which were made bearable by the skill of Pixérécourt. 'Black theatre', for which the German and British repertories provided one of the sources, benefited, like vaudeville, from the audience's disaffection from classical grandiloquence. Only the talent of François-Joseph Talma still succeeded in masking this shift in taste. Musicians became associated with the theatre in two ways: in writing choruses and in the composition of light operas. Méhul with *Le Jeune Henri* and Boieldieu with *L'Heureuse Nouvelle* emerged as masters of the genre. Instrumental music, in comparison, seemed to have ossified, in spite of the popularity of concerts among high society.

Décor

The most original expression of Directorial society crystallised less in the visual arts or theatrical entertainment than in the art of interior decoration. What has been improperly called the 'Directory style' goes considerably beyond the confines of the period 1795–1800, but it is true that in these years it achieved a sort of equilibrium. A concern for display and the revival of the life of high society explain the new expansion in cabinet-making. Around 1797 the 'Greek style' emerged under the patronage of the Jacob family, almost the only survivor (since Riesener was no longer an innovator) of the pleiad of the 1780s. Chairs combined curves and straight lines with elegance; the 'curule' model emerged discreetly, without the rigidity it was to take on under the Empire. Archaeological speculation did not exclude refinement. Designers occasionally gave beds the most extravagant appearance by an accumulation of hangings and innumerable carvings of wild animals. The 'Etruscan' and 'Greek' décor took its inspiration freely from the frescos of Tuscany and from ceramics. From both of these the dominant reds and browns, which brought out the bright colours of the marquetry, were borrowed. As for the 'Egyptian' contribution, if it is true that Bonaparte's expedition was to give it spectacular publicity, it was nevertheless already present before this epic adventure: sphinxes had joined swans and chimeras as decorative motifs. This style was not closed in on itself; it was constantly innovating, searching to unite the elegance of the *ancien régime* with the geometrical rigour of contemporary trends. The decoration of Bonaparte's apartment in the Rue de Chantereine summed up without excess the principal aspects of this style: a *tricolore* bed inspired by the design of army tents, silks decorated with flowers and ebony armchairs covered in yellow leather went to make up a somewhat discordant ensemble. Later Madame Récamier was to tire of this architectural furniture in which comfort was too much sacrificed to show. But for the moment the decorative arts delicately expressed the ambiguous modernity of the epoch and provided a small elite with the illusion of exoticism and serenity.

On none of these 'cultural fronts' did the Directory achieve convincing results. Repressive measures were unable to dislodge Catholicism; nor were the official or semi-official cults able to replace it. Civic festivals – the promise of open theatre – created only a drab liturgy without giving the French people a new common soul. The school had not become the crucible of the nation, nor of its ruling class. The arts had maintained their autonomy. The people were held at a distance from a culture proud of its certainties, which in the same breath rejected the language of others – that is to say dialect – and the language of mysticism and irrationality. Among the elite the new ideology was unable to impose itself without opposition. Directorial society was subjected to too many centrifugal pressures to unite around a common vision.

6

From expansion to decline

'Liberté-Fraternité
Franzes in carrocia, e nun a pe'

Italian distich[1]

Campoformio had settled nothing. Austria, paying more attention than ever to Italy, had not given up hope of obtaining considerable compensation for the loss of Belgium. The Directory had capitulated to Bonaparte's blackmail, but the Fructidoreans intended both to go beyond the ambiguities of the treaty and to affirm the supremacy of civil power. The lightning war of Year V and its diplomatic conclusion had aroused contradictory passions in the Italian peninsula. The patriots, buffeted but not despairing, seemed to be preparing for renewed combat. Would the 'Great Nation' resist their appeal? Would they, with her or despite her, be able to realise their other ambition – that is to say, after liberty, unity? An unremitting conflict threatened to set the strategic or economic exigencies of the tutelary power – France – against the aspirations of these patriots. And this indeed was the case, even without taking account of the fact that the war machine, now largely autonomous, had its own demands, even its own policy.

Nor had Campoformio settled the other major problem, that of the confrontation with the English. Any peace without them was illusory, but people were convinced that peace with them was impossible. The conflict, then, had to go on. But was the French navy capable of war with England? If not, there would be a great temptation to go in pursuit of easier successes in the east.

[1] 1798?

143

THE CONFLICT WITH ENGLAND

The naval war

'Let us concentrate all our activity on the navy and destroy England. Europe will then be at our feet.' Most of those in positions of authority under the Directory and, it seems, a large section of public opinion, shared Bonaparte's analysis. But in 1797 France had not yet got the means for a grand naval policy. Four years of war had cost her thirty-five ships of the line and sixty-one frigates. The quality of the crews left something to be desired. Until the law of 4 Brumaire Year IV, which defined the conditions of enrolment in the navy, recruitment had been conducted in an unsystematic way. Besides, English naval supremacy, which obliged the French squadrons to take refuge in Brest and Toulon, restricted the possibilities for manoeuvre. French sailors were undertrained. Naval officers had joined the *émigrés* in greater numbers than had their colleagues of the land armies. Many incompetent individuals had taken their place. Truguet had had to purge the chiefs-of-staff but, since the war had not revealed any new talent, most of the commands were still assigned to officers of the *Royale*, who were often elderly. Convinced of the irrevocable inferiority of the French fleet, they fostered a passive attitude, if not, indeed, one of defeatism. Admiral Pléville-le-Pelley, who had replaced Truguet in the re-organisation of July 1797, was, wrote La Révellière, 'an old man, extremely upright, disinterested, zealous and courageous'. But, aged seventy-one, he symbolised continuity more than daring. This fleet, some of whose ensigns were approaching the age of sixty-five, was hardly capable of compensating for its handicaps by qualities of dynamism or imagination.

The situation in the colonies obviously suffered from French naval weakness. Thanks to Victor Hughes, French rule had been restored in Guadeloupe, but Martinique had not been retaken. In Santo Domingo Toussaint-Louverture had greatly helped General Laveau repel the English. He intended to profit alone from his successes. For this reason he freed himself of Laveau, then Santhonax – sent back to Santo Domingo by the Directory – by having the one elected to the Council of the Five Hundred and the other to the Council of Elders. The north and west of the island were held by Toussaint, and the south by the mulatto Rigaud, except for Port-au-Prince and a few other positions occupied by the English. Toussaint negotiated their departure and a trade agreement without informing the new French leader, General Hédouville, who had to leave in the face of Toussaint's threats. The black revolutionary could write that the Republic had 'no more zealous defender than himself' and that he rejected the 'mad plan for independence'; but in fact France no longer had more than formal authority over the island. The English, absorbed by the conquest of the West Indies, had attempted no hostile action against the other French possessions. St Louis and Goree were so neglected that the Thermidoreans had, as Lefebvre pointed out, omitted to mention them in the constitution of Year III. In the Mascarene Islands the settlers repulsed the representatives of the Directory; they had not abolished slavery and feared the interference of the homeland. Under such conditions the Republic's overseas presence could be described as non-existent.

There seemed to be two ways to wipe out these 'pirates': to strike at them in their lair or to destroy their economic power. In the euphoria of the victory in Europe, the first of these seemed possible. It enjoyed, moreover, the approval of Parisian public opinion. In the police report for 30 September 1797, the public mood was described thus: 'people want a landing in England; they want the British government, driven back into a corner, to be punished for the Machiavellianism which gave it the means to tear open the breast of our *patrie*. The patriots reproach it for the Vendée, the Royalists reproach it for Quiberon.'[2] England had just lost Corsica and Leghorn, and with them the control of the western Mediterranean. What is more, the Irish revolutionaries persevered in their plans for an uprising. They had established contact with the mutineers of the fleet in April–May 1797. Parker's 'floating republic' had been crushed. But the mutiny was nonetheless an indication of something rotten in the invincible Royal Navy. France was no longer alone. She could in principle count upon the fleets of her two new allies, Spain and the Batavian Republic. In fact the Spanish fleet, defeated by Jervis at Cape St Vincent on 14 February 1797, had fallen back on Cadiz. As for the Dutch, they had attempted to leave the Helder but had been crushed off Egmond (11 October).

The Directory, however, persisted in its plans. On 26 October Bonaparte was appointed commander-in-chief of the Army of England, and when he was received in the Luxembourg on his return from

---

[2] A. Aulard, *Paris pendant la réaction thermidorienne et sous le Directoire* (5 vols., Paris, 1898–1902), vol. 4, p.25.

Rastatt this nomination was resoundingly confirmed: 'Go to London', Barras told him, 'and punish outrages which have gone too long unpunished.' He had already worked out the details of his forces and formed his staff. Truguet, prospective commander of the fleet prior to his appointment as ambassador to Madrid, and Pléville-le-Pelley were to assemble at Brest sixty-three vessels of the line and fifty-two frigates. A force of 50,000 men was transferred from the Army of Italy. To finance the operation Ramel, wanting to exploit the prevalent atmosphere of patriotism, issued a loan. It was an indifferent success; the rich failed to subscribe. On 8 February Bonaparte left to inspect the preparations for the invasion on the coasts of the Nord and the Pas-de-Calais. On 23 February he handed the Directory a report concluding that the plan was impracticable. If peace was not to be signed with England, war against her had to be waged in Hanover or Egypt. The Directors finally had to agree that a frontal attack was beyond French means.

Towards the east

Bonaparte's change of mind seemed sudden. But, anticipating the next step as was his custom, he had written to the Directory as early as 16 August 1797: 'The time is not far off when we will feel that truly to destroy England it is necessary for us to seize control of Egypt.' His Mediterranean policy was taking shape more clearly; the Ionian Islands and the Venetian settlements in Albania were organised into three *départements*. And he marked out Malta as France's next objective. At the same time he made inquiries about the Turkish attitude. There was no doubt that the Mediterranean was the focus of his new ambitions. Was he at this time thinking, as he claimed in St Helena, of following in the footsteps of Alexander as far as the Indus? This claim seems to belong to the realm of political fiction. If Bonaparte had intended, before Acre, to reserve the long term possibility of a great eastern design, he seems to have considered as more likely a relatively short stay – six months – which would have been long enough to establish a French presence in Egypt, the necessary starting point for any other operation. Above all, Bonaparte feared that by staying in France he would exhaust his popularity and lose his political liberty. In Egypt he would be his own master; distance would preserve and magnify him. 'It is necessary to go to the east', he told Bourrienne, 'it is the source of all great glory.'

He received important backing from Talleyrand, the Minister of External Affairs, who, on 26 January 1797, submitted to the Directory a report which came down in favour of an expedition to Egypt. At least two considerations led him to this conclusion. Since becoming minister he was hoping to enter the Directory and was gambling on Bonaparte to help him in this. Hence his desire to please the general. And his definite, and perhaps subsidised, anglophilia inclined him to deflect French aggression away from England. The Directors were won over by these two accomplices. Once a landing in England had been ruled out, the idea of hitting at English trade by threatening India seemed logical. According to the reports of French agents, Egypt was in a state of neglect. It was a tempting prospect to settle there and possibly develop tropical crops. It could become a new French colony to replace those which had been lost. How would the Turks react? Bonaparte and Talleyrand affirmed that Constantinople would come to an arrangement. The Directors were weak enough to believe them. It is not altogether impossible, however, that at a delicate moment they were seizing the opportunity to remove from France a general who was too popular.

The decision was taken on 5 March 1798. Bonaparte, helped by the ordnance officer Najac, speeded up the preparations; he had to be at the Nile before the floods. The expedition's destination was kept secret to mislead the English. On 19 May the fleet left Toulon. Convoys from Corsica, Genoa and Civitavecchia joined it at sea. 400 ships carrying 55,000 men made their way slowly eastwards. Bonaparte had recruited his soldiers from the Army of Italy and his subordinates from among proven generals such as Desaix and Kléber. With him he took scientists like Monge, Berthollet, Geoffroy and Dolomieu, and writers and artists like Vivant Denon. This commission of 187 scholars, artists and scientists was a striking homage to Bonaparte's reputation, although he was already, it is true, a member of the Institute. Through their presence, the conquest became also a pilgrimage and an exploration. As the mathematician Fourier put it, 'the sciences, after a long exile, again set eyes on their homeland and prepared to beautify it'. The French ships arrived in Malta on 9 June. The Grand Master of the Order, who had no doubt been 'squared', only put up a show of resistance. On 12 June the knights transferred their sovereignty to France. The English, obsessed by previous French attempts, had for a long time believed that the expedition was aimed at Ireland. Now Nelson hurried at great speed towards Alexandria. He reached it on 28 June and left disappointed. The French armada had been saved from disaster by its very slowness; it arrived outside Alexandria on 1 July. Disembarkation took place speedily through fear that the English might return. The town surrendered the next day. Bonaparte issued a proclamation declaring that he was charged with freeing the Egyptians from Mameluke domination and strongly affirming the respect of the French for Islam. Leaving Kléber and 3,000 men at Alexandria, he marched to Cairo across the desert. This was the hardest but shortest route. The soldiers suffered great hardship on this journey. They came close to believing that the Directory, by sending them into these sands, had organised a deportation rather than an expedition. After two skirmishes the decisive battle took place near Cairo. The celebrated Mameluke cavalry of Bey Murad shattered on the French squares (21 July). While Desaix pursued Murad into upper Egypt, Bonaparte defeated Bey Ibrahim, who retreated towards Syria. When Bonaparte returned to Cairo, Egypt was conquered, but the French were prisoners of their victory: Nelson had just annihilated the French fleet at Aboukir (1 August). Brueys had anchored there because he was unable to enter the harbour of Alexandria, and Bonaparte had been hesitant about being immediately separated from the squadron. Nelson attacked the French ships which were at anchor. They were outflanked along the length of the coast and caught between two lines of fire. The inexperience of the crews was enough to complete the catastrophe. Brueys, Dupetit-Thouars and Casabianca died. Only four ships, under the command of Villeneuve, succeeded in reaching Malta.

Egypt: a French colony

Bonaparte's policy consisted both of obtaining the co-operation of the local population and of modernising Egypt. Reassuring the indigenous population meant first of all respecting their beliefs. Bonaparte gave strict orders to this effect, which were largely adhered to. At one moment he even tried to persuade the sheikhs that the French might be converted – no doubt a purely tactical measure. He summed up his thinking in a letter to Kléber: 'One must lull fanaticism to sleep until one can uproot it.'[3] Besides, this policy of negotiation was needed in order to win over, for whatever purpose, the Arab world. Bonaparte was already posing as the protector of Islam and corresponding with

---

[3] Letter of 22 August 1799 quoted by A. Palluel, *Dictionnaire de l'Empereur* (Paris, 1969), p. 373.

the Bey of Tunis, the Bey of Algiers and the Sultan of Morocco. A grandiose festival was organised in Cairo for the anniversary of the birth of Mahomet. Direct administration seemed inopportune, and, moreover, impracticable. The French therefore retained the bulk of the existing judicial and financial structures. In the field of finance Bonaparte intended to make use of the experience of the Christian Copts and let them bear the unpopularity of the job. To hold the country it was enough to rally and control the elites. Thus a 'divan', composed of seven members and an 'aga', a leader of the janissaries, and an *intendant*, was created in Alexandria and in Cairo, and then in each province. These bodies acted as consultative councils to the French generals responsible for administering the districts.

The commission of intellectuals which Bonaparte had brought with him was supposed to be the instrument of a policy of enlightenment. On 22 August 1798 Bonaparte transformed it into the Institute of Egypt, to which he assigned three tasks: 'The progress and propagation of Enlightenment...research into, study and publication of natural, industrial and historical facts about Egypt...[and] the provision of advice about the different questions on which it will be consulted by the government'. Before there was any prospect of 'propagating Enlightenment' the scientists had to overcome much suspicion. According to the testimony of Bonaparte himself, they succeeded in winning the esteem of the 'ulemas' of the people, but not in instructing them. On the other hand, the Institute successfully carried out a sort of general inventory of the country, including topographical surveys, archaeological sketches, and the collection of natural and social statistics. From this collective enterprise was to emerge the admirable *Description de l'Egypte*. The new discipline of Egyptology was created, placing on a scientific basis studies which had hitherto relied simply on recollections from antiquity or on the tales of travellers. Pursuing his third objective, Bonaparte directed the work of the Institute distinctly towards applied research. He showered his collaborators with questions of immediate interest – how to purify the waters of the Nile, how to replace hops in the making of beer, etc. – or of a more long-term nature – for example, how to acclimatise the vine to Egypt. Bonaparte himself contemplated re-establishing the ancient canal between Cairo and Suez, improving navigation on the Nile and developing the road network. Together with these projects for the Egyptian infrastructure, the French attempted to break with the archaic methods of the peasants (by the introduction of windmills) and to develop tropical crops. Health

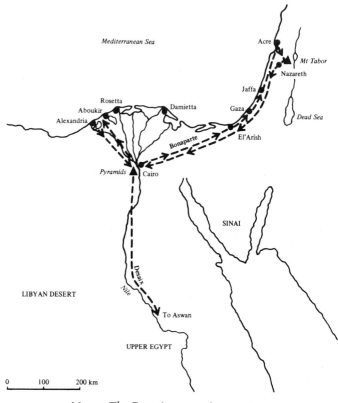

Map 4 The Egyptian campaign, 1798–9

remained their major preoccupation. Desgenettes and Larrey supervised the medical section. They set up a system of surveillance in the ports, conducted surveys of the most dangerous diseases (the plague, ophthalmia) and created centres to care for the local population. Bonaparte's extreme vigilance in this area was of course aimed at protecting his soldiers and future settlers from the risks of infection. But he was also concerned about the physiological distress of the indigenous population; his calculated policy did not exclude generosity.

Despite this policy of tolerance and reform, the Muslim masses did not cease to regard the French as infidels and invaders. This was all the more the case because the land tax, being more efficiently collected, weighed more heavily, and because new taxes (registration duties, the *patente*, taxes on houses) irritated the population of the towns.

Moreover the French had carried out massive requisitions of rice, meat and camels. When the Sultan declared holy war on France (9 September 1798) his agents and the ulemas of the mosque El Azhar incited the population to rise up. The most serious revolt broke out at Cairo on 21 October. With General Dupuy killed, the garrison almost lost control of the town. Once the situation had been restored, Bonaparte had a large number of rioters arrested and decapitated. The rebels lost several thousand men. But the French did not give way to uncontrolled repression and tried to recover the confidence of the Egyptians. The general divan, an assembly of notables chosen from the fourteen provinces, had met not long before the Cairo uprising. Bonaparte maintained his previous policy and brought even more native figures into the administration of the country, perhaps in the hope of creating a class dependent on himself.

The end of a dream

While Desaix pacified upper Egypt with difficulty (he reached Aswan on 1 February 1799), Bonaparte prepared for an expedition into Syria. Not, as he claimed at St Helena, to conquer India (with 13,000 men!) but, more prosaically, to break the blockade and attack a Turkish army which was gathering in this region. On 21 February the French troops seized El'Arîsh, which commanded the entry into Syria. They occupied Gaza and Ramleh without encountering any opposition and, on 4 March, they were within sight of Jaffa. Three days later the town was taken by storm and pillaged. Three thousand fighters had lain down their arms on a promise that their lives would be spared; Bonaparte had them massacred. Perhaps he feared having to feed them (but considerable supplies had been found in Gaza and Ramleh); above all he hoped to terrorise Djezzar, the Pasha of Syria, and make him come to terms. The siege of Acre lasted from 19 March to 17 May. The French heavy artillery, transported by sea, had been captured. And an English flotilla, under the command of Sidney Smith, was blockading the harbour and supplying and supporting the defenders. Djezzar also enjoyed the support of a French *émigré*, Phélippeaux, who had been a fellow pupil of Bonaparte at Brienne. Junot and Kléber blocked the advance of a relief army in the region of Lake Tiberias (9 April and 11 April). Bonaparte arbitrarily gave these two battles the most spectacular names of Nazareth and Cana. He himself went to back up Kléber who was in difficulties and helped him to defeat the bulk of the enemy forces at the foot of Mount Tabor on 16 April. But his army, lacking reinforcements, was growing weaker. Alarming news arrived from Egypt: a Turkish army was forming at Rhodes. Bonaparte had to raise the siege. He had lost 4,000 men and 160 officers. The retreat took place in appalling conditions. The exhausted army, exasperated by failure, was on the verge of revolt. The soldiers hit by the plague had been reassembled at Jaffa. The disease, arriving via Rosetta and Damietta, had broken out during the siege of Acre. It is reported that Bonaparte performed the heroic gesture of touching the buboes and took the drastic decision of poisoning the sick who could not be transported. A charismatic leader and a ruthless general, he attempted to mould destiny. Upon his return to Cairo on 14 June he soon had to face the landing of a Turkish army. Mustafa's 18,000 men, who had established themselves on the Aboukir peninsula, were besieging Alexandria. On 25 July they were crushed near the city by Bonaparte. This allowed him, taking slight geographical liberties, to say that: 'The name of Aboukir was fateful to every Frenchman; the day of 7 Thermidor has made it a glorious one.' Since October Bonaparte had contemplated returning to Europe. The Directory had authorised him to give up his command when he felt this would be appropriate. The news which reached him, especially of the loss of Italy, decided him to depart. He left Kléber at the head of the army and on 23 August embarked for France, accompanied by a few faithful followers, including Monge and Berthier.

EXPORTING THE REVOLUTION

The contagion of revolution

Numerous contradictions undermined the Helvetic Confederation and, after 18 Fructidor, made it vulnerable to the wave of revolution. In Zurich, for example, the authorities still had to reckon with the friends of Pestalozzi and Lavater who called the power of the patricians into question and incited the peasants to revolt against the seigneurial system. But the most explosive contradiction was that which set the feudal territories against the oligarchy of the cantons. In the Vaud, in particular, the 'patriots' were still struggling against 'despotism' and hoped to win the French over to their cause. The most notable figures among them, La Harpe and Pierre Ochs, flaunted 'Girondin' opinions.

Reubell, a friend of Pierre Ochs, and La Révellière knew that they were admirers of the Thermidorean Constitution. Moreover, the strategic position of Switzerland was enhanced by the new Rhineland–Milan axis; and for an always impecunious Directory the treasury in Berne had many attractions. Agreement was therefore possible. At a meeting on 8 December 1797, attended by among others Reubell, Ochs and Bonaparte, the principle of French intervention was accepted. The revolutionaries hoped to do without help from outside but, as Ochs said, it was above all necessary to 'kill the oppressor'. Reubell and Ochs had prepared a constitution, federal in structure, in which central power was, however, reinforced. On 24 January 1798 a general Assembly of the Vaud territory proclaimed independence. Revolution broke out in Lausanne, Berne, Lucerne and Soleure. The French had to intervene against the Bernese and protect the Vaud. Brune and Schauenbourg marched on Berne, leaving Masséna to occupy the upper valley of the Ticino. The Helvetic Constitution was proclaimed as their front advanced. But the peasants of the 'primitive' cantons (Uri, Saint-Gall, etc.) refused to adopt it. They had to be forced to do so after the Battle of Morgarden on 3 May. The Valais was in its turn shaken by a revolt which was quickly pacified (17 May). Meanwhile France had taken securities: the two enclosed territories of Mulhouse and Geneva were annexed (28 January and 15 April 1798). The wishes of the inhabitants – relatively willing in Mulhouse, hostile in Geneva – had counted for less than the strategic and economic interests of France. Thus the young Republic was from the outset the victim of a policy in which 'missionary' intentions combined with imperialist designs.

In Italy the situation was also favourable to the contagion of revolution. Piedmont, surrounded by the Cisalpine and Ligurian Republics, had difficulty in resisting the agitation orchestrated by the 'Jacobins' and by Guigéné, the new French ambassador. But the Directory did not want to dismember the kingdom and it restrained its representatives. Similarly, French policy in Tuscany worked for the maintenance of the status quo. Indeed, the triumvirate did not wish to see the setting up of a unified Italian Republic and the upsetting of the stability of the peninsula. The Directory was not ready to exchange revolution in Italy for perpetual war. But there were forces pushing it in the opposite direction and in Rome they came together successfully. The 'Jacobins' of the papal city attempted to secure the intervention of France. The French ambassador, Joseph Bonaparte, refused. But in the course of a demonstration for the 'democratisation of the town',

General Duphot, a councillor at the embassy, was killed (28 December 1797). This murder brought about Joseph Bonaparte's departure and a brutal reaction from the Directory: Berthier, commander of the Army of Italy, received orders to march on Rome, drive the Pope and Curia out of the city and instigate the setting up of the Republic. The affair did not get off to a good start; the peasants revolted and the Pope surrendered to all demands. The desired end was brought about through propaganda; on 15 February the patriots, meeting at the Forum, proclaimed the Republic. On the next day the Pope left Rome; a provisional government of seven consuls was set up under the protection of the French. In liquidating the Pope's temporal power the Directory believed that it was striking an important, even definitive, blow against Catholicism. By helping Italian Jacobins in this way it was providing itself with a master card for the home front. Finally, the contractors coveted papal wealth. Their influence also counted in the decision.

The constitutions

The constitutional organisation and political life of the sister-republics were not determined exclusively by internal plans and conflicts. They also reflected the wishes of the tutelary power – France – and the balance of forces between France and the local patriots. It was for this reason that the new constitutions, although drawn up according to different methods, were all variations upon an imposed text, that of Year III. But it is also true that they reflected to a certain extent local traditions and problems. The question of national unity provided the first source of difficulty. The demand for unity inspired some of the Batavian patriots. It was also the aspiration of the Swiss revolutionaries and, above all, the force behind Jacobinism in Italy.

With respect to Holland, the Fructidorean Directory abandoned the anti-unitary attitude which had hitherto predominated in Paris. Delacroix, the ambassador in The Hague, and General Joubert, assisted by the Dutch patriot Daendels, organised a *coup d'état* against the principal federalist deputies (22 January 1798). The constitution, approved by the people on 23 April 1798, sanctioned this act; the provinces lost all form of sovereignty. The description of this as a 'Batavian 18 Fructidor' expresses the reality of what had happened. It was the local result of events in Paris. The triumvirate had tolerated this change of direction because it saw the unification of the Low

Countries as neither a threat to France nor a cause of tension with the states of Europe. Similar considerations helped Ochs convince Reubell not to divide up Switzerland. But after having given in, the Directory changed its mind and considered carving up Switzerland into three confederated republics (27 February 1798). The unanimous opposition of the patriots, however, forced it to return to the original proposal. This hesitancy illustrated the complexity of what was at stake. Unity would result in a cohesive state and therefore a solid alliance, but it could also arouse national feelings and, consequently, a spirit of independence. The Italian patriots, who had, since the creation of the Cisalpine Republic, agitated in favour of Italian unity, came up against the irreducible hostility of the Directors. 18 Fructidor had changed nothing. La Révellière and Reubell were still mistrustful of these 'anarchists'. After the *coup d'état* of 22 Floréal Year VI it seemed to them that 'extremists' outside and inside France were fighting the same battle. They were all the more resolved not to give in. Moreover, Europe would not have stood for an over-powerful Italy.

The fundamental laws of the sister-republics reproduced the framework of the French Constitution: a two-stage electoral process, a bicameral system, a strict separation of powers. New solutions could not be expected from constitutions drawn up by the French. Daunou, a former member of the Commission of the Eleven, did not innovate when, with Faipoult, Florent and Monge, he drew up the Roman Constitution. The Ligurian Constitution, the work of Genoese patriots, was inspired by the same principles. The enlightened bourgeoisie thus conferred a universal value on the juridical structure of the Thermidoreans. In any case, their tightrope was narrow. The first Ligurian Constitution had antagonised the aristocracy and clergy. Bonaparte insisted that the text be revised in a less liberal direction. For example, the over-generous voting qualifications now reproduced the requirements of the French constitution.[4] The Batavians had a similar experience. The radicals would have liked a constitution similar to the 'Anarchic Code'. Delacroix brought them round to accept less adventurous proposals. The French model therefore seemed to draw the limits. But the constitutions did stray a little from this celebrated precedent. They reflected the conditions and traditions of the various countries either by adaptations of vocabulary (consuls, prefects and tribunate in Rome) or, more often, by recognising national particularities: thus the Cispadane Republic made Catholicism the state religion. The Batavian

[4] H. B. Hill (138).

Constitution, in emphasising social rights, retained traces of the preliminary debates. In short, each constitution had its own trademark. Overall they were distinguished from the Thermidorean Constitution by a more 'progressive' tone; suffrage was sometimes wider and the sovereignty of the people better defined. But the French advisers had themselves introduced fundamental modifications affecting the strengthening of the executive, the creation of prefects and the administrative hierarchy. The sister-republics served as testing grounds; they felt the effects of the changes in the thinking of French governing circles on constitutional issues. They provided, in a sense, the missing link between Daunou's constitution and that of Bonaparte.

Political life: imitation and reality

Similar constitutions gave rise to near-identical problems. The political life of the sister-republics was punctuated, as in France, by a series of *coups d'état*. Moderates and Jacobins, struggling for power, looked for the indispensable support of France. But the Directory's position did not always coincide with that of its civil and military representatives. French political conflicts were superimposed upon local antagonisms; the 'Great Nation' continued to tear itself apart through the proxy of the Italians or the Dutch. After a certain time-lag and with some discrepancies, the foreign patriots re-enacted the political development of the French Republic. *Coups d'état* of the 18 Fructidor variety were succeeded by coups from the right (of the 22 Floréal variety), which were themselves followed by a second wave of Jacobinism, contemporaneous with the events of Prairial Year VII.[5] Among the first series there figured, besides the Batavian coup, the test of force in the Cisalpine Republic which concluded in favour of the Jacobins who wanted unity (13 April 1798). General Brune, contrary to his predecessor Berthier, had difficulties with the democrats. He applied the orders of the Directory without hesitation. Among the right-wing *coups d'état* was that of 12 June 1798 which expelled the Dutch Jacobins from power. General Joubert was the instrument of the faction opposing Delacroix. The circumstances of this coup – the resignation or arrest of the Directors, with grenadiers entering the chamber of the Legislative Body – gave it the appearance of an '18 Brumaire'. Indeed, Sieyès was to believe that in Joubert he had found the 'sword' which he needed.

[5] J. Godechot (23), chap. 13.

In the Cispadane Republic Bonaparte distinguished three parties: 'The friends of their former government, the partisans of an independent but slightly aristocratic constitution, the partisans of the French Constitution or of pure democracy'. To rally the mass of the people, it was necessary, he explained, to support the middle party.[6] The people were indeed the stake in these rivalries between oligarchies, but, except for those in the towns, they were hardly concerned with this limited and artificial political activity. In the Roman Republic, politics were the prerogative of a restricted group of intellectuals, doctors, lawyers and priests. Around the city, the people of the countryside were in revolt. The Jacobins were everywhere recruited from the ranks of the bourgeoisie; almost everywhere the great divide between town and country continued, both in the people's behaviour and in their outlook. Some Jacobins understood that they needed to give up their 'enlightened paternalism' and, by the redistribution of land, ally themselves with the peasant masses. But they lacked the power to do this, and the spectre of an 'agrarian law' reinforced the alliance between the new dominant classes and the French. The sale of church property, demanded before the Revolution by the reformers, was, in the Romagna, carried out to the almost exclusive benefit of the middle classes and the nobility and, in the Roman Republic, to that of the *notables* and the contractors. The Church's patrimony was provisionally in the hands of 'rural traders' and bankers. In the countryside the Revolution had yet to be carried through.

The occupiers and the occupied

The peasants and the *petit peuple* of the towns, thwarted in their hopes of a new distribution of wealth and power, had at the same time to bear the weight of French occupation. Certainly it is true that, by the time that the French had looted the Swiss treasury and collected ten of the expected thirty million francs, the war tax had been levied only on the 'oligarchs' and on the religious congregations. But Lecarlier's successor as civil commissioner, Rapinat, had not been completely able, in spite of his coup of 17 June 1798, to break the influence of the Bernese *notables* on the Directory. The yield on taxes had been poor, and in the next year Masséna had to feed the Army of Helvetia by requisition. Thus discontent spread to all layers of the population. The commissioner of the Helvetic Republic noted: 'It is time that this stopped, we do

[6] Quoted by V. Giuntella (136), p. 333.

not want to be cisalpinised.' The Cisalpine Republic was indeed being bled dry. The treaty of alliance of 21 February 1798 – which forbade any prohibitive measures against French trade – imposed on the republic a tax of 18 million *livres* per annum. This stretched the economy, already in crisis, to its limits. Monthly payments had practically ceased by the end of the year.

The companies of contractors took part in the scramble for spoils. When French troops entered Rome, the Haller Company seized treasures from the Vatican under the pretext of paying itself for the expenditure incurred in supplying the troops. Following this, the Bodin Company obtained huge national domains which it resold for enormous profits, in return for services which had been largely mythical. This large-scale plunder had at least a 'legal' cover. Thus the pillage of works of art which had so disgusted the Italians and a few French artists (David, Hubert Robert, etc.) had been authorised by the armistice agreements. But the extortion of funds, precious objects and foodstuffs was also the daily practice of many soldiers. The generals took the lead, Masséna and Brune more cynically than the others. To the despoiled populations, the mutiny of Masséna's soldiers and the incessant conflicts between the Directory's commissioners and the military chiefs seemed to be merely episodes in a process of settling old scores in which booty was the stake.

The exactions of the occupiers prepared the ground for the uprising of the occupied. At the root of all the revolts were the peasants. They had profited little from an urban revolution – a revolution in the towns for the towns. When they opposed the war taxes or the anti-religious policy, they demonstrated their total rejection of revolution. Their uprisings, which did not necessarily take on a 'national' tinge, reflected above all the traditional resistance to unsettling innovations. Only a catalyst was needed. In Belgium this was provided by Jourdan's conscription law of 1798. Upon the announcement of this measure, the peasants of Campine, northern Flanders and German Luxemburg rose up against the French (12 October 1798). This area, formally integrated into the territory of the Republic, saw its annexation as an occupation and resented it. But the 'War of the Peasants' had more the air of a 'Vendée' than of a war of national liberation. Even the linguistic question did not play a determining role.[7] These bands of armed peasants terrified the bourgeoisie. Towns closed their gates on the approach of the 'Catholic army'. Isolated and deprived of foreign

[7] Cf. R. Devleeshouwer (135).

support, the *jacquerie* was broken in two months. The war courts executed hundreds of rebels. Out of 8,000 priests condemned to deportation, only 500 could actually be apprehended, and these were sent to join the French refractories on the Ile de Ré and the Ile d'Oléron. In the Roman Republic, in Tuscany and in several Swiss cantons the peasants also waged an active guerrilla campaign against the occupying troops. In the summer of 1799 this became more violent: the war revealed the weakness of the French while simultaneously increasing their demands.

The causes of these various uprisings were to be found in the pre-Revolutionary societies which had now been overturned. There were, on the other hand, other movements, born out of national aspirations, which turned France's own mystique against her. Disappointed Italian patriots had gathered together after Campoformio into a secret society. The original group had very quickly received the support of Lombard patriots and former companions of Buonarroti. The society, organised like the Babeuf plot, took as its aims first the liberation of Italy from all occupiers, and then her unification. In February 1799, after the enforced abdication of the King, a rigged plebiscite had proclaimed the unification of Piedmont with France. The Turin committee sparked off an insurrection which was finally crushed by Grouchy. Significantly, portraits of Lepeletier and Marat were found on the rebels. The friends of Lahoz, Cerise and Fontoni had wanted to reconcile independence with revolution by force of arms.

The example of Naples

The Neapolitan Republic, the last of the sister-republics to come into being, took these contradictions and ambiguities to an extreme. Ferdinand IV, advised by Austria and by Nelson, had believed it possible to profit from French difficulties – three months after Aboukir – by seizing Benevento and re-establishing the Papacy. His army, commanded by the Austrian, Mack, marched on Rome and occupied the city on 27 November. Championnet, following a tactical retreat, moved on to the offensive, re-entered Rome on 13 December and pursued Mack into Neapolitan territory. On the approach of the French, Ferdinand IV abandoned his capital and took refuge in Sicily. Mack signed a compromise armistice, but an uprising of the poor, the *lazzaroni*, gave the Neapolitan patriots the pretext for which they had been waiting. On 26 January they proclaimed the Republic, with the assent of Championnet but against the wishes of Faipoult. From this point on it was war between the Jacobin general and the commissioner, who was anxious to preserve the rights of the Directory. A definitive rupture occurred on 6 February; Faipoult was expelled from Naples for having opposed Championnet's policy of independence. It is not clear whether the French general was a disinterested champion of Jacobinism or a political adventurer, a pale imitator of Bonaparte. A Soviet historian has recently tried to rehabilitate him by showing the influence exercised over him by the French Marc-Antoine Jullien, a friend of Buonarroti and Secretary-General of the Neapolitan government.[8] Whatever the truth about this ambitious and complex personality, the patriots in power were not able, or did not want, to adopt a bold policy. Instead of 'reducing the large properties', as Jullien had requested them to do, they contented themselves with abolishing feudal dues. And even then the peasants had to buy back their 'real' rights. Similarly, their lukewarm social reformism did not win over the urban masses. On the French side, Faipoult's departure had not, as his adversary claimed, freed the Neapolitans. Pillaging, arbitrary taxation and trafficking of all kinds finally discredited a republic which depended on protectors of this sort. Moreover, the Directory, alerted by Faipoult, decided to dismiss Championnet, and, given the gravity of the case, to bring him before a court martial. The Neapolitan deputation which came to Paris to plead the cause of the republic was dismissed; the Directors did not want to present Europe with a *fait accompli* nor to ratify the collusion of the Jacobins and the generals. The Italians were, once again, victims of the fluctuations of French policy. Championnet's glorious rehabilitation after 30 Prairial was negative proof of this. The final feature of this exemplary tale was that the poor peasants, who, following the appeal of the King, were in revolt against the French and their allies, were in fact waging their own struggle – a merciless class struggle against the rich, whether Republican or not. Cardinal Ruffo, their leader, had to take account of this anti-seigneurial hatred and include these savage revolts in his counter-revolutionary strategy.

[8] V. Daline (133).

The second coalition

The Treaty of Campoformio had sketched the outlines of a possible agreement. Before the Franco-Austrian agreement could become effective, it had to be ratified by the Imperial Diet, which was supposed to determine, in collaboration with the French plenipotentiaries, what compensation was due to those princes who held possessions on the left bank. Bonaparte and Treilhard, joined by Bonnier, the head of the Directory's diplomatic bureau, embarked on the negotiations in November 1797. Reubell had given them formal instructions: to obtain all the left bank of the Rhine, including the Cologne region which had been clearly excluded from the bargaining of Campoformio. The Diet resigned itself to voting for the transfer in principle (9 March 1795). But, in conformity with the previous agreement, the Austrian representatives insisted on some compensation for this. Treilhard replied that the Cologne region was not a new acquisition since the Rhineland was already French by right of conquest. Indeed the Directory had without further ado organised its annexation. After the death of Hoche, his ephemeral Rhineland Republic had been gradually transformed into French territory through the efforts of Rudler, a friend of Reubell. The laws, courts and language of the French Republic were introduced into the Rhineland. On 23 January 1798 these various measures were sanctioned by decree; the Rastatt negotiators were confronted with a *fait accompli*. At the same time France carried out two major operations: the creation of the Roman Republic and of the Helvetic Republic. This was to negotiate one policy and carry out another; the truce of Campoformio had clearly been broken. Austria had hoped for compensation in Italy; instead she was confronted with further encroachments. The negotiations dragged on, but the Court of Vienna no longer thought about anything other than reconstructing an alliance against France. A diplomatic incident led to the first crisis. Bernadotte, the new ambassador in Vienna, had been the object of a hostile demonstration. He demanded his papers and left Austria (15 April). It was believed that war would break out and Bonaparte feared that he would have to abandon his Egyptian expedition. The two governments made an attempt at conciliation. François de Neufchâteau and Cobenzl met at Seltz and recognised that their positions were irreconcilable (7

July) The Directory persisted in maintaining simultaneously both a policy of natural frontiers and a policy of Girondin-style expansion, leaving Austria only the choice between capitulation and war. But by increasing its ambitions it widened the circle of its enemies. This transition from a Rhineland strategy to an Italian strategy and thence to a Mediterranean strategy gave Austria the support of Russia and Turkey, both of whom were now implicated in any confrontation. Aboukir sealed the reconciliation of Paul I and the Porte. It was possible to counter-attack. A Russo-Turkish squadron retook Cerigo, Zante and Cephalonia. The French garrisons of Malta and Corfu were in danger. The eastern adventure precipitated Russia into the war. The lack of subsidies alone prevented her intervention in Europe; this was remedied by the Treaty of London. The Russians promised to send a contingent into Italy provided the Austrians raised no objection, to participate with the English in a landing in Holland and even to plan an expeditionary force for the invasion of Brittany. In exchange, the English bound themselves to provide an initial lump sum of £225,000, followed by £75,000 each month as long as the war lasted (29 December 1798).

The Directory therefore turned towards Prussia. Was it not possible to make an ally of her? Sieyès was charged with the mission. No worse choice could have been imagined. As a defrocked priest and a regicide, he symbolised all that monarchical Europe detested. But his failure was essentially a result of Prussia's political and ideological crisis, which inclined her more than ever towards security.[9]

At Rastatt Jean de Bry (replacing Treilhard, who had been elected a Director on 15 May), Bonnier and a new envoy of the Directory, Roberjot, were set the task of presenting new demands. France wanted the Rhine islands and some points on the right bank. Six months of discussion and an ultimatum overcame resistance (9 December 1798). This was a very belated victory for French diplomacy at a moment when the King of Naples was attacking Rome, English ships were entering Leghorn and the ports of Sardinia, and Russian troops were moving into Galicia with the complicity of Vienna. On 12 March 1799 the Councils declared war on Austria and on the Austrian Grand Duke of Tuscany.

[9] On the theme of Franco-Prussian friendship, see J. Droz, 'L'Idéologie, facteur de politique internationale. La neutralité prussienne et l'opinion publique de 1795 a 1806' in *Mélanges Pierre Renouvin* (Paris, 1966).

The French military effort

Meanwhile the Republic had been preparing for war. The volunteers of 1793 could not be counted upon indefinitely. It was necessary to move beyond provisional and improvised arrangements. Faced with these mounting dangers it was universally felt to be urgent to guarantee stable recruitment for the armies. The conscription law, known as the 'Jourdan law', which had been under discussion since January 1798, was passed on 5 May 1798. All Frenchmen aged twenty had to be enrolled on recruitment lists and remain on them until the age of twenty-five. Military service was thus theoretically compulsory for all males for five years. But these conscripts, divided into five annual classes, would not all be called up. The Minister of War would take the youngest conscripts to make up the required quota, before calling up the next classes. Only registered sailors and men married before 1798 were exempt from service.

The Legislative Body immediately asked that 200,000 men be raised. Administrative chaos, sabotage and the action of the recruiting boards reduced the number of young men from the first class who were declared fit for service to 143,000. Only 96,000 set off; the rest ignored the call up or failed to join their depots. The *départements* of the east were outstanding for their civic virtue: in the Haut-Rhin 67% of the quota called up had appeared at the assembly points.[10] This exceptional rate contrasts with the uncooperative attitude of the *départements* of the south-east, the Pyrenees and the Massif Central, and the coolness of the rest of the country. It was thought prudent to exempt the west – but not Belgium! – from this call up. To complete the numbers the Councils decided to call up 150,000 men, chosen by lot, from the second and third classes, to act as possible replacements (17 April 1799). This produced 57,000 men. When the military situation deteriorated, the fourth and fifth classes were called up. France was eventually to raise 400,000 men against the coalition powers. The war effort was coupled with psychological preparation. The French complex about encirclement again proved its usefulness and the language of revolutionary war was rediscovered. The assassination of Bonnier and Roberjot on their departure from Rastatt, carried out by subordinates of Archduke Charles, stirred up an indignation which was carefully orchestrated. Throughout France, funeral ceremonies, held in an atmosphere of patriotic exaltation, called the population to vengeance.

[10] F. L'Huillier (8).

Defeats

The allies' plans combined an Austro-Russian advance into Italy, followed by an offensive into eastern France, with the landing in Holland of an Anglo-Russian force which was to invade Belgium and northern France. The Directory had also chosen to take the offensive, although its objectives were above all to defend its frontiers.[11] According to his instructions, Jourdan was to march on Vienna via southern Germany and the Danube. But he had only 25,000 men against the 78,000 of Archduke Charles. The same handicap affected Masséna's progress through the Grisons and the Tyrol: the opposing army was three times larger than his. Finally Schérer, with 32,000 troops, was to confront 95,000 Austrians and 20,000 Russians on the Piave and in Tuscany. The Army of Italy was also facing a threat on the southern front where Macdonald was in command of the Neapolitan sector. Many of the French troops were held back in the rear by garrison and surveillance duties. In such conditions the idea of an offensive in all directions was a considerable risk. This error of judgement was punished by a series of defeats. Jourdan crossed the Rhine at the beginning of March but his way was blocked at Ostrach (21 march) and he was defeated at Stokach (25 March). He had to fall back and, in a rage, he resigned, as did Bernadotte. Masséna, who had entered the Vorarlberg, thus found himself exposed. Archduke Charles attacked him outside Zurich on 3 and 4 June. The French resisted from well-placed positions to the west of the city. As for Schérer, his offensive had foundered. At the end of March he had lost 8,000 men in a battle on the Adige. On 5 April the Austrians attacked near Rivoli. Schérer fought a bloody but indecisive battle at Magnano. He judged it essential to retreat and did not halt until reaching the Adda, from where he could protect Milan. Then he gave up his command in favour of Moreau. Kray, the Austrian general, awaited the arrival of the Russian contingent led by Suvorov, famous for his campaigns against the Turks. The allied army, 100,000 men strong, attacked 28,000 Frenchmen. Suvorov drove his adversaries off the field, entered Milan on 28 April and took Turin on 27 May. The rump of the French troops regrouped in the region of Genoa. Drawing a lesson from these failures, the Directory modified its strategy. Since Masséna had been able to stabilise the Swiss front, it seemed sensible to make an exceptional effort to save Italy. Macdonald would abandon Naples and attack the Austro-Russian

[11] S. T. Ross (142), pp. 170–87.

forces on their flank, synchronising his action with an offensive by
Moreau. This brilliant plan required impeccable execution. Unfortunately Macdonald had to take the impact of the allied army alone
and was defeated on the Trebbia (19 June).

At sea, the French objective was to regain control of the eastern
Mediterranean, lifting the blockade of Malta and Egypt. Bruix was to
take a fleet of twenty-four ships and ten frigates from Brest to Toulon;
from there he would sail to Egypt and bring back Bonaparte. The
English were puzzled by the departure of this expedition and uncertain of its destination. Was it to be Ireland, Portugal or Sicily?
They dispersed their fleet and Bruix was able to reach Toulon without
fighting. According to the Directory's plans, the Spanish squadron
ought at this point to have met up with the French. In fact, Bruix made
contact at Cartagena but was unable to persuade Admiral Mazarredo
to follow him towards Malta (29 June). The Court of Madrid expressed
its reservations; even Paris hesitated. Bruix dared not act alone.
Ultimately the joint fleets moved into the Atlantic and returned to
Brest. The appointment of Bernadotte to the Ministry of War and of
Joubert to Italy raised hopes that events would now move in France's
favour. But Joubert wasted an opportunity to attack Suvorov when
the Russian general was distracted by the siege of Alexandria. He
allowed Suvorov to recover and his army was defeated and he himself
killed at Novi on 15 August. In this succession of missed opportunities
the Directory could at least rejoice at the success of the Franco-Dutch
army in the Helder, under Brune, which resisted the Duke of York's
25,000 English and 15,000 Russian troops. The threat of an invasion
of Belgium, which would perhaps have resulted in an uprising, was
thus removed.

Recovery

Three factors explain the French recovery in the autumn of 1799: the
divisions between the allies, a skilful plan and an incomparable ex-
ecutant. The victories of the allies had whetted appetites and given
rise to competing plans. The Court of Vienna had found it difficult
to accept the sight of the Russians entering Italy and upholding against
them the unity of the Kingdom of Piedmont–Sardinia – all the more
since Paul I's designs on Malta were taking shape and seemed to
foreshadow Russo-Turkish hegemony over the western Mediterranean.
In addition, after Novi, the Austrians no longer wanted to leave

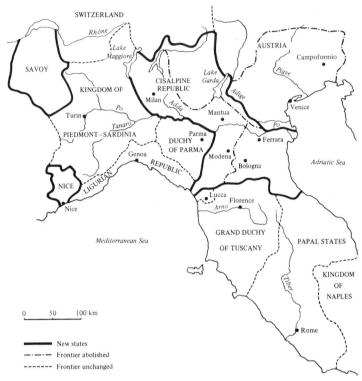

Map 5   The Swiss campaign, 1799

Belgium to the influence of the English in return for their own freedom of manoeuvre in Italy. Thugut now wanted to invade Belgium by the Rhine, before the predictable collapse of the French front in the north should give Belgium to the Duke of York.

It was therefore agreed to make various changes to the original plan: Archduke Charles would head for the Rhine; he would be replaced in Switzerland by Suvorov, who, together with Korsakov, already on the spot, would have the honour of making the breakthrough towards Paris. The Archduke, in a hurry to take up his new position, left Switzerland and took Mannheim on 18 September. The Directors at this point saw the full advantage that they could derive from the situation: the Austrians had left, Suvorov had not yet arrived. Victory had to be sought during this hiatus. Masséna, positioned in Switzerland, the allies' weakest point, was reinforced. While Lecourbe slowed down

Suvorov's advance and Soult blocked the way forward towards an Austrian corps, Masséna attacked Korsakov near Zurich on 25 September. The Russians, who were crushed, retreated northwards. Rid of Korsakov and the Austrians, the French turned to meet Suvorov, who was making painful progress along the St Gotthard road. In several actions they forced the Russian general to fall back towards the upper Rhine. The pugnacity of Masséna and his subordinates had contributed outstandingly to the success of the manoeuvre.[12] In Holland the Duke of York beat the Franco-Dutch at Alkmaar (2 October) but was unable to carry the day at Castricum (6 October). Brune finally received reinforcements while the bad weather prevented the Anglo-Russians from obtaining assistance by sea. The Duke of York negotiated his re-embarkation (18 October). The Republic was saved.

The strength of the recovery should not let us overlook the failure of the second Directory's foreign policy. England had not succumbed and Mediterranean expansionism had created an anti-French coalition which remained threatening. The Directory was condemned, in Denis Richet's felicitous phrase, to perpetual war. One might conclude that the nature of the regime predisposed it to favour war. There is no doubt that the contractors and generals, and perhaps some merchants, as well as some sections of public opinion, all pressed for expansion. In this sense also, war engendered war. And without an external threat, how could the revolutionary constraints be maintained? At St Helena Bonaparte settled the question: 'The Directory was overpowered by its own weakness; to exist it needed a state of war as other governments need a state of peace.' But this was to make light of the irreducible hostility of the monarchies, and the forces supporting them, to the Republic – even the Republic of Daunou – and to overlook in each country the revolutionary dynamic and the social contradictions which encouraged and were stoked up by war. When Bonaparte landed at Fréjus on 9 October 1799 the crucial battles had been won, but to a nation sick of war he alone appeared capable of guaranteeing the Revolution while simultaneously making peace.

[12] The conception of which S. T. Ross (142) attributes solely to the Directory.

7

The fall

'Imperceptibly everything is going to pieces, everything is decomposing'
Police report, Paris, 19 Prairial Year VII

THE UNION OF THE REPUBLICANS

The Fructidorean Terror

The police operation of 18 Fructidor and the laws adopted on 19
Fructidor opened a phase of repression against the right-wing opponents
of the regime. This return to revolutionary violence has been dubbed
the 'Fructidorean Terror'. Although the term is pithy, it risks masking
the original features of the period. Far from expressing the exasperation
or fears of the masses, this was instead a 'cold' Terror, less bloody than
its precursor, more reasoned, almost administrative. In 1797 the return
of the *émigrés* and refractories had been the most spectacular and most
threatening manifestation of the reaction. The repressive measures
therefore aimed to eliminate these implacable enemies of the Republic.
By the terms of the law of 19 Fructidor, returned *émigrés* had to leave
French territory within fifteen days, even if they had been provisionally
'struck off'. If they did not obey they would be liable to the death
penalty, by virtue of the law of 1793. Many fled abroad; others took
to hiding. But a number were seized, mainly in Paris and the south-east.
Over one hundred were executed. And the relatives of *émigrés* who held
public offices had to relinquish their posts.

This hunting out of *émigrés* was not enough for the more intransigent.
On the instigation of Sieyès, Boulay de la Meurthe put forward a
radical proposal. The nobles would be considered to be foreigners and
consequently would be excluded from political activity unless they
obtained naturalisation. In addition, former members of the *parlement*,

governors and *intendants* of the *ancien régime* would be banished for life. Exceptions were envisaged in favour of Directors, deputies, generals and nobles who had rendered important services to the Revolution. In spite of this conciliatory clause, Barras himself was under threat. There was intense opposition to this 'inhuman' law. The Councils would do no more than deprive the nobles of their right of residence. Even these measures were not applied, but this vigorous campaign showed the persistence of the Thermidoreans' passionate feelings against the nobility. As for the clergy, we have seen the effects of the rigorous measures taken against them; the reviving Church returned to the catacombs. As a result, the second Directory secured itself a year of tranquillity. The priests, the hounded *émigrés* and the rebels, deprived of the support of the hitherto conniving municipalities, no longer constituted a danger. In arresting forty-two Parisian printers and numerous journalists, the government had stifled all expression of reactionary opinion. The hostile press of Year V gave way to a conformist press. The executive had obtained this success by methods which were often illegal: arbitrary arrests, searches, the surveillance of correspondence, raids and beatings became common practice. The Legislative Body, even had it so wished, was no longer in a position to prevent these many violations of individual liberties. France was at this time under a police regime. But this arbitrariness was tempered by the relative inefficiency of Directorial administration. The newly promoted officials did not always carry out their orders with much enthusiasm. Sometimes it proved necessary, as in the Sarthe, to take back part of the 'Fructidorised' personnel. In the west, in Belgium and the frontier zones, the population protected the hunted priests. The Royalists maintained their networks; the Philanthropic Institutes survived the storm. Should military difficulties combine with internal discontent, this underground agitation might once again break out into the open.

The problems of the purge

The triumvirate had dealt with the most urgent problem by hitting at the Legislative Body, but it had to extend the purge to every level. If not, the state would continue to elude its grasp. Besides nullifying certain elections – in the *départements* and the municipalities and in the judiciary – it was necessary to ensure that the public servants who remained in office were loyal: a flood of dismissals therefore rained down upon the civil and military personnel. Those whose recent attitude had appeared suspect paid for their lukewarm republicanism. Thus Generals Moreau, Kellermann and Beurnonville, the three Lille negotiators (Letourneur, Maret and Colchen) and two of the Treasury's commissioners were all relieved of office. Nineteen of the Directory's commissioners and hundreds of *agents communaux* were driven out of their posts. The central administrations of sixty-three *départements* (including the Sarthe, the Côte-d'Or, the Haute-Loire) were also victims of a rigorous 'weeding out'.

This spiralling purge, which in places affected even office clerks, was, then, carried out with systematic thoroughness. But its implementation, on the other hand, seems to have been fairly confused and chaotic. One becomes aware, in this period of tension, of the slowness of the administrative machine, of the central authorities' difficulty in gaining total control over it and also of the intrusion of local political rivalries into national problems. Apart from exceptional cases, the government had no source of information other than its commissioners, and when these were unreliable it depended on information provided by people from the region involved. For its judgements about existing personnel, Paris often had at its disposal only individual denunciations or petitions emanating from Jacobins. What allowance had to be made for private antipathies and feelings of revenge? How could the real adversaries of the regime be located through these partisan judgements? Distance, isolation and problems of language also slowed down communication. J. R. Suratteau has shown this for the *département* of the Mont-Terrible – this *terra incognita* within France – but examples could be found of less marginal regions which suffered from similar time-lags.

Repression occurred generally in three phases. At first, following the *coup d'état*, sackings took place in the *départements*: the most prominent personalities and the 'revanchists' of Year V were thus eliminated. Then, during Vendémiaire and Brumaire, the provinces became calm; the moderates breathed again. But the purge created new victims in the following month and intensified during the winter. This periodisation stemmed from several causes. The respite was perhaps a result of hesitation on the part of the government and its agents in widening the circle of those who were to be 'Fructidorised'. The operation threatened to overstep its objective by hitting authentic Republicans and undermining the very working of the state. Replacements were not available in every case. This first halt in the purge no doubt also resulted from various gaps in information in Paris, and, locally, from a particular balance of political forces. But one can also assume that this period of inactivity resulted from a phenomenon typical of the Directory: the flexibility of the authorities. The local administrations which did not hail the Fructidor coup with unanimous messages of approval, whether through conviction (the minority), or through conformism (the majority), were rare indeed. This large-scale rallying to the regime partly defused any policy of severity and dispelled divisions. The situation had then to settle before new groups began to denounce these belated conversions and set the movement off again. This second wave was the work of the Jacobins.

No enemies on the left?

The risk, glimpsed for a moment, of a restoration of the monarchy had silenced the divisions between the Republicans. Directorials and neo-Jacobins were provisionally united by the royalist threat. Once the clubs had been authorised to reconstitute themselves, 'constitutional circles' emerged to support the policy of republican defence. These were not always spontaneous creations; rather, they were set up with the help of the authorities as a semi-official infrastructure. In the Sarthe and the Loir-et-Cher the constitutional clubs spread cell by cell: a club which was already in existence organised a move towards a neighbouring locality and set up a sister-society there. And from this new base missionaries set off to create yet more republican cells.

The Jacobins profited more than the Directorials from this strategy of encouraging the spread of the clubs. The 'men of '93' – local Terrorists and former members of revolutionary committees – began to take their revenge. Many were appointed to posts that had fallen vacant. Sotin surrounded himself with Jacobins; left-wing journalists started to write again, as in *Le Défenseur de la Constitution* in which the former Hébertist Ballois expressed the hopes of his friends. But the label 'Jacobin' often had only an emotional sense and disguised a whole variety of positions. In Paris – and seen from Paris – the Jacobinism of Year VI consisted of a confused amalgam of terrorism, the popular movement and Babouvism. But in fact the Jacobin movement everywhere had not been made up of the same elements and only rarely conformed to the Parisian 'model'. In Metz, for example, one of the leaders was seen as a Babouvist. But he was at most a left-wing Jacobin, concerned less with political and social upheaval than with the anti-religious and anti-royalist struggle. His friends maintained that they were partisans of the constitution of Year III which they feared might be revised with an oligarchical bias. They were preservers of the Revolution, not anarchists. Thus in the reconstituted Constitutional Club there was peaceful coexistence between the Jacobins and the moderate Republicans. The Jacobins of Toulouse governed the city with great even-handedness: given the absence of the Directorials from this region where the White Terror was still active, they were the almost inevitable incarnation of republicanism. To take the Haute-Loire as a final example: here the Jacobins were distinguished by their enthusiasm for repression, not by their demands for greater democracy.

Yet neo-Jacobinism did constitute a potential danger to the regime, even if it had sworn allegiance to it. There was a danger that the advanced Republicans would link up with the people. A start to this process was seen after Fructidor in Metz where, in tandem with the meetings of the constitutional clubs, meetings were held in cafés at which workers discussed the problems of the day with bourgeois Jacobins. Without necessarily having any subversive intentions, the Jacobins nevertheless threatened political stability since they wanted to pursue the policy of the defence of the Republic to its ultimate conclusion by taking the risk of reintroducing the people into politics.

The action of the Directory

The Directorial clan attempted for its part to consolidate the victory of Fructidor. Two new Directors were elected in place of Carnot and Barthélemy. Merlin de Douai – 'Merlin the suspect' – joined the Directory with an established reputation as a jurist: while in office he was to show evidence both of his capacity for work and of his authoritarian tendencies. François de Neufchâteau, less 'political' than his colleagues, was ambitious to contribute to the common task of regeneration. Lambrecht replaced Merlin de Douai (henceforth Merlin) at the Ministry of Justice and, at the Ministry of the Interior, Letourneur took the post that François de Neufchâteau had filled for a few weeks. The other ministers – Ramel, Talleyrand, Sotin, Schérer (War) and Pléville-le-Pelley – remained in office. The conflict which had started between the Directory and the Councils had stimulated certain Directorials to ponder a reform of the constitution. Should the executive be reinforced by, for example, giving it the right to dissolve the Legislative Body? Was it wise in a period of revolution to renew one-third of the deputies every year? These were the questions that excited political circles in Paris. The entourage of Barras and the friends of Mme de Staël took the risk of raising them in articles or speeches. But these not-disinterested suggestions came to nothing, as did Sieyès' attempts at undermining the constitution. Bonaparte, questioned by Talleyrand, had indicated the impossible reform: 'Governmental power, in the full latitude which I attribute to it, ought to be considered as the true representative of the Nation.' The 'revisionists' were not yet ready to take the plunge. In any case the Directory wanted neither to alienate the Councils by diminishing their power, nor to appear to be criticising the institutions after having just fought to protect them. But it was necessary to prepare for the elections without waiting to be forced into another test of strength, the outcome of which might be doubtful. The first precaution to be taken was to reserve to the Legislative Body, in its present composition, the task of checking the credentials of the newly elected deputies. This proposal, put forward at the end of November, was accepted by the Five Hundred, and then, belatedly, by the Elders (31 January 1798). To justify the abandonment of the procedure employed in Year V, it was explained that the new deputies should not be judges in their own cases. But the system of validation adopted had the equally serious disadvantage that the results of the elections were to be checked by those very people who were going to be replaced. The real problem, as in Year III, was to avoid a royalist majority in the Councils. Finally, on 12 February, another safeguard was put in place: it was decided that the outgoing Director would give up his office on 27 Floréal; it would therefore fall to the Councils to choose a successor to him before the arrival of the new third on 1 Prairial. The ruling group was thus protected against the election of a new Barthélemy.

The preparation of the elections was inspired by the same principles. In the name of revolutionary legitimacy it was intimated that unsatisfactory results would be annulled. As a commissioner of Château-du-Loir put it bluntly: 'Just let the elections of Year VI be the same as those of Year V! The newly elected deputies will all be inhabitants of Madagascar or Guyana!'[1] The constitutional clubs and the commissioners of the Directory drew up lists of 'recommended' candidates. The Five Hundred had even planned to change the places in which the forty-five electoral assemblies met in order to remove them from the influence of the Royalists (1 January 1798). The Elders opposed this exorbitant measure; it already seemed to the Directory's

---

[1] Quoted by M. Reinhard (10), p. 315.

party that the Jacobins were gaining strength dangerously and that it was time to thwart their progress.

The turning point of Pluviôse

The extent of the Jacobin upsurge began to worry the partisans of the government during Frimaire. Had the regime been saved from the royalist peril only to let the friends of Hébert and Babeuf resume their propaganda? In Nice, in the Doubs, the Allier, the Jura and the Haute-Vienne, the 'anarchists' no longer concealed themselves. Two parliamentary initiatives seemed particularly alarming. The first, by Lamarque, was to give an indemnity to the Babouvists acquitted at Vendôme. The Council of the Five Hundred ratified this proposal (6 December 1797) which foundered in the Council of the Elders. Baudin, spokesman for the Directorials, had strongly opposed it. The other bill, put forward by Pons de Verdun, proposed the reopening of the electoral registers. Republicans who had been pursued in Year V by the White Terror would be able to enter their names. Pons also demanded that 'voluntary enrolment' on electoral registers be possible (the quid pro quo being the payment of a tax equal to three days' work) even outside the month of Messidor to which the constitution restricted such voluntary registration. This provision would have brought into the primary assemblies poor citizens who were normally excluded from them. The Jacobin minority on the Legislative Body had gone beyond the limit and their proposals aroused among conservative supporters of the government an obsessive fear of 'equalising anarchy'. The Elders rejected this project twice. At the end of February 1798 the republican coalition was crumbling. Except for Barras, who was always careful not to cut himself off from the democrats, the Directors were inclined towards a break. La Révellière trembled to see the return of the 'drinkers of blood' and Reubell would not tolerate being outflanked by extremists, but it was Merlin who embodied the reversal of policy. Showing himself to be at once the most determined and the most active, he put all his energy into setting obstacles in the path of the Jacobins. The partisans of the Directory moved to alert the electors. In a speech delivered to the Constitutional Club of Paris, Benjamin Constant declared war on the 'revival of Babouvism' (27 February). His remark was extensively reproduced by the government press. Two weeks earlier Sotin, considered too Jacobin, had been replaced as Police Minister by Fondeau, a protégé of Merlin. This simultaneous change in the attitude of the Directorial deputies, the Paris press and the government seemed to give cohesion and clarity to the anti-Jacobin reaction. But J. R. Suratteau has rightly emphasised the lags between Paris and the provinces, between France and the outside world.[2] At the moment when Merlin was preparing measures against the democrats, the Directory's commissioners in the *départements* had only just assimilated the previous policy and were concentrating their blows against the right. Similarly, the 'Batavian Fructidor' of 22 January 1798 was out of step with events in France.

The preparation for the elections

Merlin had the idea of using the commissioners responsible for inspecting the highway toll gates to obtain information outside the official channels. Thanks to these secret observers, by Ventôse the Directory knew the pre-electoral geography of France. In the super-ficially anodyne correspondence of the commissioners, mention was often made of impassable roads, of work requiring to be carried out, of necessary expenditure. These were all pieces of coded information on the extent of Jacobin strength and the need for funds to support the Directorials. Taken together, these reports, emanating from the nine regions, confirmed Merlin's prediction. Except in Belgium, the counter-revolutionaries would not manifest themselves at the elections. On the other hand, many *départements* were won over to the die-hard Republicans. This was the case, among other places, in the Corrèze, the Ardèche, the Dordogne, the Hautes-Pyrénées, etc. The government acted at two levels. Publicly the executive denounced the anarchist threat and the collusion of the Royalists of the 'white cockade' and the Royalists of the 'red cap' (7 March). It closed the Jacobin clubs, arrested the leaders and sacked the suspect commissioners and ad-ministrators. Papers were closed down; Lyons, Saint-Etienne, Marseilles and Périgueux were placed under martial law. What is more, pro-paganda tried to frighten the property owners by reviving the memory of the Vendée trial. The authorities gave secret orders to the com-missioners to promote orthodox candidates and to help them with all the weight of the administration. They were asked to draw up frequent

[2] J. R. Suratteau (153).

pictures of the public mood in their *département* and to dissuade the electors from voting for deputies with over-pronounced views, such as Bentabole, Lamarque or General Jourdan. Merlin and François de Neufchâteau surveyed this correspondence vigilantly and prepared dossiers. While in Germinal Year V it was only the Philanthropic Institutes which had meticulously prepared for the elections, this time it was the government which set up a system of official candidatures. The contest was indeed of vital importance. The elections of Year VI constituted a sort of 'deciding round'. The final third of the members of the Convention were about to confront the electors. Seats vacant since Fructidor also had to be filled. There were therefore 437 deputies to elect. In a free competition, the Thermidoreans risked being beaten. This is why Merlin took a supplementary precaution. He suggested to the Directory's commissioners that they provoke secessions in the electoral assemblies where the government's supporters were in a minority. The Legislative Body would then have no more to do than to validate the results of the 'loyal assemblies'; this meant that the executive would not have to intervene after the event as in Fructidor. The new validation procedure was turned, quite legally, against the Jacobins.

The change in policy came a little late. The Directory did not entirely succeed in making itself obeyed by an administration whose new adversaries had only just rejoined it, nor in making the new direction in its policy understood everywhere. While certain commissioners refrained from influencing the electors and while the administrators of the *départements* still considered the right to be the main enemy, the Jacobins resisted the measures of intimidation. In the Sarthe they were even well-enough implanted to supervise the polling.

Disappointing results

Secessions, very numerous in the primary assemblies, also affected twenty-seven secondary electoral assemblies. Four of the 'mother assemblies' were of royalist persuasion; some represented the Directorial party; most were held by 'anarchists'. The moderate Republicans had therefore followed Merlin's instructions strictly. In the Seine electoral assembly the majority, composed of former members of the revolutionary committees, clashed with the partisans of the government. The latter left the Oratoire, in which the assembly was meeting, and installed themselves in the Institute. The length of time over which the polling took place encouraged not only electoral manoeuvres but also the spread of rumours about results in certain places. This information, arriving in no particular order, interfered with the functioning of the assemblies. The offices of the Ministry of the Interior and the Directory were apprised daily about the developing situation in the assemblies. Through the immense efforts of its administration the government thus knew the details of the results. There was only one month – Floréal – in which to act. After 1 Prairial the new deputies would take up their seats by right.

The Jacobins triumphed in their old zones of the Pyrénées and the Massif Central, in the Bouches du Rhône, the Doubs, the Nord, the Sarthe and the Seine. The regions favourable to the Directorials included the east, the west and the eastern edge of the Massif Central. But many of the assemblies had been undecided. In all, about forty *départements* had fallen into the hands of the die-hards; five had opted for counter-revolution; the rest formed a block which was apparently docile towards the government. The official campaign had not been able to stop almost one-third of the elected deputies from being pronounced Republicans. The elections of Lucien Bonaparte, of Lindet and even more of Barère were acts of defiance against the government. Yet in spite of these warning shots the situation of the Directory was not seriously compromised. Suratteau has calculated that after these elections the Directory still disposed of about four hundred votes in the Legislative Body. But the Directors did not intend to allow so many of their adversaries to enter the Councils. In the elections of Year VII the government would be definitively disavowed. It was important to act to prevent this as early as possible.

The coup of 22 Floréal

On 3 Floréal the Councils embarked upon the validation of the elections. From this moment the Directorials were gripped by panic. Creuzé-Latouche and Hardy wanted to prevent the 'wild beasts' from entering the Legislative Body. The majority would undoubtedly use the secessions to chose 'good' deputies. But the scruples of some and the resolute opposition of Lamarque and Jourdan slowed this process down. Besides, the validation procedure, case by case, proved to be very cumbersome. By 15 Floréal only fifteen *départements* had been examined. The events which occurred during the Seine elections had indicated the bias of the Directorials. While the reporter of the validation commission proposed to annul the decisions of the two competing assemblies, the deputies adopted the results of the elections of the seceding assembly which met at the Institute and which was considerably in a minority. Time was running out. On 15 Floréal a limited commission, led by Bailleul, was charged with drawing up a general list which could be speedily adopted *en bloc*. In spite of protests from the left, there was, then, a move towards collective action. The government collaborated very closely in the drawing up of the lists of admissions and exclusions. Without the help of its administration the commissioners would not have been able to see their task through in time. Finally all disputes were settled in a law passed by the Five Hundred on 18 Floréal and by the Elders on 22 Floréal (11 May). In forty-seven *départements* the elections were validated. In nine other cases annulment affected only administrators and judges. In nineteen *départements* preference was shown for seceding assemblies. Elsewhere, in places where secessions had not occurred, those elected were selected arbitrarily (thirteen cases). Eight *départements* were deprived of all parliamentary representation as a result of the annulment of all the results. In most cases the other electoral results – besides parliamentary ones – were also affected. The law excluded one hundred and six deputies and only replaced fifty-three; 30% of the choices made by the electoral assemblies – at every level – were annulled. In doing this the Councils had exercised their legislative power. It fell to them to lay down the law. The term '*coup d'état*' is therefore technically inaccurate. But it is clear that the deputies had acted under pressure from the Directors. Crassous, an acolyte of Bailleul, did not hesitate to dramatise the situation: 'The guillotine is ready', he told his colleagues, 'do you want to mount it?' The vote was, then, to some extent extorted by blackmail. The motives advanced lacked consistency; the drafters of the law made no effort to convince: thus Chapelle was an 'intriguing banker', Villain 'a correspondent of Poultier', Giot a 'turbulent revolutionary'. By way of justification it was claimed that the Councils had to exclude professed opponents of the constitutional settlement, since an oath of loyalty to the constitution was required at every level, from the primary assemblies to the Legislative Body. The deputies in a sense formed a special category of public servant. Moreover, many of them were dependent on the government as administrators, commissioners and judges. The very idea of national representation was called into question. The second Directory, on which François de Neufchâteau had just been replaced by Treilhard, had won the contest, but the conditions in which its victory took place irremediably discredited the regime. Many Directorials regretted having joined in a manoeuvre which once more debased the legislature. Moreover, some fifty Jacobins had slipped through the censors' net. And since only the new third had been subjected to the purge, the Jacobins elected in Year IV and Year V retained their seats. Thus there were approximately one hundred and ten left-wing deputies who were prepared to accept any alliance as a way of making the executive pay for the events of Floréal.

THE DIRECTORY ON THE DEFENSIVE

The revolt of the deputies and the elections of Year VII

The Jacobin minority, led by Marbot and Jourdan, waged an unremitting guerrilla campaign against the Directory. On several occasions the left-wing deputies found themselves backed by certain Directorials annoyed at the encroachment of the executive. For example, during Messidor a majority came together in the Five Hundred to deny the Directory the right to fill vacant places on the Appeal Court. The Elders restored this prerogative to the Directory, but the incident was significant. A similar alliance formed on the issue of General Schérer. The Minister of War was accused of having profited from state contracts. In fact it was his protector, Reubell, who was being attacked through him. On this occasion Lucien Bonaparte emerged as the leader of a current of opinion which, without, properly speaking, being Jacobin, developed a left-wing stance. These skirmishes, in a regime based on the separation of powers, had no immediate consequences. They expressed, however, the alarming disaffection of many deputies from the Directory, at a time when the diplomatic situation of France was again deteriorating. On the approach of the elections, the government no longer believed itself in a position to set up as thorough an organisation as in the previous year. It considered that it would be more skilful to gamble on appeasement and continuity. A proclamation by François de Neufchâteau, once again Minister of the Interior, did certainly evoke the memory of 'the murderers carrying Féraud's bleeding head on a pike', but on the whole his tone remained moderate: 'No more anarchy but also no hatred, no vengeance, above all no reaction.' Nevertheless the commissioners received orders to secure the election of candidates approved by the Directory. The electoral assemblies only accepted one-third of them. This was an undeniable setback for the government. Moreover the assemblies were poorly attended; the electors showed no enthusiasm to meet. In Alsace participation in the elections fell from 30% in Year VI to an average of 15% in Year VII. The Directorials and the Jacobins were no more than tiny factions fighting for power in the face of the indifference of the French people. The assemblies were less disrupted than in Year VI, and out of twenty-seven secessions the Councils ratified the decisions of twenty-five 'mother assemblies', thereby disavowing the policy pursued in 1798. The conspicuous failure of numerous government candidates caused it to be believed that the Jacobins had triumphed. And thanks as much to the rebellious Directorials as to the military defeats, the Jacobins were now provisionally going to get the upper hand.

A 'parliamentary journée': 30 Prairial

The military defeats provided the Directory's opponents with a pretext to launch their attack. Schérer was again given severe treatment. He symbolised the incompetence, corruption and favouritism for which Lucien Bonaparte reproached the executive. But these skirmishes counted for little compared to the major event: on 9 May Reubell left the Directory; on 16 May Sieyès was elected to it. The accession to power of this illustrious member of the Constituent Assembly marked the end of an era. A majority had been obtained to elect the most constant of the 'revisionists'. His election to the Directory, with the consent of Barras, signified that the institutions were going to be profoundly modified. Two questions now had to be faced: how would this change be carried out? And to whose benefit?

The parliamentary base of the second Directory had narrowed yet further. The most active groups – Jacobins, friends of Sieyès, repentant Directorials (such as Génissieu) – seemed certain to be successful to the extent that the *Plaine*, impressed by the resurgence of the left, made no effort to block the planned operation. Rumours of a *coup d'état* put the deputies on the ready; they did not want to be victims of a new Fructidor. It is hard to see which general the Directory could have used when the military situation was so disastrous. But this hypothetical threat was enough to mobilise a spirit of resistance. A message from the Five Hundred to the Directory on 17 Prairial had demanded a report on the military situation. On 28 Prairial, since no answer had been received, Poullain-Grandprey persuaded the Five Hundred to reiterate this demand and to sit in permanent session as a way of forcing the Directory to reply. The Elders took the same decision. But the executive, paralysed by its divisions, could come to no agreement. On the same evening Bergasse, a Jacobin deputy, delivered the decisive blow in accordance with a plan which had no doubt been squared with Sieyès. He explained that Treilhard was in violation of the constitution because less than a year – four days less – had elapsed between his departure from the Legislative Body and his election to the Directory. This slight infringement of the constitution had already been raised during a previous debate. On that occasion it had been decided not to consider the date of his election but that of his taking up of office. La Révellière, irritated by this underhand manoeuvre, urged Treilhard not to give in. But the latter believed that resistance was useless and resigned on the same evening. Without a majority, the Directory was powerless against the Councils. To replace Treilhard the Elders picked Gohier, a somewhat dull Jacobin, out of a list put forward by the Five Hundred. Encouraged by this first success the Councils resumed the offensive. Boulay de la Meurthe, one of the deputies closest to the government, accused La Révellière and Merlin of having prepared a *coup d'état* in order to prolong the 'enslavement' of the Legislative Body. While a commission – on which sat, among others, Boulay, Lucien Bonaparte, Bergoeing, friends of Barras and Jacobins – was preparing a response to the Directory's message, Sieyès and Barras tried to secure the resignation of their colleagues. Their attempts were less effective than the solemn intervention of a group of Directorial deputies who implored the two Directors to give way. Merlin was the first to succumb and La Révellière could not but follow suit (18 June 1799). The Councils had carried off their '9 Thermidor'. Would the coalition which had formed to avenge the Floréalists be able to maintain itself once the objective had been attained? In the long term the programmes of the Jacobins and dissident Directorials were not compatible. But in the enthusiasm of revenge they believed this alliance to be durable. On the Directory, Moulin, the Jacobin general, would support Barras; and Roger-Ducos would align himself with his friend Sieyès. The latter appeared as the real winner of an operation which he had first sought and then conducted in a masterly fashion. Barras' only political principle was survival. Although protected by his skill, he was supported by no political force, since he avoided linking himself with the democrats and was unable to contest Sieyes' leadership of the moderates. Finally, to the extent that Reubell and La Révellière had attempted to limit the autonomy of the generals, the fall of the second

Directory consecrated the victory of the military. With Championnet free, it represented a striking disavowal of civil power.

The illusion of Jacobinism

The ministerial reshuffle brought into the government friends of Sieyès (Cambacérès as Justice Minister, Reinhard as Minister of External Affairs) and acknowledged Jacobins like Bernadotte and Lindet. The Jacobins also moved into the administration of the *département* of the Seine and into the Bureau Central in Paris. Given that Marbot had replaced Joubert at the head of the 17th division, the left wing of the coalition seemed to have secured a firm position. During Messidor and Thermidor the Jacobins turned their attention towards legislative action. Having obtained the repeal of the law of 19 Fructidor, which limited the freedom of the press, they passed three great public safety laws. On 10 Messidor of the 'Jourdan law' reorganised national defence. At the same time a forced loan of 100 million francs was adopted to finance the war effort. Finally, on 12 July, it was decided to set up a system of hostages. The intention was to end the situation of political banditry which victimised public servants, soldiers and purchasers of national property. At the same time the Jacobins of Paris set up a club in the hall of the Manège where all the previous assemblies had sat. Presided over by Drouet, this club quickly enjoyed massive success. Speeches of Babouvist or 'Terrorist' inspiration were made; in the face of the threat to France's frontiers, speakers rediscovered the rhetoric of Year II. The bourgeoisie became frightened and their newspapers raised the spectre of new September massacres. Each camp was thus mimicking the Great Terror; clashes occurred near the Manège and in several provincial towns; the *jeunesse dorée* went back into action in Bordeaux, Amiens, Rouen and Caen. Sieyès became irritated and worried by these embarrassing allies. On the anniversary of 14 July he gave a warning. Then he embarked on a campaign of denunciation against the Club du Manège (speeches of 9 Thermidor and 10 August). Finally, helped by Fouché, who had just been appointed Minister of Police, he replaced Marbot by Lefebvre (11 August) and closed the Manège (13 August). This rupture of the Prairial coalition took place without harming its instigator. The faubourgs did not react and the Jacobins on the Councils were unable to intervene effectively. Sieyès removed a future obstacle by demonstrating that the weight of the left had been over-estimated.

The royalist uprisings

After Fructidor the royalist movement had gradually reconstituted itself. Initiatives were co-ordinated from two centres. The 'Swabian Agency', with Précy, Dandré and Imbert-Colomès, took particular responsibility for action, leaving political tasks to the 'Royal Council', which included Collard and Montesquiou. The remarkable network of Philanthropic Institutes had, overall, survived the repression. They only needed to be re-activated. The Royalists set about doing this, especially in Bordeaux, Narbonne, Montpellier and Toulouse. Each institute formed 'elite companies', but the military chiefs lacked rifles for their recruits. Furthermore, the leaders misjudged the quality of some of the new members, whose adhesion was more formal than real. Their 'lists of numbers' encouraged them to prepare over-ambitious plans. Even so, it was considered advisable to wait until the coalition armies had reached the frontiers. Towards mid-August 1799 the offensives of the Anglo-Russians in Holland, of the Austrians in Germany and of the Austro-Russians in the south-east were expected to create the optimum conditions for the success of the Counter-Revolution. The royalist leaders would then simultaneously spark off uprisings in the west and south-west. But the situation came to a head faster than the strategists had predicted. From the autumn of 1798 clashes increased between Royalists and Republicans in the Toulouse region. The royalist movement seemed to have reached a new threshold; rural cantons swung towards the rebels. The Jourdan law infused this endemic agitation both with a powerful motive and with new reinforcements. The call up of April 1799 had indeed caused a flood of desertions. In the Haute-Garonne, in the Ariège and in the Lot-et-Garonne the commissioners reported, during July, that the bands of deserters had grown considerably and were becoming aggressive. This seemed like the genesis of another Vendée. The civil and military authorities of the south-west had alerted the Directory, which had been unable to release regular troops to prevent an uprising. Everything rested, then, on the civic virtue and capabilities of the local Republicans. Unlike the south-east, the administrative infrastructure of the Garonne region held firm, especially in Toulouse where the fate of the area was decided. The Jacobins, whose control of the municipality had been confirmed by the last elections, led the resistance and gathered information on the activities of the Royalists. On 5 August General Rouge, who commanded the royalist companies of the Haute-Garonne, hurriedly gave the order to move on to the attack. The rebels no doubt believed that they held sufficient trump cards. Moreover, with their forces mobilised, it would have been dangerous to wait; their plans risked being compromised if the Republicans had the time to react and obtain relief. The rebels did not enjoy the advantage of surprise: on the evening of 5 August their partisans in Toulouse failed to gain control of the gates of the city. But Rouge's ten thousand men occupied the surrounding countryside. A sortie by the Republicans on 8 August miscarried. On the next day a second and better-conceived attack broke the encirclement of the city.

In Bordeaux the Royalists, led by Dupont-Constant, the founder of the Philanthropic Institute, had not planned to move before 5 August. The premature action of the Toulouse Royalists left them in an exposed position; their uprising came to little more than a disorganised agitation. Similarly, on the news of the uprising in Toulouse, the Landes and the Basses-Pyrénées were thrown into a seething turmoil which the Republicans managed to contain. Yet, on 10 August, most of the Gers, the Ariège and the Haute-Garonne were in a state of insurrection. On 20 August, as soon as they had received reinforcements from the Lot and the Tarn, the Republicans counter-attacked. In a few days they had without difficulty defeated the badly equipped and badly led royalist bands. The failure of the royalist leaders to concert their action had saved the Republic.

The repression was restrained. Thousands of insurgents had been arrested during the course of these events. Few of them came before the war councils. The Directory freed 'farmers' who could prove that they had been forcibly conscripted. In this way large landowners like the Comte de Villèle escaped conviction; prior to 18 Brumaire only eight people had been executed. This spectacular clemency – who did not remember Quiberon? – obviously had political significance. The government lacked the means for prolonged repression; it had to appease the peasantry. Besides, Sieyès and Fouché had no intention of creating a void around the Jacobins of Toulouse. They mistrusted these 'pronounced' Republicans and did not want to create a pole of revolutionary attraction in the south-west. The Republicans of the Haute-Garonne hoped that revolutionary measures would be taken. The calculated caution of the Directory disappointed them and increased their disaffection from the regime.

BRUMAIRE

A respite

The state of war encouraged Sieyès to treat his political enemies without indulgence. Having struck at royalist printers and journalists, he turned against the main organs of the Jacobin press, *Le Journal des hommes libres*, *Le Défenseur de la patrie* and *Le Démocrate*. With their propaganda restricted in this way, the Jacobins were no longer successful at imposing themselves in the Councils. In the face of the mass of governmental or undecided deputies, they needed real popular support. But the Parisian *sans-culottes* no longer counted as a political force and did not see their own problems reflected in these quarrels among *notables*. Moreover the troops stationed within the 'constitutional belt' ostensibly had the task of preventing a new '31 May'. The policy of the left also lacked clarity. The Jacobin leaders for a long time believed that they could induce Barras to join their camp. But the same people also envisaged resorting to a military intervention to set up a 'dictatorship of public safety'. It was a sign of the times that on this point they received a very evasive answer from Bernadotte.

The Jacobins drew their strength from neither their numbers nor their relative weight, but rather from the military difficulties of the Republic. In these circumstances they could plausibly demand revolutionary measures. This is why their last offensive coincided with the Anglo-Russian victories in Holland. Belgium was on the point of being invaded. Paris believed itself to be threatened. On 13 September Jourdan asked the Five Hundred to proclaim that the country was in danger. If this appeal evoked epic memories, it also revived old fears. Daunou, in the name of the Thermidoreans, declared that the constitutional regime would not survive such a measure. He refused to sacrifice the institutions and social peace in order to put into motion the irresistible mechanism of exceptional laws. Furthermore, he went on, France had an executive which was quite capable, providing that it was supported, of organising victory itself. Was it not perhaps the case that the danger, as in 1792, came from within, and that the left was preparing a new '10 August'? On this same evening Sieyès, in collusion with Barras, forced Bernadotte to resign as a security measure. Discussion resumed on the next day; Jourdan's proposal was rejected by 245 votes to 171. The victories of Masséna and Brune freed the

Directory from foreign threats and Jacobin pressure. The royalist danger remained. The third uprising, that of the west, broke out in mid-October. Under the command of Bourmont, the Chouans briefly invested Le Mans, Nantes and St Brieuc. But as soon as General Hédouville had assumed command of the republican troops and organised mobile columns, following the example of Hoche, the insurrection collapsed. The internal and external situation was not favourable to it. On the eve of Brumaire the Chouan bands were ruthlessly hunted down.

Bonaparte and the revisionists

The Directory had succeeded, in part thanks to its adversaries, in gaining time. But was the government to be endlessly condemned to sealing up breaches in its support? Could the regime survive this system of annual elections in which the whole structure was called into question on each occasion? Bourgeois opinion pined for certainties, for rationality. Since Prairial the government was both isolated and assailed from within. The Jacobin and royalist oppositions kept up their pressure. But most worrying of all was the growing hostility of the elites upon which the Thermidorean regime rested. Business circles blamed it for the return of the economic crisis and criticised the most recent financial measures: the auditing of the debts of the contractors and the establishment of a forced loan. From 9 Brumaire a parliamentary offensive developed against the terms of this loan. The spokesmen for the financial interests secured a re-examination of the bill. 'The Counter-Revolution is achieved', cried the left-wing deputy Lesage-Senault, thereby emphasising the importance of the debate. As for the Idéologues, they progressively distanced themselves from the second Directory. In *La Décade philosophique* one can follow the burgeoning of this crisis of confidence. The coup of 30 Prairial had seemed to be the beginning of a recovery, but in fact the regime was becoming caught up in petty quarrels and moving in alarming directions (the law on hostages, the forced loan). Faced with the rising tide of dangers, it was clearly incapable of defending the common good. Thus the elites turned against it both for its arbitrariness and for its incompetence. Purchasers of national property, administrators assailed by the Chouans and traders ruined by the consequences of banditry all blamed their misfortunes on it. Discredited by the corruption of its ruling circles as much as by its failures, the Directory had ceased to be 'credible'.

The constitutional arrangements of Year III needed fundamental revision. The constitutional practice of the sister-republics indicated the path that should be followed. Stability implied a reinforcement of the power of the executive, and, as its corollary, a reduction in legislative power. The *journées* of 18 Fructidor and above all 22 Floréal had helped to turn many people against the regime. The Directory's inability to impose its policies – especially upon the Treasury – was a condemnation of the constitution constructed in Year III. The balance of powers had only led to their reciprocal neutralisation. Furthermore the elections, or rather the annual upheavals, allowed too many mediocre individuals to enter the Councils. The antiparliamentarianism of the *notables* echoed the people's long-standing mistrust of the 'perpetual' members. Sieyès once again took up familiar themes. And those who wanted change had to reckon with him; they would be forced to accept the new Director as their partner. It was Sieyès who, when La Révellière suggested to him in Year III that he present his own constitutional proposals, had replied 'I would not be listened to.' But the slowness of the revision procedure prevented any hope of a peaceful transition. Force would be needed to extract the consent of the Councils. This was to re-enact Fructidor – against the republican deputies. A supposed Jacobin plot would provide an opportunity to remove the Councils from the capital. This is why Sieyès attempted to stir up a fear of anarchists among property owners; without such a psychosis nothing would be possible. Which general would fall in with the scheme? Their camarilla was, as G. Lefebvre has said, violently hostile to the 'lawyers of the Directory'. To the contempt of professionals for '*péquins*'* (the word itself was recent) was added the military's bitterness against a government that it held responsible for the defeats. But this hatred covered contradictory political intentions. Augereau, Bernadotte and Jourdan had publicly ranged themselves on the left. Any one of them could become the secular arm of the Jacobins. This is why Sieyès turned to Joubert, who was emerging as increasingly hostile to the 'anarchists'. He had even described certain orators at the Manège as 'escaped convicts'. Furthermore he had precious experience: in Holland he had learnt the techniques of a *coup d'état*. The general was a convinced revisionist. On 17 Messidor he had written to the Directory that without profound reforms 'the Republic would perish with the Republicans'. Sieyès proposed to him that he join his scheme. An agreement was made. But Joubert, who was unknown to the public,

* Civilians. [Trans.]

had first to acquire 'the reputation necessary for the mystique of the role' (Fouché). Sieyès secured for him the command of the Army of Italy. As we know, the Battle of Novi put an end to his career.

Since Macdonald refused to replace Joubert in the plot, Sieyès attempted to win over Moreau who was hesitating. The revisionists had reached a dead end, when the news was learnt of Bonaparte's arrival in France.

From Fréjus to Paris Bonaparte was acclaimed as a saviour. At each stage of his journey the constituted authorities took pains to pay homage to him; fervent crowds greeted the general who would save France from invasion, the politician who had gained stature by his 'exile'. Arriving in Paris on 16 October, he was immediately approached from all quarters. His return introduced another unknown factor into politics. Everyone rushed to 'situate' him. Bonaparte made inquiries, but gave little away. In his largely mendacious proclamation of 18 Brumaire, the first phrases, which evoke this period, do ring true: 'On my return to Paris', he announced, 'I found division in all sources of authority, and agreement on only this one truth, that the constitution was half-destroyed and could not save liberty. All parties came to me, confided their plans in me, unveiled their secrets and demanded my support: I refused to be the man of any one party.'

He quickly realised that there was, in practice, a power vacuum. Lucien explained Sieyès' plans to him and asked for his agreement. Bonaparte detested and feared Sieyès. He had little desire to be the 'sword' of this ambitious man; but to accede to power, the assistance of a Director was unavoidable. Barras had no future; the Jacobins no longer represented more than a muddled and negative faction. The only possible axis was to be found in the revisionist camp in which repentant Directorials (Daunou, Boulay, Benjamin Constant) sat side by side with Cabanis and Volney. This party, whose exact nature was still undefined, represented the hopes of all enlightened conservatives. Bonaparte had no option but to come to an understanding with them, that is, with Sieyès. The two men occupied the same political ground and neither could do anything without the other. But they took a long time to recognise this. Talleyrand served as intermediary. Eventually Bonaparte met the Director at the house of Lucien. He accepted the idea of a *coup d'état*, in return for one modification which almost proved fatal to it: when the Councils were transferred to Saint-Cloud, all the deputies, and not only followers of Sieyès, were to have access to the château. But there was an altogether deeper divergence over the objective of the coup: was the intention to impose Sieyès' constitution on the Councils, or was it, as Bonaparte demanded, to form a provisional government of three consuls – including himself – who would draft a new charter with the assistance of a few deputies? Sieyès understood that in this case he might well be supplanted. Was he being naive or was he playing along? In any case, he had no alternative and had to give in.

Paris

Bonaparte was still not sure of support from two sources. First, from business circles. The conspirators needed both funds to buy complicity and the public support of bankers to remain in power. Collot gave several million *livres* on the morning of the coup, and Ouvrard promised his help. Other powerful business men were probably sounded out, but it seems that they did not contribute financially to the enterprise. Part of the necessary money no doubt came from the Ministry of Police. Second, the support of Bonaparte's comrades was questionable. The plan would be put at risk if certain generals, through principle or jealousy, stood in the way. Augereau, Jourdan and Bernadotte remained uncommitted. Moreau accepted an unobtrusive role. At this moment the conspirators could only count on themselves. Only later would people rally to their cause.

As agreed, the Elders were summoned on the morning of 18 Brumaire (9 November) – suspect deputies having been 'forgotten' – to decide the transfer of the Councils to Saint-Cloud and to entrust Bonaparte with the command of the Paris troops. This second measure, in fact, fell within the prerogatives of the Directory; the illegality was overlooked through fear of anarchists. Once the decree had been secured, Bonaparte went to greet the Elders and then headed for the Palace of Luxembourg. Sieyès and Roger-Ducos resigned, but the Directory could have continued without them and still have obstructed the operation. All depended on Barras. Since Bonaparte's return the Director had been requested by various intermediaries – including Réal and Fouché – to come to an agreement with the general. But Barras still believed himself to be indispensable and did not want to become involved in a small clique, preferring to be sought out in case of crisis. As for Bonaparte, even putting aside his personal resentments, he had come to realise that Barras, in spite of his intrigues, represented only a survival from the past, not a political force. Moreover, in the eyes of the public, Barras symbolised all the defects of the regime. It would have been foolhardy for Bonaparte to form an alliance with him and risk tarnishing his own image. At the very most he agreed, on Talleyrand's advice, to allow the Director an honourable exit. The latter, surprised by the speed of the conspirators, consented to sign the letter of resignation which Talleyrand and Bruix had brought with them. He had not considered resisting; the balance of power was no longer in his favour. Moreover, in the preceding weeks he had come to understand the power of the Napoleonic myth. 'All the civil and military population and all the people of the faubourgs', he would write in his *Mémoires*, 'flocked to Bonaparte as if to a new existence.' Perhaps also he was tired of political life. Did Bonaparte's envoys buy Barras' departure as many historians have claimed without proof? According to Barras' latest biographer, Jean-Paul Garnier, it is impossible to be sure.[3]

In retiring to Grosbois Barras 'escaped from history' (Vandal). His two colleagues, Gohier and Moulin, refused to desert their posts. They were left as prisoners of Moreau. Paris was calm; the plan seemed to be well under way.

Saint-Cloud

On 19 Brumaire at 2 p.m. the Councils, meeting in the Château of Saint-Cloud (occupied by the Council guards and troops from Paris), began to react. In the Five Hundred the Jacobins demanded that an oath of fidelity to the constitution be taken by roll call. Lucien, who was presiding, had to accept this. Moreover, it won the conspirators a respite. But their plan was faltering. Legislative initiative lay with the Council of the Five Hundred. How could such a recalcitrant assembly be made to ratify their schemes? In the Council of the Elders there were protests from those deputies who had not been summoned on the previous day; the others became increasingly worried. The best course seemed to be to appeal to the Directory for advice. Lagarde, the Secretary-General, anticipating events, replied that the Directory had ceased to exist. A peaceful solution – the election of new Directors – now presented itself. The *coup d'état* would be reduced to a ministerial crisis. Bonaparte, nervous, decided to intervene. To the Elders he made a brutal and incoherent speech, whose effect was disastrous. The interruptions disconcerted him and he withdrew having achieved nothing. His reception by the Five Hundred was yet more hostile. To cries of 'outlaw', Jacobin deputies surrounded and jostled him. Murat and Lefebvre helped their leader to leave the hall.

[3] J-P. Garnier, *Barras, le roi du Directoire* (Paris, 1970).

While Bonaparte seemed devastated by this unexpected resistance, Lucien remained cool. For a moment he stood up to the furious deputies, then, protected by soldiers, he retired from the presidency in order not to have to take note of the 'outlawing' of his brother. As for Sieyès, he convinced Bonaparte to move up the troops since intimidation had not sufficed. Lucien and Bonaparte harangued the soldiers. With the authority of his office, the President of the Five Hundred denounced the 'representatives of the sword' who had attempted to kill his brother. The legend of an assassination attempt was thus created. The soldiers of the Paris garrison were outraged and the Council guards shaken. Immediately, Murat, marching at the head of a column, drove the Five Hundred out of the Orangerie. The *coup d'état* was complete. Without a murmur the Elders voted the replacement of the Directory by an executive of three members – the 'Consuls', Bonaparte, Sieyès and Roger-Ducos – the adjournment of the Councils until 1 Ventôse and the setting up of a legislative commission. To drape these measures with an appearance of legality Lucien rounded up the deputies of the Five Hundred. Towards 11 p.m. he assembled less than a hundred of them in the hall of the Orangerie. This rump Council confirmed the previous decisions but substituted the planned commission by two commissions of twenty-five members. Then the Elders ratified the law and invited the Consuls to take the oath. On 20 Brumaire (11 November), at 3 a.m., everyone returned to Paris.

Contrary to Sieyès' hopes, the transition of power had not taken place smoothly. The revolutionary bourgeoisie was clearly not going to escape a military dictatorship, even if it was by the 'most civilian member of the military'. From 20 Brumaire Sieyès understood that Bonaparte would be the master. In front of the Brumarian elite – Chazal, Talleyrand, Boulay, Roederer and Cabanis – the man who had personified the Revolution militant and triumphant formally acknowledged this: 'In the deplorable situation in which we find ourselves, it is better to submit than to excite divisions which would bring certain downfall.' Bonaparte became the legatee of the Revolution. Would he be better able than the Thermidoreans to preserve its inheritance?

Conclusion

Power was for the taking: on the evening of 19 Brumaire the rumours which came from Saint-Cloud did not surprise Paris. The military reverses which had only belatedly been stemmed, the economic crisis, the return of civil war – all these represented failure. The regime's destiny had no doubt been settled on 22 Floréal Year VI. By invalidating a portion of the newly elected deputies the Directory had recognised that the representative system was not viable, since for the second time the executive had had to violate the constitution. What could be presented as a measure of defence during Fructidor, this time took on the appearance, in the eyes of the Republicans, of an arbitrary act. No doubt this won the Directory a respite; but it lost it the minimum consensus without which a regime cannot survive. The rest was a matter of time. Bonaparte took felicitous advantage of the situation, but deserved no credit for it: the Directory gave way at the first sign of pressure. In fact the regime collapsed above all under the weight of its own contradictions: the contradictions of a liberal system which could only survive by violating its own legality, which needed war – at any rate since Fructidor – to satisfy the contractors and generals and to provide itself with income, and which, through war, alienated its freedom of manoeuvre and justified the accusations of its adversaries at home and abroad. Neither the war nor the Revolution was over; in fact, the Revolution developed yet further. The undisguised domination of the bourgeoisie had developed new awareness among the people. Ultimately it matters little that in the immediate term only a handful of activists had carried out a radical critique of the system. With an impeccable class instinct the new owners of property had certainly felt the danger. This is why the 'anti-anarchist' obsession dominated – paralysed – even the most reflective among them. Was the Directory entirely reassuring on this score? The weakness of its state apparatus stemmed, among other things, from its ambiguous nature:

its public servants were both employed by the state and elected. As for the ideological hegemony which would have ensured the domination of the *notables* more effectively than force, the Directory had in this area conducted an interesting but doomed experiment. It was clear that the bourgeois anticlericals were caught in an impasse. Bonaparte came to understand this and drew the appropriate conclusions. Finally, the regime's opponents could plausibly claim that it had itself nurtured a current of social subversion. Had it not on several occasions allowed, if not encouraged, Jacobins, even democrats, to express themselves? These spasmodic upsurges of revolution were full of danger; they risked reviving the popular movement.

Furthermore, the Directory, as a consequence of its imperialist policy, continued to export the Revolution into Europe, gradually weakening old regimes which were already being undermined from within. We know how French expansion rebounded on France politically and economically. It also gave birth, in the conquered territories, to nationalist–revolutionary feelings, which were hardly compatible with the interests of the tutelary power, if not, indeed, directed against them. At the same time the presence of the occupier tended to exacerbate these conflicts and to restore strength to the most traditional sectors of these societies in crisis. But if the foreign policy of the Republic had contradictory consequences, it above all sharpened the fundamental division which set revolutionary France against monarchical Europe. The Directory thus created for itself irreducible opponents on every front, and led to the inevitable emergence of a regime which could resist this twofold class struggle.

In these circumstances, the regime's longevity is paradoxical. How was it able to survive? One must not underestimate the tenacity of its much-disparaged political class, which, in the image of Barras, fought all the harder since it made no distinction between its own personal interests and the common interest. As long as there appeared to be no alternative solution within a republican framework, these profiteers of the Revolution had no intention of relaxing their grip. But the Directory derived its strength even more from the weakness of its adversaries. On the left, the popular movement did not recover from the disaster of Year III: the new regime benefited from the experience of the Thermidoreans. Its police did not, however, give up the hunt for former leaders of the *journées*. But these were no longer in a position to stir up the people. The movement was atomised, effectively dissolved. The royalist enemy seemed more formidable. The Republic was in danger on at least three occasions: during the summer of 1795 at the moment of the Quiberon landing; between Germinal and Fructidor Year V when parliamentary counter-revolution threatened to link up with an armed coup by Pichegru; and finally, during the summer of 1799, when the south-west flared up. But this list reminds us also of the Royalists' numerous failures. Their operations which could have had deadly consequences if they had been better conducted, collapsed through lack of preparation and co-ordination. But such 'technical' errors derived ultimately from a political cause: the fundamental heterogeneity of the royalist movement. In each, or almost each, of these operations, one finds elements of internal conflict: Vendémiaire was exclusively the work of the constitutional monarchists; the quarrels between Puisaye and the absolutists contributed to the Quiberon defeat. Finally, in Year V, the majority in the Councils was paralysed by dissensions between 'white Jacobins' and 'Feuillants'. Above all, the royalist camp was weakened by the extreme positions taken up by the Pretender. A more conciliatory attitude would have rallied the majority of the country. On the counter-revolutionary basis of the Verona Manifesto, the monarchy could only hope for a restoration through the defeat of France. This situation left opportunities for the Orléanist party; it is all the more regrettable that the study of this current of opinion has not been properly carried out.

The last adversaries of the Republic were the foreign armies. The Directory's strength rested partly on the quality of the military instrument forged in Year II, partly on the talent of the generals, and partly on the number and on the abnegation of the soldiers. But the divisions within the opposing alliances eased France's task. Prussia's policy in the first coalition, and the rivalries of Austria and Russia in the second all contributed to the triumph of the Republican government.

After Brumaire the long denigration of the Directory began. Historians have gradually abandoned this black legend in favour of a more balanced study of the period. If the regime founded by the Thermidoreans could not pride itself on numerous successes, it did nonetheless prepare the way for many of the achievements of the Consulate. The reorganisation of the tax system and of the financial administration were begun, we have seen, by Ramel-Nogaret. François de Neufchâteau contributed to the economic recovery and gave a much-needed stimulus to efforts at innovation. Besides these two areas which are often mentioned, we should add that of the administrative infrastructure. The commissioners of the Directory who watched over the authorities in the *départements* partly held the role which was later taken by the prefects. The regime's evolution in an authoritarian direction in its final phase and the people's lack of enthusiasm for elective office reinforced the powers of these government agents, and thereby its tendency to centralisation. These fragmentary achievements were not enough to enhance the credit of the regime. They were at one and the same time too precarious – at the mercy, therefore, of any change in the economic situation – and too slow to impress contemporaries. For example, the slight take-off in the cotton industry did not compensate for the stagnation of traditional textiles. The improvement of farming techniques had not yet resulted in visible progress. In other words, the reformism of Year VI had not had time to prove itself. The Consulate inherited schemes which were in the process of fulfilment – and took credit for them. In politics only the short term counts.

The Directory's achievement was not, therefore, insignificant. In spite of the final catastrophe, it had been able to preserve the bourgeois revolution. Taking up once again the aims of the members of the Constituent Assembly, the Thermidoreans had wanted to complete the process of reconstructing the new society for which the previous century had been a preparation. Circumstances and their own weaknesses had prevented them from succeeding. Bonaparte would set about the same task. It would fall to Bonaparte to 'terminate the Revolution', to heal the nation.

Bibliography

REFERENCE WORKS

Since the previous volumes in this series have introduced the main reference works on revolutionary history, we will only mention here two works devoted exclusively to our period.

Kuscinski, A. *Les Deputés aux Corps législatifs, Conseil des Cinq-Cents, Conseil des Anciens, de l'an IV à l'an VII*, Paris, 1905. A useful but sometimes inaccurate dictionary. Correct against the works of J. R. Suratteau

Massin, J. *Almanach du premier Empire du 9 Thermidor à Waterloo*, Paris, 1965

SOURCES

Aulard, A. *Paris pendant la réaction thermidorienne et sous le Directoire*, 5 vols., Paris, 1898–1902. Police reports and extracts from newspapers

Babeau, A. *La France et Paris sous le Directoire. Lettres d'une voyageuse anglaise suivies d'extraits de lettres de Swinburne*, Paris, 1888

Barras. *Mémoires*, Paris, G. Durruy, 1895–6

Debidour, A. *Recueil des Actes du Directoire exécutif*, 4 vols., Paris, 1910–17. This publication stops in February 1797

La Révellière-Lépeaux. *Mémoires*, Paris, 1895. Published by his son

Mallet Du Pan. *Correspondance avec la Cour de Vienne 1794–1798*, Paris, 1884

BASIC WORKS

General history of the period

1 Deville, G. *Thermidor et Directoire*, Paris, n.d. Socialist history directed by Jaurès. Still valuable thanks to its many documents

2 Furet, F. and Richet, D. *La Révolution*, vol. 2, *Du 9 Thermidor au 18 Brumaire*, Paris, 1966. Trans. S. Hardman, London, Macmillan, 1970

3 Lefebvre, G. *Le Directoire*, Paris, 1947. Sorbonne lectures. Trans. R. Baldick, London, 1965

4 Reinhard, M. *La France du Directoire*, Paris, 1946. Deals only with 1796
5 Sciout, Ph. *Le Directoire*, Paris, 1895–7. A detailed account

Regional studies

6 Clémendot, P. *Le Département de la Meurthe à l'époque du Directoire*, 1966
7 Lefebvre, G. *Les Paysans du Nord pendant la Révolution française*, reissue, Bari, 1959
8 L'Huillier, F. *Recherches sur l'Alsace napoléonienne*, 1947. The first chapter presents 'L'Alsace au lendemain de la Révolution'
9 Pirenne, H. *Histoire de la Belgique*, vol. 6, *La Conquête française*, Brussels, 1926
10 Reinhard, M. *Le Département de la Sarthe sous le régime directorial*, Saint-Brieuc, 1935
11 Suratteau, J. R. *Le Département du Mont-Terrible sous le régime du Directoire*, Paris, 1964
12 Verhaegen, P. *La Belgique sous domination française*, vol. 1, *La Conquête (1792–1795)*, Brussels–Paris, 1923

SPECIALISED STUDIES

Chapter 1 A difficult transition

13 Boussoulade, *L'Eglise de Paris, du 9 Thermidor au Concordat*, Paris, 1950
14 Cobb, R. 'Notes sur la répression contre le personnel sans-culotte de 1795 à 1801', *Annales historiques de la Révolution française* (1954), pp. 23–49
15 Cobb, R. *Reactions to the French Revolution*, Oxford University Press, 1972
16 Cobb, R. 'Quelques aspects de la crise de l'an III en France', *Bulletin de la Société d'histoire moderne*, 1966
17 Cobb, R. *The Police and the People. French Popular Protest (1789–1820)*, Oxford, 1970. A brilliant essay in social psychology
18 Dubreuil, L. *Histoire des insurrections de l'Ouest*, vol. 2, Poitiers, 1930. Dated
19 Festy, O. *L'Agriculture pendant la Révolution française: les conditions de production et de récolte des céréales (1789–1795)*, Paris, 1947
20 Fryer, W. R. *Republic or Restoration in France (1794–1797)*, Manchester, 1965
21 Fuoc, R. *La Réaction thermidorienne à Lyon*, Lyons, 1957
22 Garrone, A. Galante. *Gilbert Romme*, Turin, 1959. French translation, Paris, 1971
23 Godechot, J. *La Grande Nation. L'Expansion révolutionnaire de la France dans le monde (1789–1799)*, Paris, 1956
24 Godechot, J. *La Contre-Révolution (1789–1804)*, Paris, 1961. Trans.

S. Attanasio as *The Counter-Revolution: Doctrine and Action, 1789–1804*, London, 1972

25 Guillemin, H. *Benjamin Constant muscadin (1795–1799)*, Paris, 1958

26 Harris, S. E. *The 'Assignats'*, Cambridge, Mass., 1930

27 Hufton, O. H. *Bayeux in the Late Eighteenth Century*, Oxford, 1967

28 Hutt, M. 'La prétendue pacification de l'an III. Considérations critiques sur la situation en Bretagne à la veille de Quiberon', *A.h.R.f.* (1966), pp. 485–521

29 Kaplow, J. *Elbeuf during the Revolutionary Period: History and Social Structure*, Baltimore, 1964

30 Latreille, A. *L'Eglise catholique et la Révolution française*, vol. 1, Paris, 1946

31 Lefebvre, G. *Les Thermidoriens*, Paris, 1937. Trans. R. Baldick as *The Thermidoreans*, London, 1965

32 Lefebvre, G. *Etudes orléanaises*, vol. 2, *Subsistances et maximum (1789–an IV)*, Paris, 1963

33 Marion, M. *Histoire financière de la France depuis 1715*, vol. 3, Paris, 1921. A polemical and confused, but nonetheless irreplaceable, work

34 Mathiez, A. *La Réaction thermidorienne*, Paris, 1929. A long commentary on the title

35 Mitchell, M. 'Vendémiaire, a Re-evaluation', *Journal of Modern History* (1958), pp. 191–202

36 Reinhard, M. *Le Grand Carnot*, vol. 2, *L'Organisateur de la victoire*, Paris, 1952

37 *Gilbert Romme (1750–1795) et son temps. Actes du Colloque de Riom-Clermont*, Paris, 1966

38 Rudé, G. 'Les Sans-culottes parisiens et les journées de vendémiaire an IV', *A.h.R.f.* (1959), pp. 332–46

39 Soreau, E. 'Contribution à l'histoire du ravitaillement en Loir-et-Cher pendant la Révolution', *A.h.R.f.* (1934), pp. 481–527

40 Tarlé, E. *Germinal and Prairial* (trans.), Moscow, 1959

41 Tönnesson, K. D. *La Défaite des sans-culottes: mouvement populaire et réaction bourgeoise en l'an III*, Paris, 1959

42 Vidalenc, J. 'L'Affaire de Quiberon', *Actes du 87ᵉ Congrès national des Sociétés savantes (Poitiers, 1962)*, Paris, 1963

43 Zivy, H. *Le 13 Vendémiaire an IV*, Paris, 1898

Chapter 2 On two fronts

See also nos. 18, 20, 24, 27, 29 and 36

44 *Babeuf et les problèmes du babouvisme. Colloque international de Stockholm, 1960*, Paris, 1963

45 Beyssi, J. 'Le Parti jacobin à Toulouse sous le Directoire', *Annales historiques de la Révolution française* (1950), pp. 28–54, 109–33

46 Brelot, C. *Besançon révolutionnaire*, Paris, 1966

47 Brelot, J. *La Vie politique en Côte-d'Or sous le Directoire*, Dijon, 1932
48 Caudrillier, G. *L'Association royaliste de l'Institut philanthropique à Bordeaux*, Paris, 1908
49 Church, C. 'The Social Basis of the French Central Bureaucracy under the Directory', *Past and Present* (April, 1957), pp. 59–72
50 Coe, R, 'La Théorie morellienne et la pratique babouviste', *A.h.R.f.* (1958), no. 1, pp. 38–50. The article is followed by a debate between J. Dautry, A. Saitta and the author
51 Dautry, J. 'Le Pessimisme économique de Babeuf et l'histoire des utopies', *A.h.R.f.* (1961), pp. 215–33
52 Desgranges, F. *La Centralisation républicaine sous le Directoire: les municipalités de canton dans le département de la Vienne*, Poitiers, 1954
53 Dommanget, M. *Sur Babeuf et la conjuration des Egaux*, Paris, 1970. A collection of articles
54 Fremont, G. *L'Administration municipale de Verdun sous le Directoire (1795–1799)*, Nancy, 1964
55 Godechot, J. *La Propagande royaliste aux armées sous le Directoire*, Paris, 1933
56 Marx, R. *Recherches sur la vie politique de l'Alsace pré-révolutionnaire*, Strasburg, 1966. An attempt at electoral sociology
57 Mazauric, C. *Babeuf et la Conspiration pour l'Egalité*, Paris, 1962
58 Mazauric, C. 'Babouvisme et conscience de classe' in *Sur la Révolution française*, Paris, 1970, pp. 147–62
59 Meynier, A. *Les Coups d'état du Directoire*, vol. 1, *Le Dix-huit Fructidor*, Paris, 1927
60 Parker, H. T. 'Two Administrative Bureaux under the Directory and Napoleon', *French Historical Studies* (1965), pp. 150–69
61 Saitta, A. 'Autour de la Conjuration de Babeuf. Discussion sur le communisme (1796)', *A.h.R.f.* (1960), pp. 426–35
62 Suratteau, J. R. 'Les Elections de l'an IV', *A.h.R.f.* (1951), pp. 374–93; (1952), pp. 32–62
63 Suratteau, J. R. 'Les Elections de l'an V aux Conseils du Directoire', *A.h.R.f.* (1958), no. 5, pp. 21–63
64 Tönnesson, K. 'L'An III dans la formation du babouvisme', *A.h.R.f.* (1960), pp. 411–25
65 Tulard, J. 'Le Recrutement de la Légion de police de Paris sous la Convention thermidorienne et le Directoire', *A.h.R.f.* (1964), pp. 38–64
66 Woloch, I. 'The Revival of Jacobinism in Metz during the Directory', *Journal of Modern History* (1966), no. 1, pp. 13–37
67 Woloch, I. *Jacobin Legacy. The Democratic Movement under the Directory*, Princeton, 1970

Chapter 3 Conquests

See also nos. 23, 36 and 55

68 Bonnel, U. *La France, les Etats-Unis et la Guerre de course*, Paris, 1961

69 Bourdeau. *Les Armées du Rhin au début du Directoire*, Paris, 1902

70 Cessi, R. 'Da Leoben a Campoformio', *Rendiconti della Classe di Scienze morali, storiche, e filologiche dell'Accademia nazionale dei Lincei* (1954), pp. 558–86

71 Dejoint, G. *La Politique économique du Directoire*, Paris, 1951. In spite of its title, it deals essentially with French economic relations before 18 Fructidor

72 Droz, J. *L'Allemagne et la Révolution française*, Paris, 1949

73 Giuntella, V. 'L'Esperienza rivoluzionaria', in *Nuove Questioni di storia del Risorgimento e dell'unità d'Italia*, Milan, 1961, pp. 311–43. An excellent up-to-date assessment

74 Godechot, J. 'Les Aventures d'un fournisseur aux armées: Hanet-Cléry', *Annales historiques de la Révolution française* (1936), pp. 30–41

75 Godechot, J. *Les Commissaires aux armées sous le Directoire*, Paris, 1937

76 Guyot, R. *Le Directoire et la Paix de l'Europe*, Paris, 1911

77 Nabonne, B. *La Diplomatie du Directoire et Bonaparte*, Paris, 1951

78 Reinhard, M. *Avec Bonaparte en Italie, d'après les lettres inédites de son aide de camp Joseph Sulkowski*, Paris, 1946

79 Reinhard, M. 'Les Négociations de Lille et la crise du 18 fructidor', *Revue d'histoire moderne et contemporaine* (1958), pp. 39–56

80 Sagnac, P. *Le Rhin français pendant la Révolution et l'Empire*, Paris, 1918

81 Saitta, A. 'Struttura sociale e realtà politica nel progetto costituzionale dei giacobini piemontesi (1796)', *Società* (1949), no. 3, pp. 436–75

82 Stern, J. *Le Mari de Mademoiselle Lange, Michel Jean Simons (1762–1833)*, Paris, 1933

83 Stuart-Jones, E. H. *An Invasion That Failed. The French Expedition to Ireland of 1795*, Oxford, 1950

84 Vaccarino, G. *I Patrioti 'anarchistes' e l'idea dell'unità italiana*, Turin, 1956

Chapter 4 Economic activity

See also nos. 70, 73 and 81

85 Ballot, C. *L'Introduction du machinisme dans l'industrie française*, Paris, 1923. Remains fundamental

86 Bergeron, L. 'Profits et risques dans les affaires parisiennes à l'époque du Directoire et du Consulat' *Annales historiques de la Révolution française* (1966), pp. 359–89

87 Bouloiseux, M. *Le Séquestre et la vente des biens des émigrés dans le district de Rouen (1792–an X)*, Paris, 1937

88 Causse, H. 'Un Industriel toulousain au temps de la Révolution et de l'Empire: François-Bernard Boyer-Fonfrède', *Annales du Midi* (1957), pp. 121–33

89 Chabert, A. *Essai sur les mouvements des revenus et de l'activité économique en France de 1798 à 1820*, Paris, 1949

90 Crouzet, F. 'La Ruine du grand commerce', in F. Pariset (ed.), *Bordeaux au XVIIe siècle*, Bordeaux, 1968

91 Darquenne, R. 'Histoire économique du département de Jemmappes', *Annales du cercle archéologique de Mons, 1962–1964* vol. 65 (Mons, 1965), pp. 1–379

92 Delcambre, E. *La Vie dans la Haute-Loire sous le Directoire*, Rodez, 1943

93 Demougeot, A. 'La Vie difficile à Nice au temps du Directoire (1795–1799)', *Recherches régionales* (1968), no. 1, pp. 1–37

94 Dubreuil, L. *La Vente des biens nationaux dans le département des Côtes-du-Nord (1790–1830)*, Paris, 1912

95 Lebrun, P. *L'Industrie de la laine à Verviers pendant le XVIIIe siècle et le début du XIXe siècle*, Liège, 1948

96 Lefebvre, G. 'Les mines de Littry (1744–an VIII)', article reprinted in *Etudes sur la Révolution française*, Paris, 1963, pp. 159–96

97 Leleux, F. *A l'Aube du capitalisme et de la révolution industrielle. Liévin Bauwens, industriel gantois*, Paris, 1969

98 Leon, P. *La Naissance de la grande industrie en Dauphiné*, part 2, section 2, chapter 3, 'La Crise industrielle (an III–an VII)', Gap, 1954

99 Leuilliot, P. *L'Alsace au début du XIXe siècle*, vol. 2, *Les Transformations économiques*, Paris, 1959. Lots of information on the metallurgical and textile industries under the Directory

100 Marion, M. *Histoire financière de la France depuis 1715*, vol. 4, Paris, 1925

101 Marion, M. *Le Brigandage pendant la Révolution*, Paris, 1934

102 Richert, G. 'Biens communaux et droits d'usage en Haute-Garonne pendant la réaction thermidorienne et le Directoire', *A.h.R.f.* (1951), pp. 274–88

103 Rouvière. *L'Exploitation des mines nationales du Gard (1792–1800)*, Nîmes, 1901

104 Saint-Leger, A. de *Les Mines d'Anzin et d'Aniche pendant la Révolution*, Paris, 1935–9

105 Schmidt, C. 'Un Essai de statistique industrielle en l'an V', *Bulletin de la Commission de recherche et de publication des documents relatifs à la vie économique de la Révolution* (1908), pp. 11–205

106 Schnerb, R. *Les Contributions directes à l'époque de la Révolution dans le Puy-de-Dôme*, Paris, 1933

107 Schnerb, R. 'La Dépression économique sous le Directoire après la disparition du papier-monnaie an V–an VIII', *A.h.R.f.* (1934), pp. 27–49

108 Sentou, J. 'La Fortune immobilière des Toulousains et la Révolution française', *Commission d'histoire économique et sociale de la Révolution française* (Paris, 1970)

109 Soreau, E. 'Les Ouvriers en l'an VII', *A.h.R.f.* (1931), pp. 117–24

110 Vermale, F. 'Les Dettes privées sous la Révolution et le remboursement en assignats', *A.h.R.f.* (1933), pp. 160–6

111 Viard, P. 'Vers l'Ajustement légal des prix (métal et papier) dans l'Hérault à la fin de l'an V', *A.h.R.f.* (1928), pp. 243–63

112 Viard, P. 'Quelques faillites à Dijon sous le Directoire', *La Révolution dans la Côte-d'Or* (1929), pp. 91–106

Chapter 5 Beliefs, rituals and language

See also nos. 13 and 30

113 Barbé, J. J. 'Le Théâtre à Metz sous la réaction thermidorienne et le Directoire', *Annales historiques de la Révolution française* (1928), pp. 247–65

114 Barnard, H. C. *Education and the French Revolution*, Cambridge, 1969. A rapid survey

115 Bois, B. *La Vie scolaire et les Créations intellectuelles en Anjou pendant la Révolution (1789–1799)*, Paris, 1929

116 Bois, B. *Les Fêtes révolutionnaires à Angers, de l'an II à l'an VIII*, Paris, 1929

117 Boussoulade, J. 'Le Presbytérianisme dans les Conciles de 1797 et de 1801', *A.h.R.f.* (1951), pp. 17–37

118 Carlson, M. *The Theatre of the French Revolution*, Ithaca, 1966. A study of Parisian theatres

119 Francastel, P. *Le Style Empire. Du Directoire à la Restauration*, Paris, 1939

120 Gaulmier, J. *L'Idéologue Volney*, Beirut, 1951

121 Janneau, G. *Le Style Directoire*, Paris, 1938

122 Kitchin, J. *Un Journal 'philosophique'. La Décade (1794–1807)*, Paris, 1966

123 Leith, J. A. *The Idea of Art as Propaganda in France (1750–1799)*, Toronto, 1965

124 Leon, A. *La Révolution et l'Enseignement technique*, Paris, 1968

125 Mathiez, A. *La Théophilanthropie et le Culte décadaire*, Paris, 1903

126 Ozouf, M. 'De Thermidor à Brumaire: le discours de la Révolution sur elle-même', *Revue historique* (1970), pp. 31–66

127 Picavet, F. *Les Idéologues*, Paris, 1891

128 Plongeron, B. *Conscience religieuse en Révolution. Regards sur l'historiographie religieuse de la Révolution française*, Paris, 1969

129 Trenard, L. *Lyon, de l'Encyclopédie au Préromantisme*, vol. 2, *L'Eclosion du mysticisme*, Grenoble, 1958

130 Viaux, J. *Le Meuble en France*, Paris, 1962

131 Vial, F. *Trois siècles d'histoire de l'enseignement secondaire*, Paris, 1936. Celebrates the Ecoles Centrales

Chapter 6 From expansion to decline

See also the bibliography for chapter 2

132 Charles-Roux, F. *Bonaparte gouverneur d'Egypte*, Paris, 1936

133 Daline, V. 'Marc-Antoine Jullien après le 9 Thermidor', *Annales histor-iques de la Révolution française* (1966), no. 3, pp. 390–412. A Babouvist in the entourage of Championnet

134 de Felice, R. *La Vendita dei beni nazionali nella Repubblica romana*, Rome, 1960. A study towards an economic history of Italy under French influence

135 Devleeshouwer, R. 'Le Cas de la Belgique' in *Occupants et occupés (1792–1815)*. *Colloque de Bruxelles 1968*, Brussels, 1969, pp. 43–65

136 Giuntella, V. *La Giacobina repubblica romana (1798–1799)*, Rome, 1950

137 Herold, C. *Bonaparte in Egypt*, London, 1963

138 Hill, H. B. 'Les Préliminaires de la Constitution ligurienne de 1798', *A.h.R.f.* (1958), no. 4, pp. 51–7

139 Lacour-Gayet, G. *Talleyrand*, Paris, 1929–39

140 Marcelli, U. 'La Crisi economica e sociale a Bologna e le prime vendite dei beni ecclesiastici 1797–1800' in *Atti e memorie della deputazione di storia patria per la provincia di Romagna*, 1953–4

141 Rodger, A. B. *The War of the Second Coalition (1798–1801). A Strategic Commentary*, Oxford, 1964

142 Ross, S. T. 'The Military Strategy of the Directory. The Campaign of 1799', *French Historical Studies* (1967), pp. 170–87

143 Suratteau, J. R. 'Occupation, occupants et occupés en Suisse de 1792 à 1814' in *Occupants et occupés (1792–1815)*. *Colloque de Bruxelles 1968*, Brussels, 1969, pp. 165–216

144 Vallée, G. *La Conscription dans le département de la Charente (1798–1807)*, Paris, 1937

145 Verhaegen, D. *L'Influence de la Révolution française sur la première Constitution hollandaise du 23 avril 1798*, Utrecht, 1949

146 Zaghi, C. *Bonaparte e il Direttorio dopo Campoformio*, Naples, 1956

Chapter 7 The fall

See also nos. 18–45, 48, 52, 54, 56, 66, 121 and 125

147 Delcambre, E. *Le Coup d'état du 18 fructidor et ses répercussions dans la Haute-Loire*, Rodez, 1942

148 Guyot, R. 'Du Directoire au Consulat : les transitions', *Revue historique* (1912), pp. 1–31

149 Lacouture, J. *Le Mouvement royaliste dans le Sud-Ouest*, Hossegor, 1932

150 Meynier, A. *Les Coups d'état du Directoire*, vol. 2, *Le Vingt-deux Floréal an VI et le Trente Prairial an VII*, Paris, 1928

151 Meynier, A. *Les Coups d'état du Directoire*, vol. 3, *Le Dix-huit Brumaire et la Fin de la République*, Paris, 1928

152 Olliviet, A. *Le Dix-huit Brumaire*, Paris, 1959. An impressionistic history

153 Suratteau, J. R. 'Les Elections de l'an VI et le Coup d'état du 22 Floréal', unpublished thesis, Paris, 1971

154 Vandal, A. *L'Avènement de Bonaparte*, vol. 1, *La Genèse du Consulat. Brumaire*, Paris, 1903

ADDITIONAL WORKS

155 Brunel, F. 'Les derniers Montagnards et l'unité révolutionnaire', *Annales historiques de la Révolution française* (1977), pp. 385–404

156 Lefebvre, G. *La France sous le Directoire (1795–1799)*, Paris, 1977. The full reissue of these lectures is accompanied by considerable bibliographical updating and a discussion of recent scholarship by J. R. Suratteau

157 Lyons, M. *France under the Directory*, London, 1975

158 Godechot, J. *La Vie quotidienne en France sous le Directoire*, Paris, 1977

159 Church, C. H. 'In search of the Directory' in *Essays in memory of Alfred Cobban*, London, 1973

160 Suratteau, J. R. 'Le Directoire comme mode de gouvernement' in *Actes du colloque international Mathiez-Lefebvre (1974)*, Paris, 1978

161 Homan, G. D. *Jean-François Reubell, French Revolutionary Patriot and Director (1747–1807)*, The Hague, 1971

162 Bergeron, L. *Banquiers, négociants et manufacturiers parisiens du Directoire à l'Empire*, Paris, 1978

163 Woronoff, D. 'Les Problèmes de la sidérurgie à l'époque du Directoire', *Actes du colloque international Mathiez-Lefebvre (1974)*, Paris, 1978

164 Geyl, P. *La République batave (1795–1798)*, French translation, 1971

SUPPLEMENTARY BIBLIOGRAPHY

There is not a great deal of new work on this period: the following is a list of the major articles only. (Quite a number of the post-1970 books are already in the main bibliography.)

Bruhat, J. *Gracchus Babeuf et les Egaux, ou le 'premier parti communiste agissant'*, Paris, Perrin, 1978

Elliott, M. *Partners in Revolution. The United Irishmen and France*, Yale University Press, 1982

Gendron, F. *La Jeunesse dorée*, Presses Universitaires du Québec, 1979

Higonnet, P. *Class, Ideology, and the Rights of Nobles during the French Revolution*, Oxford, Clarendon Press, 1981

Hunt, L. 'The Failure of the Liberal Experiment in France, 1795–1799', *Journal of Modern History*, 51 (1979)

Jones, C. *Charity and Bienfaisance: the treatment of the poor in the Montpellier region 1740–1815*, Cambridge University Press, 1983

Lewis, G. *The Second Vendée. The Continuity of Counter-Revolution in the Department of the Gard, 1789–1815*, Oxford, Clarendon Press, 1978

Lewis, G. and Lucas, C. (eds.) *Beyond the Terror*, Cambridge University Press, 1983

Lucas, C. 'The First Directory and the Rule of Law', *French Historical Studies*, 10 (1977)

Ozouf, M. *La Fête révolutionnaire, 1789–1799*, Paris, Gallimard, 1976

Rose, R. B. *Gracchus Babeuf: the First Revolutionary Communist*, London, Arnold, 1978

La Statistique en France à l'époque napoléonienne, papers of symposium held in Paris, 14 February 1980, Centre Belge d'étude des sociétés contemporaines, Brussels, n.d.

Vovelle, M. *De la cave au grenier*, Paris, Fleury, 1980

Index